# The Inexhaustible Gospel

Neal A. Maxwell

A Retrospective of
Twenty-one Firesides and Devotionals
Brigham Young University
1974–2004

Order from
Speeches
218 UPB
Brigham Young University
Provo, UT 84602
http://speeches.byu.edu

# CONTENTS

# Family Perspectives

Neal A. Maxwell

I commend Brigham Young University for its special commitment to family life, reflected not only by this special week of substance and counsel, and not only by its continuing curricular concern and the nearly unique College of Family Living but also for the commitment to the family by this University expressed in so many other ways. Other universities and colleges teach about the family, but sometimes others view the family as a transitory, economic unit in human history—not as an eternal unit. Curricula elsewhere deal with the need for certain skills in family life (which none of us doubts) and with the interrelationships among humans who are temporarily collected as families—but not with individuals as eternal realities. This University and its College of Family Living act from an entirely different point of view and even though the form may parallel the academic form elsewhere, the operating assumptions and the theological foundations produce a deep and pervasive commitment to the family, making what happens on this campus unique.

---

*This devotional address was given at Brigham Young University on 15 January 1974.*

I am grateful for the faculty and students alike at this University, who understand the tandem relationship between theology and identity, between family and eternity. At this University there is coequal concern with that nutrition pertaining to the body and that nutrition pertaining to the spirit. We certainly share with the secular world concern over diets required for our physical health, but we also assert to a sick and undernourished world that a divine diet has been prescribed for the soul of man, and further, that the primary source of his succor should be the family.

## DIVINE REVELATION ABOUT THE FAMILY

In 1902 President Joseph F. Smith said that it is "family life, on which the government of the Church is based and perpetuated" ("Editor's Table," *Improvement Era* 5 [February 1902]: 308–9). I know of no parallel institutional commitment to the family anywhere else in the world. The prophets of the Church have all drawn on the same divine well; therefore, their doctrines and teachings are the same. Seers see not only farther but deeper than other men, taking into account the relationships of truths and realities. Our late President, Harold B. Lee, counseled us with the same kind of specificity when he said, ". . . remember that the most important of the Lord's work that you will ever do will be the work you do in the walls of your own home" ("Strengthening the Home," p. 7). It is significant that the summation of his counsel focused, again, on the family and on the home.

President Spencer W. Kimball focused on the family as he offered this advice: "I like to compare the home evening, family prayer, and other associated activities of the Church for the saving of the family, when they are conscientiously carried out, with an umbrella. If the umbrella is not opened up, it is little more than a cane and can give little protection from the storms of nature. . . . The umbrella spread out makes the silken material taut. When the rain falls, it runs off; when the snow falls, it slides off; when the hail comes, it bounces off; when the wind blows, it is diverted around the umbrella" (*Conference Report*, October 1969, p. 23).

We are at a point in human history when, unfortunately, it is no longer merely sprinkling; the rains have begun to fall, and at this very point in history, ironically, many umbrellas are being folded up and put away.

## SECULAR FALLACIES ABOUT THE FAMILY

Isn't it ironical that some of those who are most vigorous in taking the American family apart are also among those who are the first to complain because, then, the family does not work? Isn't it ironical that in an age when we are learning almost feverishly about what is most ecologically sound, what are the most efficient and economic ways to produce energy or protein in order to help other human beings, that we should be so incredibly blind—because like ancient Judah, we are "looking beyond the mark"—when it comes to pursuing those processes which are best for the production of good human beings? The relative spiritual, as well as the physiological efficiencies of systems are a justifiable concern. Beef cattle foraging on a poor range require twenty pounds of food in order to produce one pound of gain. Chickens with a good balanced diet produce one pound of gain for every two pounds of feed. One approach is many times more efficient than the other, just as (so far as human goodness is concerned) the social and spiritual sum of our political, educational, and economic institutions is usually not sufficient to offset the deficits in the home.

Analogously, we have far too many lonely humans foraging on deficient "homesteads" and too many governmental programs which attempt abortively to substitute a less efficient system of helping humans than the home; it is the home that we must rescue, repair, and sustain. Only when homes are full of truth, warmth, and trust, can our other institutions perform their tasks, and when too many homes are defective, then the deterioration becomes contagiously interinstitutional, affecting schools and governments. If we are really concerned about the most economical way of achieving happiness for ourselves and/or our fellowmen and about those skills that are needed in successful human enterprises, then we should seek these gains through the family, with the help, of course, of other institutions.

Otherwise, we shall always be investing dollars and hopes in less efficient ways of helping mankind. Just as the wheel does not have to be reinvented perpetually, we do not have to reinvent the family, a divine institution.

Yet so many fail to hear the crash of the surf of statistics generated by an abundance of research about the importance of early life and of family influence. There is in the secular world either a failure to generalize from the research or, when generalizations emerge, the generalizations are not acted upon. It is almost as if the secular world condemned itself to act like Sisyphus, who was condemned to roll a huge boulder to the edge of the mountain top only to have it come tumbling back down whereupon the process is repeated endlessly. Indeed, the sincere Sisyphus syndrome is all about us. The eternalism approach of the gospel of Jesus Christ lays great stress, for instance, on the innocence of the newborn and on the importance of helping that individual "streamlet," nearest its source, so it can achieve identity and maintain purity. Secularism, on the other hand, tends to become fascinated with building vast purification plants downstream; but, ironically, secularists have difficulty agreeing on what dirt is—on what is to be filtered out.

If you prefer a different analogy, we are witnesses to a rather bizarre game of human chess in which there is strange value placed on the various pieces on the chess game. The kings and queens, the parents, are thought of as being inconsequential; the castles, or homes, get traded off for pawns with great casualness; the bishops, which might represent religion, remain largely unused in responding to the challenge. Yet, in the midst of this strange pattern of play, the world wonders why it cannot checkmate human misery.

While more research and information are almost always desirable, how much more research do we need before we begin to accept the realities of how, almost relentlessly, parental patterns are projected into their posterity? How much more research do we need with regard to the sources and the importance of self-esteem? There is an ecology that pertains to the world of man's spirit and his self-esteem. We must begin to think about the deprivation of the individual storehouse of self-esteem as a vital community concern. We have a stake in each other's self-esteem.

How much more research does the world need before we can accept parents as pivotal and before we focus on the family without apology and half-heartedness? Of course, there are rogue parents just as there are rogue policemen. Of course, there are some people, through no fault of their own, who do not marry. Of course, there are some, who, through no fault of their own, experience defective and broken homes, but these exceptions are not reasons for abandoning this remarkable resource, the family. The family is the tilt point for a vast number of souls who can go either way—to alienation and anger or to sweetness and service.

## LATTER-DAY SAINTS TO PRESERVE TRUTHS ABOUT THE FAMILY

Alas, it may be true that those who do not believe in God, who is a loving parent and who is the Father of the human family, will also never be able to accept the eternal importance of the institution of the family, except as something that is socially useful—little wonder we arrive at different conclusions or that we have different priorities. How important, therefore, it is that we remain at our posts as sentries over doctrines and teachings like that concerning the family, even if the world in its mistaken, but sincere way, seems to be headed in entirely different directions. The Latter-day Saints ought to understand, for instance, that the wars of tomorrow are this day being forged in the overheated families of today. How many dictators or assassins do we need to study in order to understand the consequences of distortion in the home? How many more examples do we need, including the energy crisis, where a few control the resources needed by many, before realizing that food and fiber are not the real challenge? Rather, it is selfishness and our human delivery systems. And where, indeed, can one learn, first-hand, selflessness and sharing? In the home, where such skills and attitudes tend to be learned, if they are learned at all.

Many citizens today, for instance, are alarmed, and rightfully so, when they see a vast oil slick develop which may be headed for the habitat of wildlife or a culinary water resource. Isn't it interesting that only the seers seem to be able to see the approaching tide of effluence flowing from parental permissiveness that is now in the process of engulfing so many? So few other voices are raised in alarm. The ears of the secular world are attuned to the messages that come from the Paul Reveres, not the prophets. There appear to be so many Paul Reveres riding about, issuing so many jeremiads and warnings, that the crucial warnings are being drowned out.

Isn't it interesting that at a time when we ought to know better about the limitations of what legislation can do to change human behavior, that some women prefer legal power to righteous influence? Some may choose to ignore or to rechannel the maternal instinct, but they cannot rise above it. Isn't it interesting that the secular world now directs our attention (with certain justifications to be sure) to the unmet needs of women, when the most common tragedy in the modern home is the malfunctioning father who so often leaves his post untended and who is so often insensitive to the needs of his wife? Isn't it interesting with regard to the matter of individual fulfillment, a natural and basic human need, that some fail to observe that one of the great advantages of being fulfilled is that one does not have to spend all of his or her time thinking about being fulfilled? Those I know and admire, who have deep and abiding testimonies, do show differences in certain preferences and in some dimension of their lifestyles, but on things that really matter, they are incredibly alike!

Isn't it interesting that at a time when patriotism is called into question, that some fail to realize that one cannot really have a sense of country without a sense of kinship, that one cannot have a sense of kinship without family, and one cannot have a sense of family without parents?

Isn't it interesting that in a time when we want to demand increasing accountability from each other that so many fail to realize that no deep-seated sense of accountability can exist without reference to absolute values and truths, such as the brotherhood of man?

Isn't it, of course, simply that the gospel of Jesus Christ contains all the correct principles for human conduct, but it is also the way in which these principles are interwoven with each other. Secularism so often seizes upon a single true principle and elevates it above all others. This act of isolation does not make the principle seized upon any less true, but to isolate any principle is to make it monastic. How many today live within the prison of just one principle? Elevating any correct principle to the plane of a religion is poor policy; just as one person makes a poor church, one principle makes a poor religion. Principles can become "prodigal" as well as people and can be estranged in "a far country" and be "spent" with little to show.

Most every secular cause about which I know anything at all usually focuses on a single principle or concern, but it is an act of isolation, not of correlation. It is the orthodox orchestration of the many principles found in the gospel of Jesus Christ that is necessary for human happiness. One would be amused at the so-called new "moral geometry" with its alien angles, fluid lines, and restless unfixed points, if the human consequences were not so tragic.

Insofar as he has it, where does man suppose he gets his inborn sense of righteous indignation anyway? And if our sense of righteous indignation does not rest on some divine moral absolutes, why should anyone pay any attention to us? When he sees the imperfections all around him, the disciple of Jesus sees such imperfections as an invitation to help. But for those who see life, man, and the universe (without looking through the lens of the gospel), imperfection means rejection. When we hate ourselves, the defects of others loom especially large. Where better can we learn how to forgive, how to love, and how to cope with our failures than at home? Strategically speaking, the choices are clear: family or anomie!

Isn't it ironical that those who have been described as the "new impuritans" in their iconoclasmania not only reject the existence of God but also the existence of Satan himself, and, in their celebration of sensual things, they end up in the employ of the very adversary whose existence they scoff at? The great trap is sprung because Satan's most powerful desire is that "all men might be miserable like unto himself." However few we may be, we must hold up to the world the true picture of mankind, "things as they really are" and "as they really are to come."

We can best learn that we are children of God by experiencing that kind of relationship and teaching in the home; we can best learn in the home that we are important, that we matter, and that there are at least some others who love us.

Those who have not known love are more likely to have a special struggle accepting the existence of a God whose greatest attribute is his love and all of whose laws hang on the first two commandments with their high requirement of love. Those who have not known forgiveness are more apt to have difficulty forgiving others. Those who have never had to be accountable will have greater difficulty learning to be accountable themselves and are apt to be more shrill in the demand about the accountability of others. Those who have not been trusted will find it more difficult to trust others. Those who have not known peace, both in their homes and in their souls, will find it more difficult to fashion a world in which there is peace, because conflict will seem so normal. Those who do not know specifically what the conditions of righteousness are as described by God will find it more difficult to become righteously indignant at the human conditions that do cry out for change. Those who have not known the rigors of repentance in family life are less apt to be able to cope with the stress of change.

Several years ago, an astute friend of mine, Dr. Jack Adamson, concluded a commencement address by recalling John Milton's phrase concerning England's legendary image about how St. Michael, the warrior, would appear off Cornwall to save England from her external menaces, chiefly Spain. Milton's counsel was that the angel, and England, had for too long been looking seaward, for England was soon to be engulfed in a civil war. Milton's poetic plea was: "Look homeward, angel, now and with pity and compassion." That counsel is appropriate for Americans, and others, today in yet another sense— for too long we have looked outside ourselves, and beyond our homes, in trying to improve the human conditions. But the message of poets, as well as prophets, is "Look homeward, now!" That we may do so I pray in the name of Jesus Christ. Amen.

# *But for a Small Moment*

### Neal A. Maxwell

I am delighted to be with you tonight, my brothers and sisters, to partake of the spirit that is here and of that marvelous music. I wish you knew how much as a generation you inspire those of us who have the privilege of working with you. I want you to know that I regard you highly—collectively and all here whom I know individually—and have great expectations for you. The highest compliment I can pay to you is that God has placed you here and now at this time to serve in his kingdom; so much is about to happen in which you will be involved and concerning which you will have some great influence.

It is because you will face some remarkable challenges in your time; it is because the Church has ceased to be in the eyes of men a mere cultural oddity in the Mountain West and is now, therefore, a global church—a light which can no longer be hid; it is because you have a rendezvous with destiny that will involve some soul stretching and some pain that I have chosen to speak to you tonight about the implications of two things we accept sometimes quite casually. These realities are that God loves us and, loving us, has placed us here to

---

*This fireside address was given at Brigham Young University on 1 September 1974.*

cope with challenges which he will place before us. I'm not sure we can always understand the implications of his love, because his love will call us at times to do things we may wonder about, and we may be confronted with circumstances we would rather not face. I believe with all my heart that because God loves us there are some particularized challenges that he will deliver to each of us. He will customize the curriculum for each of us in order to teach us the things we most need to know. He will set before us in life what we need, not always what we like. And this will require us to accept with all our hearts—particularly your generation—the truth that there is divine design in each of our lives and that you have rendezvous to keep, individually and collectively.

God knows even now what the future holds for each of us. In one of his revelations these startling words appear, as with so many revelations that are too big, I suppose, for us to manage fully: "In the presence of God, . . . all things . . . are manifest, past, present, and future, and are continually before the Lord" (D&C 130:7). The future "you" is before him now. He knows what it is he wishes to bring to pass in your life. He knows the kind of remodeling in your life and in mine that he wishes to achieve. Now, this will require us to believe in that divine design and at times to accept the truth which came to Joseph Smith wherein he was reminded that his suffering would be "but a small moment" (D&C 121:7). I'd like to talk to you about some of those small moments that will come your way in life and that come to each of us.

Let me begin by reminding you that we so blithely say in the Church that life is a school, a testing ground. It is true, even though it is trite. What we don't accept are the implications of that true teaching—at least as fully as we should. One of the implications is that the tests that we face are real. They are not going to be things we can do with one hand tied behind our backs. They are real enough that if we meet them we shall know that we have felt them, because we will feel them deeply and keenly and pervasively.

## THE LESSONS OF THE ATONEMENT

Christ on the cross gave out the cry "My God, my God, why hast thou forsaken me?" That cry on the cross is an indication that the very best of our Father's children found the trials so real, the tests so exquisite and so severe, that he cried out—not in doubt of his Father's reality, but wondering "why" at that moment of agony—for Jesus felt so alone. James Talmage advises us that in ways you and I cannot understand, God somehow withdrew his immediate presence from the Son so that Jesus Christ's triumph might be truly complete.

From Gethsemane and Calvary there are many lessons we need to apply to our own lives. We, too, at times may wonder if we have been forgotten and forsaken. Hopefully, we will do as the Master did and acknowledge that God is still there and never doubt that sublime reality—even though we may wonder and might desire to avoid some of life's experiences. We may at times, if we are not careful, try to pray away pain or what seems like an impending tragedy, but which is, in reality, an opportunity. We must do as Jesus did in that respect—also preface our prayers by saying, "If it be possible," let the trial pass from us—by saying, "Nevertheless, not as I will, but as thou wilt," and bowing in a sense of serenity to our Father in heaven's wisdom, because at times God will not be able to let us pass by a trial or a challenge. If we were allowed to bypass certain trials, everything that had gone on up to that moment in our lives would be wiped out. It is because he loves us that at times he will not intercede as we may wish him to. That, too, we learn from Gethsemane and from Calvary.

It is interesting to me, brothers and sisters, to note that among the qualities of a saint is the capacity to develop patience and to cope with the things that life inflicts upon us. That capacity brings together two prime attributes—patience and endurance. These are qualities, in the process of giving service to mankind that most people reject or undervalue. Most people would gladly serve mankind if somehow they could get it over with once, preferably with applause and recognition. But, for the sake of righteousness, to endure, to be patient in the midst of affliction, in the midst of being misunderstood, and in the midst of suffering—that is sainthood!

I am struck quite forcibly by the idea that no man has yet become President of the church of him who suffered so much who has not himself undergone some special challenges previous to that moment. The challenges vary from President to President, but the ways in which these men have coped with these challenges are strikingly similar.

If we use Jesus as a model in the midst of the suffering about which we're speaking, then it is also noteworthy that even in the midst of his exquisite agony he managed to have compassion for those nearby who were then suffering much, though much less than he—those on the adjoining crosses or about him below the cross. How marvelous it is when we see people who are not so swallowed up in their own suffering that they cannot still manage sympathy, even empathy, for those who suffer far, far less. How many of us here may have undergone the embarrassment of being comforted by those who had more reason to be comforted than we? Yet we recognize in that act of theirs a saintliness to which we would so gladly aspire.

If we at times wonder if our own agendum for life deliver to us challenges that seem unique, it would be worth our remembering that, when we feel rejected, we are members of the church of him who was most rejected by his very own with no cause for rejection. If at times we feel manipulated, we are disciples of him whom the establishment of his day sought to manipulate. If we at times feel unappreciated, we are worshipers of him who gave to us the Atonement—that marvelous, selfless act, the central act of all human history—unappreciated, at least fully, even among those who gathered about his feet while the very process of the Atonement was underway. If we sometimes feel misunderstood by those about us, even those we minister to, so did he, much more deeply and pervasively than we. And if we love and there is no reciprocity for our love, we worship him who taught us and showed us love that is unconditional, for we must love even when there is no reciprocity.

Most of our suffering, brothers and sisters, actually comes because of our sins and not because of our nobility. Isn't it marvelous that Jesus Christ, who did not have to endure that kind of suffering because he was sin-free, nevertheless took upon himself the sins of all of us and experienced an agony so exquisite we cannot comprehend it? I don't know how many people have lived on the earth for sure, but demographers say between 30 and 67 billion. If you were to collect the agony for your own sins and I for mine, and multiply it by that number, we can only shudder at what the sensitive, divine soul of Jesus must have experienced in taking upon himself the awful arithmetic of the sins of all of us—an act which he did selflessly and voluntarily. If it is also true (in some way we don't understand) that the cavity which suffering carves into our souls will one day also be the receptacle of joy, how infinitely greater Jesus' capacity for joy, when he said, after his resurrection, "Behold, my joy is full." How very, very full, indeed, his joy must have been!

I should like, therefore, to speak to you on the premise that it is a part of discipleship for us to be prepared for the kind of rigors that Jesus always leveled his disciples. He said, "My people must be tried in all things, that they may be prepared to receive the glory that I have for them, even the glory of Zion; and he that will not bear chastisement is not worthy of my kingdom" (D&C 136:31). That is hard doctrine. Peter made it even more rigorous. Peter didn't want us to take any credit upon ourselves for the suffering we endure because of our own mistakes. He was willing to see us take credit for the suffering we endure because of discipleship, but not because of our own stupidity or our own sin (1 Peter 2:20). Then Moroni reminded us, "For ye receive no witness until after the trial of your faith" (Ether 12:6). That's the rigorous path of discipleship, brothers and sisters, about which I wish to speak at least in this one dimension tonight, giving you some examples, if I may.

If God chooses to teach us the things we most need to learn because he loves us, and if he seeks to tame our souls and gentle us in the way we most need to be tamed and most need to be gentled, it follows that he will customize the challenges he gives us and individualize them so that we will be prepared for life in a better world by his refusal to take us out of this world, even though we are not of it. In the eternal ecology of things we must pray, therefore, not that things be taken from us, but that God's will be accomplished through us. What, therefore, may seem now to be mere unconnected pieces of tile will someday, when we look back, take form and pattern, and we will realize that God was making a mosaic. For there is in each of our lives this kind of divine design, this pattern, this purpose that is in the process of becoming, which is continually before the Lord but which for us, looking forward, is sometimes perplexing.

### TRAPS IMPEDING THE ABILITY TO MEET CHALLENGES

I should like to suggest some traps into which we can fall, if we are not careful, as we try to meet the challenges that life delivers at our doorsteps. The *first* temptation that we must resist, brothers and sisters, is the Jonah response, in which we sometimes think we can escape the calls that come to us, that we can somehow run away from the realities that will press in upon us. Jonah, you recall, had been called to go to Nineveh. He didn't want to go to that urban center that was so big. We are told it took the people hours to walk across that city. He tried to find a ship going to Tarshish. He "paid the fare thereof," hoping to leave the presence of the Lord. You and I will one day know, if we do not know now, there is no way we can escape from God's love, because it is infinite. However many times in our lives we might rather go to a Tarshish than a Nineveh, he will insist that we go to Nineveh, and we must pay "the fare thereof."

Recently a young man was called to his Nineveh. The president of the Salt Lake mission home, President Rawson, told Sister Maxwell and me that not too long ago a young man came in on a Saturday to the Salt Lake mission home and said, "President, may I see you?"

The president said, "Surely, son, come into my office."

He came in and said, "I need a blessing."

"Why do you need a blessing?"

"I need a blessing because I am the only member of my family who is a member of the Church. Yesterday, when I went to leave home, one parent told me never to come back again, the other wouldn't speak to me, and the only person who said goodbye was my little brother, who came to the front gate to say goodbye to me. I'm on my way overseas and I need a blessing."

Now, brothers and sisters, that is the kind of devotion we must have in preparation for the Ninevehs of life to which we are called. However rigorous the circumstances are, we must, as this young man did, be willing to go, to trust and to surrender ourselves to our Father in heaven, who knows why in his divine plans it must be so.

A *second* trap into which we can fall is the naïveté that grows out of our not realizing that the adversary will press particularly in the areas of our vulnerabilities. It ought not to surprise us that this will be so. The things that we would most like to avoid, therefore, will often be the things that confront us most directly and most sharply. Some of you may recall that the British military planners who built the fortress of Singapore, which was supposed to be invincible, fixed the guns of Singapore so that they would fire only seaward. The Japanese very cleverly came from behind on land. Churchill and others were stunned that this citadel and fortress had fallen so quietly and so simply. Some of us have guns that fire only in one direction. We are vulnerable, and our vulnerabilities will be probed by the vicissitudes of life. One of the great advantages of life in the Church (in which the gospel is at the center) is that we can overcome these vulnerabilities; otherwise, we shall be taken by surprise and swiftly.

A *third* trap into which we can fall, if we are not careful, is to fail to notice that at the center of many of our challenges is pride, is ego. In most emotional escalations with which I am familiar, if one goes to the very center of them, there is ego asserting itself relentlessly. The only cure for rampant ego is humility, and this is why circumstances often bring to us a kind of compelled or forced humility—so that we may recover our equilibrium. Humility can help us to dampen our pride. Ironically, for those of us who most need to serve to develop our capacity to love, our very egos often make us unapproachable so far as others are concerned. We, therefore, are underused and we wonder why. And this is typical of the trials that we impose upon ourselves.

A *fourth* trap into which we can fall is that we may at times assume that the plan of salvation requires merely that we endure and survive when, in fact, as is always the case with the gospel of Jesus Christ, it is required of us, not only that we endure, but also that we endure *well*, that we exhibit "grace under pressure." This is necessary, not only so that our own passage through the trial can be a growth experience, but also because (more than we know) there are always people watching to see if we can cope, who therefore may resolve to venture forth and to cope themselves. Every time we navigate safely on the strait and narrow way, there are other ships that are lost which can find their way because of our steady light.

A *fifth* trap, and a major one, is the trap of self-pity. One man has said that "hell is being frozen in self-pity." Indeed, at times when we think our lot is hard or when we feel our selves misunderstood, it will be so easy for us to indulge ourselves in feeling some self-pity. A contrasting episode comes to us out of ancient Greece: Several hundred Spartans were holding the pass at Thermopylae, that narrow pass, and the Persians came in overwhelming numbers and urged the Spartans to surrender. Hoping to intimidate them further, the Persians sent emissaries to the Spartans, saying they had so many archers in their army they could darken the sky with their arrows. The Spartans said, "So much the better. We shall fight in the shade."

Now, brothers and sisters, the disciple has to be ready to fight in the shade of circumstance. One of the ways we can have perspective that will permit us to fight in the shade of circumstances is to read the scriptures and have involvement—intellectually and spiritually—with the case studies in the scriptures of those men and women who have coped, and coped successfully, who have undergone far more than you and I are asked to undergo. When we understand these models, we may then understand that God is totally serious about his purpose "to bring to pass the immortality and eternal life of man," that his chief concerns are not real estate and political dominion, but the growth of souls, the celestializing of the souls with whom he works.

I am one of those, for instance, who does not believe the Mormon colonies in Mexico and Canada had much to do in the Lord's eyes with real estate or physical empire, but I feel rather that these colonies were established for the preparation of a people. I call your attention to the fact that two members of the First Presidency and the wife of President Kimball have come out of those colonies in Mexico and Canada—individuals prepared beforehand for the mighty roles they now carry on in the kingdom. I don't think God's too interested in real estate. He owns it all anyway. He does seem to be incredibly interested in what happens to us individually and will place us in those circumstances where we have the most opportune chances to grow and to carry out our purposes.

A *sixth* trap into which we can fall quite easily, brothers and sisters, is the trap in which we sense that something special is happening in our lives but are not able to sort it out with sufficient precision and clarity that we can articulate it to someone else. That is so often true of the gospel. Its truths are too powerful for us to manage on occasion. Let me give you this simple illustration of how we can know something and yet not be able to communicate it fully without the help of the Spirit. If I were to bring one of you into this hall and if, instead of all of you, it were filled with fifteen thousand mothers and if I were to say to you, "Somewhere in that audience is your mother; find her," you could do it, and I suspect it wouldn't take you very many minutes. But if I said to you, "Wait outside. There are fifteen thousand mothers in there and one of them is your mother. Now, you describe her to me with sufficient precision and clarity so that I can go find her," you couldn't do it. You would still know what she looked like, but tongue could not transmit what you knew. It is that way often with the gospel. That is why we are so in need of the Spirit–so that knowledge can arc like electricity from point to point, aided and impelled by the Spirit—aid without which we are simply not articulate enough to speak of all the things which we know.

It would be interesting, for instance, if I were to ask one of you to describe to the satisfaction of all here the color yellow. Yellow, of course, is a primary color, but it would be difficult for you to describe it to us without comparing it with other colors. Yet you have no difficulty recognizing yellow when you see it. We know more than we can tell! Sometimes the things we know take the form of knowledge about what is happening to us in life in which we sense purpose, in which we sense divine design, but which we cannot speak about with full articulateness. There are simply moments of mute comprehension and of mute certitude. We need to pay attention when these moments come to us, because God often gives us the assurances we need but not necessarily the capacity to transmit these assurances to anyone else.

I would like to share with you at this moment a highly personal experience. I will not mention the name of the man involved. I mention the experience only because of one of my own tendencies (those on the stand and elsewhere who know me know that I am often too verbal and silence does not come easily to me). Fortunately, on this occasion there was a kind of mute comprehension on my part that the most important thing I could do was to be still.

A few days after April conference, a very bright, able professional man called my secretary for an appointment. Fortunately she gave it to him, and fortunately it was of sufficient duration that there was time for the chemistry of this experience to operate. He came in and we greeted each other. I, frankly, was not sure of the purpose of his visit. I assumed it might even be that he had come to complain about something. There are portions of our time as General Authorities that are given over to being ombudsmen. But I said little and sat down. I resisted the temptation to fill the silence that then ensued. Tears welled up, filling his eyes. It seemed to me we must have sat there for ten minutes, but I am sure it was only three or four. I kept still, resisting the natural temptation to rush in with supporting words, and simply let the Spirit operate. Then out it came—a marvelous, manly confession, in which he said for him to become active in the kingdom again it was necessary that he set certain things right. Over the years he felt he had been unfair to me and unkind to me, and he wanted to come and to ask for forgiveness. I again largely resisted the temptation, which by then was strong, to rush in with some quick reassurances that might put him at ease. As thoughts tumbled on thoughts and verbalizations on verbalizations, this sweet man cleansed his soul. Indeed, I had *not* felt injured by him. I was not aware of his concerns, but it would have been folly for me to have so said before there was full closure in the matter at hand.

He is a marvelous, sweet man. I admire his courage. He said even that morning he had wondered if he could come, or if he shouldn't cancel his appointment. I love him. We embraced and have stayed in close contact since. He is able and is making marvelous progress in the kingdom. I'll always be grateful for that sensing of mute comprehension that something special was about to happen which I couldn't describe but in which my role for that occasion was mostly to be still and to listen. There are times when life will visit us with challenges in which we will have a mute comprehension of what is underway but cannot transmit it fully to someone else.

A *seventh* trap, brothers and sisters, is that some of us neglect to develop multiple forces of satisfaction. When one of the wells upon which we draw dries up through death, loss or status, disaffection, or physical ailment, we then find ourselves very thirsty because, instead of having multiple sources of satisfaction in our lives, we have become too dependent upon this or upon that. How important it is to the symmetry of our souls that we interact with all the gospel principles and with all the Church programs, so that we do not become so highly specialized that, if we are deprived of one source of satisfaction, indeed we are in difficulty. It is possible to be incarcerated within the prison of one principle. We are less vulnerable if our involvements with the kingdom are across the board. We are less vulnerable if we care deeply about many principles—not simply a few.

An *eighth* trap to be avoided, brothers and sisters, is the tendency we have—rather humanly, rather understandably—to get ourselves caught in peering through the prism of the present and then distorting our perspective about things. Time is of this world; it is not of eternity. We can, if we are not careful, feel the pressures of time and see things in a distorted way. How important it is that we see things as much as possible through the lens of the gospel with its eternal perspectives.

I should like, if I may, to share with you on this point the fine writing of your own A. Lester Allen, a dean and scientist on this campus. This is what I have come to call the "Allen Analogy" about time. Let me read you these lines, if I may. Their application will be obvious. Dean Allen writes:

> *Suppose, for instance, that we imagine a "being" moving onto our earth whose entire life-span is only 1/100 of a second. Ten thousand "years" for him, generation after generation, would be only one second of our time. Suppose this imaginary being comes up to a quiet pond in the forest where you are seated. You have just tossed in a rock and are watching the ripples. A leaf is fluttering from the sky and a bird is swooping over the water. He would find everything absolutely motionless. Looking at you, he would say: "In all recorded history nothing has changed. My father and his father before him have seen that everything is absolutely still. This creature called man has never had a heartbeat and has never breathed. The water is standing in stationary waves as if someone had thrown a rock into it; it seems frozen. A leaf is suspended in the air, and a bird has stopped right over the middle of the pond. There is no movement. Gravity is suspended." The concept of time in this imaginary being, so different from ours, would give him an entirely different perspective of what we call reality.*
>
> *On the other hand, picture another imaginary creature for whom one "second" of his time is 10,000 years of our time. What would the pond be like to him? By the time he sat down beside it, taking 15,000 of our years to do so, the pond would have vanished. Individual human beings would be invisible, since our entire life-span would be only 1/100 of one of his "seconds." The surface of the earth would be undulating as mountains are built up and worn down. The forest would persist but a few minutes and then disappear. His concept of "reality" would be much different than our own.*

That's the most clever way I have seen time and intimations of eternity dealt with. *It is very important that we not assume the perspective of mortality in making the decisions that bear on eternity!* We need the perspectives of the gospel to make decisions in the context of eternity. We need to understand we cannot do the Lord's work in the world's way.

## THE CHURCH'S BASIS IN CHRIST

Now, brothers and sisters, may I prepare to close with these thoughts: The Church is fully *Christ-centered*. The Church is also *Christ-powered*, and it is also designed to help its members become more *Christlike*. Since the gospel of Jesus Christ focuses on the truths that deal with everlasting things and not on obsolescent realities, it is very important for us, brothers and sisters, to recognize that the truths in which we traffic as members of the kingdom pertain to eternity as well as to this life.

I am surprised (I would be amused if the cost were not so great) that people think they can remove the foundations of our social structure—things like work, chastity, and family and then wonder why other things crumble. You can't remove the foundation of a building while standing inside and not be hit with falling plaster. We are now in the interesting position in the kingdom of trying to warn about what is happening in the world and, at the same time, of keeping ourselves personally secure. We must be Christ-centered individually. We must have his and God's power to do our work, and we must take seriously the challenge of becoming more Christlike. You're soon going to go out into a world full of marshmallow men. Like the act of putting a finger into a marshmallow, there is no core in these men, there is no center, and when one removes his finger, the marshmallow resumes its former shape. We are in a world of people who want to yield to everything—to every fad and to every fashion. It is incredibly important that we be committed to the core—committed to those things that matter, about which our Father in heaven has leveled with us through his Son, Jesus Christ, and his prophets.

I saw an interesting cartoon not too long ago that bears on this point of marshmallow men. It showed two multicolored desert lizards conversing. One said to the other, "Of course you're going through an identity crisis. You're a chameleon."

Of course the world is going through an identity crisis. Of course it's adrift: it's got no anchor. It does not have core principles upon which to decide all other things. I am grateful that our beliefs are related to the principles of the gospel of Jesus Christ. I am grateful that God has told us that we must be ready for the trials that life will bring our way.

I speak to this generation with some sense of vicarious anticipation in your behalf of what lies ahead—urging you to pour out your hearts in supplication and prayer. There is nothing more powerful than prayer, nothing more masculine or more feminine (at the same time) than prayer. There was more power processed and expended on that single night in Gethsemane, in that small garden, than all the armies and navies have ever expended in all the battles on the land and sea and in the air in all of human history. The catalyst of prayer helped Jesus to cope with suffering, and by his suffering he emancipated all men from death and made possible eternal life. This cardinal fact about the central act of human history, the Atonement, ought to give us pause, therefore, as we face our challenges individually.

I believe it was George Macdonald who reminded us that the only door out of the dungeon of self is the love of one's neighbor. How proud we ought to be, in a quiet way, that we are members of the church of the most selfless being who ever lived. How proud we ought to be to belong to a church that makes specific demands of us and gives us specific things to do and marks the strait and narrow way, lest we fall off one side of the precipice or the other. I am so grateful that God loves us enough to teach us specifically. Had secularists written the Ten Commandments, they might have said, "Thou shalt not be a bad person." Note what the Ten Commandments say: "Thou shalt not steal, thou shalt not covet, thou shalt not take the name of the Lord thy God in vain, thou shalt not commit adultery," and so on. The gospel of Jesus Christ is specific because God cares specifically for each of us and, caring for us, will mark the way carefully lest we fall out of happiness.

A vague creed is fitted only for a vague God. We have a Father who loves us specifically and gives us things to do and, because he loves us, will cause us, at times, to have our souls stretched and to be fitted for a better world by coping with life in this world.

May God bless us with that kind of commitment, with the capacity to be serious disciples and to accept both the agendum that he has prepared for each of us because he loves us and the curriculum, prepared for each of us, which he has customized to teach us the things we most need to know, because he loves us.

There is a man I hope someday to meet—a brother of yours and mine in the kingdom. He lives somewhere behind the Iron Curtain. Another man, a priesthood leader behind the Iron Curtain, was told that there was such a man, who had not seen another member of the Church for many years. This good brother, moved by the Spirit, saved his money (which he didn't have much of), made his way through the red tape of crossing borders, and found this brother of yours and mine; he learned that he who was found had not seen another member of the Church for over twenty years. And when the man who was the finder indicated that it was possible, because he had been so authorized, to give this brother a patriarchal blessing, this good brother demurred momentarily until he got the tithing which he had saved for over twenty years and gave it to this other man so that he would be fully worthy of that blessing!

I don't know what the divine design is in the challenge of that kind of solitude. I know that this man, our brother, is meeting that challenge. Some of us will have to be most courageous, not when we're alone, but when we're in a crowd. Whatever the form the test takes, we must be willing to pass it. We must reach breaking points without breaking. We must be willing, if necessary, to give up our lives—not because we have a disdain for life as some do, but even though we love life—because we are the servants of him who did that in such an infinite way for all of us.

I testify to you in the solemnity of my soul that we are prophet-led, that this is the church of Jesus Christ, presided over by a prophet who himself knows a great deal about suffering. We are all the servants of him who suffered most that we might have with him a fullness of joy. May we be committed to that task this day and always I pray in the name of him whose church this is, even Jesus Christ. Amen.

# Taking up the Cross

―――◆―――

Neal A. Maxwell

I have been delighted, brothers and sisters, as you no doubt have been, with the quality of the music tonight. I always anticipate that portion of the program when I come. I appreciate the hospitality of your stake presidents—the able high priests who preside over the twelve stakes here—with whom we have just had a few brief, informal moments in a reception. I am grateful for these men and for the outstanding women who are ever at their sides. I appreciate, too, every chance I have to be with my colleagues, Dallin Oaks and Bob Thomas, and others who are here representing the faculty and administration. Most of all, my young brothers and sisters, I appreciate the privilege of being with you.

I need to alert you to two possible problems in the course of what I say tonight. First, I write very illegibly, and I have been trying to finish this speech in airports and elsewhere this weekend. My style of writing presently was once characterized by President Lee as unreformed Egyptian. More recently, I passed President Kimball a note on the stand at sacrament meeting to tell him that our school in

*This fireside address was given at Brigham Young University on 4 January 1976.*

Tonga had "burned" down. In his own sweet, courteous way, reluctant to embarrass me, and having studied my inscrutable inscribings as long as he could, he sent back a note and said, "Did you mean 'buried' or 'burned'?" Second, I have deliberately tried to leave myself open to the Spirit, in particular as I reach that point of closing my remarks tonight.

### THE ROLE OF WOMEN IN THE CHURCH

I appreciate, more than I can say, this opportunity to be with you as you begin the Winter Semester. I am grateful that my wife, son, daughters, and son-in-law are here also. Since my wife and daughters are here, that creates a moment when, before proceeding to my text, I wish to observe that the role of women in the Church has never been more important than it is now, because never has the Church been so directly important and influential to so many as it is now. While the Church will always be priesthood-led and priesthood-centered, we must not make the mistake of drawing wrong conclusions from that reality. I hope the young women of the Church will do all they can to develop their God-given talents and to stretch themselves intellectually and spiritually during their youth and young adult years, for the learning process is scaffolding for the soul.

We desire our women to be unarguably superb individuals, wives, and mothers, and they can contribute so much to this outcome by making the most of their educational opportunities, both now and by having a posture of lifetime learning. A short time ago, during one of the few times at our own ward sacrament meeting, our bishop called attention to a brochure describing a local Church Education program which he then placed at the side of the pulpit. Significantly, after the benediction, the first person to get a brochure was Sister Camilla Kimball, the wife of the prophet, who has rightly been called "Lady of Constant Learning." She continues to be involved spiritually; she has been a Relief Society spiritual living teacher for more than twenty years—until recently she continued to be involved. Educationally she has taken classes of one kind or another every year since she has been married, except for the last two years when traveling has precluded this kind of participation. She was the first pace-setting child of that family of eighteen high-achieving children in her father's and mother's family.

I remember a BYU movie a few years ago in which there was a line something like this: "Some men never recover from the ignorance of their mothers." Conversely, one cannot fully appreciate the Prophet Joseph Smith without noting the remarkable qualities of his outstanding mother, Lucy Mack Smith. We give to our children what we are. The more a mother brings to a nest, the more nutritive the nest.

It is very important that we genuinely encourage the full development of women in the Church, so that they can carry out their unique roles effectively and articulately—in the nursery and neighborhood, and in the classroom as well as in cookery.

Brethren, marry a woman who is your better in some respects; and, sisters, do likewise, so that your eternal partnership is one of compensating competencies. This is certainly the case in my own marriage, so far as certain attributes are concerned. I am gladdened—not threatened—by my wife's superior qualities. I am grateful for her traits and qualities that excel my own in some critical dimensions of our partnership.

I hope that our young sisters will not only acquire the vital skills of homemaking, therefore, but also that they will not neglect their natural talents in literature or language and in science, just as I hope our young men will study the facts of fatherhood, as well as physics or fine arts, and put their hands to that plow without looking back. Education involves the preparing of the person, and that is usually what matters—more than the particular calisthenics that are used.

Remember, we take our knowledge, skills, and attributes with us not only into marriage—but also into eternity. Knowledge rises with us in the resurrection, and the limitations on our luggage then will not be limitations of volume but of kind.

Finally, I have never sung Eliza R. Snow's lyrics of 1845 in the anthem of appreciation "O My Father" without being touched by its reverence for womanhood, which is light years ahead of some current attempts to dignify womanhood. The inspired truths for those lyrics came through the Prophet Joseph Smith, but the inspired poetry was Eliza's, as President Joseph F. Smith once observed.

Sisters, if there are some prophetic sayings you do not fully understand, do what a magnificent Mary did—keep those sayings in your heart and ponder them. Meanwhile, push out your own borders, just as the borders of the kingdom are being pushed out. Let LDS women show the real way to womanhood, preening not for the praise of the world or pressing for passing political preeminence. Male or female, we must not fail to see the simple truths because we are forever "looking beyond the mark."

### THE CHALLENGES OF MORTALITY

The bulk of what I wish to say tonight focuses on the need, individually and collectively, to summon all our skills and our strengths to life and then to carry the challenging cross each of us has been called to shoulder.

The specific strategic statements of divine intent about mortality are rare and profound. We know that the work of God is to "bring to pass the immortality and eternal life of man" (Moses 1:39). We also know that God places a premium on our having righteous experience, for "all these things shall give thee experience, and shall be for thy good" (D&C 122:7). *These are most fundamental perceptions about life!* Without a correct understanding of these realities by great men and women, there could not have been the faith, trust, and courage needed at Gethsemane and Golgotha, or a battered but prevailing Job, or a willing Prophet Joseph Smith who went to Carthage "like a lamb."

Correct conduct under stress is more likely when one has correct expectations about life.

To err by having naive expectations concerning the purposes of life is to err everlastingly. Life is neither a pleasure palace through whose narrow portals we pass briefly, laughingly, and heedlessly before extinction, nor is life a cruel predicament in an immense and sad wasteland. It is the middle (but briefest) estate of the three estates in man's carefully constructed continuum of experience.

One day we will understand fully how complete our commitment was in our first estate in accepting the very conditions of challenge in our second estate about which we sometimes complain in this school of stress. Our collective and personal premortal promises will then be laid clearly before us.

Further, when we are finally judged in terms of our performance in this second estate, we will see that God, indeed, is perfect in his justice and mercy. We will also see that when we fail here it will not have been because we were truly tempted above that which we were able to bear. There was always an escape hatch had we looked for it! We will also see that our lives have been fully and fairly measured. In retrospect, we will even see that our most trying years here will often have been our best years, producing large tree rings on our soul, Gethsemanes of growth! Mortality is moistened by much opportunity if our roots of resolve can but take it in.

Just as no two snowflakes are precisely alike in design, so the configuration of life's challenges differs also. Some of our experiences are not fully shareable with others. Thus, others, try as they may, cannot fully appreciate them. They must trust us, our generalizations and testimonies concerning these experiences. A few of our experiences should not even be shared. But it is useful to ponder the past examples of our partners on the pathway.

In the midst of some of these individualized challenges, however, we may cry out on our small scale as the Savior did on the cross, or as the Prophet did in Liberty Jail. Being in agony, we will pray more earnestly, for cries of agony are not the same as cries of despair.

Our individual experiences may not always be unique, but they are always authentic. God will even take into account our perceptions of, as well as our responses to, our trials. For those of us who do not, for instance, find claustrophobia a challenge, it is difficult to measure the terror that comes to those for whom it is such a challenge. Thus, a friend may seem to struggle unnecessarily long before finally prevailing with regard to a particular principle of the gospel. But for that individual, the struggle was real enough! We need, particularly, to understand with kindness those who are asked to go out to do battle again on a familiar field—on the very battleground where they have already suffered defeat several times. Yet some of our most difficult victories will occur on new terrain—like Joseph's in Egypt—when we do not have the equivalent of a "home court" advantage.

We must remember that, while the Lord reminded the Prophet Joseph Smith that he had not yet suffered as Job, *only the Lord can compare crosses!*

## IMMORTAL MOMENTS IN THE SCRIPTURES

As I review some "case studies," I will leave it to you to make the relevant application to your own life, if there be such, from the examples to which I turn now. To begin with, there is always more drama about us than we can drink in. Mortal minds cannot fully measure the immortal moments we are about to consider. For instance, in terms of learning impact, there is simply no comparison between what you and I thought of when we last heard a rooster crow and what Peter thought that once when he heard the soul-piercing sound of a cock crowing—especially the third time! That sound, no doubt, sent a shudder of sorrow through Peter—but it was godly sorrow, the kind that causes a cleansing and sends us inward to scrub our soul. You and I have heard roosters crowing many times in our lives, but for him that moment was special.

When we see each other in the morning, our sleep has often not been the same, even though we usually each say the same "Good morning!" Uriah apparently slept very well when, as a loyal lieutenant of King David, he slept with the servants on the floor at King David's door. Uriah was loyal to both his men "in the open fields," to his king, and to his wife, Bathsheba. By contrast, one cannot help but wonder how well the conspiring and adulterous David slept that same night! The later lamentations of David indicate many sleepless nights following his sending the uncompromised Uriah to his death—in the "forefront of the hottest battle," where the "valiant men were" (see

2 Samuel 11:15–16). Uriah fell, but David plummeted from the privileged place portioned for him in the next world.

Thus, there are certain mortal moments and minutes that matter—certain hinge points in the history of each human. Some seconds are so decisive they shrink the soul, while other seconds are spent so as to stretch the soul.

Contemplate a tale of two kings: There was a brief moment when King Agrippa was genuinely stirred by Paul's preachment. Paul discerningly knew that Agrippa knew; he even asked Agrippa the ultimate question: "Believest thou?" But Agrippa would not own up to his intimations and spiritual stirrings, probably computing the cost were he to do more than smoothly say he "almost" believed (see Acts 26:27–28). In my opinion, Agrippa's comment was not just flippant feedback. He had received a measure of the witness of a special witness, and some part of that king knew that what he had been told was true.

By contrast, another king, Lamoni's father, heard Aaron's preachment and owned up to as much truth as he then understood. He was willing to acknowledge the spiritual stirrings within him. Trustingly, he said in reply to the interrogatory "Believest thou that there is a God?" "And if now thou sayest there is a God, behold I will believe" (Alma 22:7). What great words from a great moment! Time in such settings is measured not by clock seconds, but by soul seconds! Those individuals who are free enough to acknowledge the first feelings of faith are true to themselves—and are surely those whom the truth makes free.

Contemplate two walks up, and then down, the slopes of two adjacent mountains—Mount Moriah and the Mount of Olives. Up one mountain came Judas "with a great multitude" to kiss and to betray the Master. One wonders what the walk *down* the mountain that night was like for Judas and which was more searing—his lips on Jesus' face, or Jesus' words to him, "Betrayest thou the Son of Man with a kiss?" (Luke 22:48). Few scenes of pathos rank with that of a guilty Judas trying to give back the thirty pieces of silver and seeing how those who had used him fiendishly were devoid of mercy and empathy for him. Judas' soul-slide was not a sudden thing, and his subsequent suicide ranks as perhaps the most self-contemptuous in history.

In contrast, early in the morning—centuries before—an obedient Abraham walked up and then down nearby Mount Moriah with his son, Isaac: "They went both of them together." Abraham had been told, "Take now thy son, thine only son Isaac, whom thou lovest." We do not know what, if anything, the father and son conversed about on the way up Moriah, but ponder what marvelous moments when father and son walked down that mountain!

Significantly, Abraham did not see the substitute ram on Mount Moriah—until *after* the moment that mattered—when he obediently "stretched forth his hand, and took the knife" (Genesis 22:2–13). Sometimes the cross must be taken up decisively. There is no time for an agonizing appraisal.

Shadrach, Meshach, and Abednego did not know if God would spare them from the fiery furnace. They simply said:

> *If it be so, our God whom we serve is able to deliver us from the burning fiery furnace, and he will deliver us out of thine hand, O king.*
>
> *But if not, be it known unto thee, O king, that we will not serve thy gods, nor worship the golden image which thou hast set up.* [Daniel 3:17–18]

Note the words "but if not"—these are words of unconditional commitment.

Sometimes we must "take the heat" even if we are not certain the thermostat of trial will soon be turned down. *We must decide before anything else is really decided!*

When we have that kind of courage, neither will we walk alone in our own "fiery furnace," for as is recorded in Daniel, there was a fourth form in that fiery furnace with the valiant threesome, and the form was "like the Son of God." Peter gave us wise counsel when he said to the disciples, which each of us aspires to be, the following words: "Think it not strange concerning the fiery trial which is to try you, as though some strange thing happened to you" (1 Peter 4:12).

When we carry the cross we must expect to share, in some measure, in the sufferings of Christ. But he will be near us even in the "fiery furnace."

Sometimes the learning process is prolonged. It was only—to use a felicitous phrase describing Enoch's people, "in the process of time" (Moses 7:21)—that the reconciliation of Esau and Jacob occurred. How one warms to the later meeting of those two matured men and their immense caravans in the desert—years after the earlier struggle over status, when "Esau hated Jacob." How magnanimous are the words then of a secure Esau in declining Jacob's proffered gift. The scriptures say, after Jacob made his offering: "And Esau said, I have enough, my brother; keep that thou hast unto thyself" (Genesis 33:9).

Much time also ensued between the walk of Joseph's brothers back from the pit into which they had thrown Joseph and their later walk back (with much-needed corn) from Egypt to Canaan, when all the brothers who had treated him so terribly were saved by a generous Joseph. If we wonder today why, when individuals in groups become unprotesting participants in a veering toward evil, no one seems to speak up; and if we are perplexed that when some speak up it is only in a weak Reuben-type dissent (which makes "I told you we shouldn't have done that" a likely utterance),—if we wonder why those things happen, it is because individuals, in this case Joseph's brothers, failed. It is always the same, brothers and sisters. Our failures are individual. You and I, therefore, have an obligation to grasp those opportunities for truth saying and for restraining evil. If we do not, we will tumble, as Joseph's brothers did, collectively. Weak individuals make great dominoes!

Perhaps a young Joseph, of whom his brothers could not even speak peaceably, might even have given them some small cause for jealousy. But a matured, magnanimous, and highly spiritual Joseph (significantly and modestly) did not at first even reveal his identity to his poverty-stricken brothers. The tree rings on Joseph's soul must have been large, indeed, including the year when he was in the pit and was then sold into a strange culture in the beginning of a great adventure. Joseph was victorious "on the road."

The same basic substance, for instance, chemically two parts hydrogen and one part oxygen, left Pilate's hands very dirty when he washed them (he thought) of the affair concerning Jesus of Nazareth. He would not listen to feedback. But notice how water was used cleansingly by Naaman, the Syrian military commander who listened to feedback (and from less statusful servants) and as a result was willing to be washed in the Jordan River and was healed of his leprosy.

Thus, the scenery, the sounds, the substance are often similar—but the consequences are immensely different, depending on how we use our mortal micromoments. As George MacDonald warned: "The moment which coincides with the work to be done, is the moment to be minded; the next [moment] is nowhere till God has made it."

There are some decisions we make when we have a reasonable understanding of the consequences that will flow from such decisions. Jesus knew and Joseph Smith knew about their impending martyrdom.

There are other times when we are swept along by events and must simply trust the Lord. For instance, Paul may not have known that his judicial appeal to Caesar would finally take him to Rome and to precious points in between. But the Lord wanted him to go to Rome, and Paul was swept along on wants of divine design and making.

### DEVELOPMENT OF PERSONAL STRENGTH

There are still other times when we can see the consequences of our decisions, but we deliberately try to repress them because we do not want to face them. David's relationship with Bathsheba could have both started *and* stopped with his view from the terrace. But it did not, for David not only saw, but sent for Bathsheba.

What, then, are some of the skills and strengths other than those now noted which enable us to lift and then to carry the cross?

*First*, we must realize that the weight of the cross is great enough without our carrying burdens that we could jettison through the process of repentance. Paul gave us wise counsel in this regard when he said, "Let us lay aside every weight, and the sin which doth so easily beset us, and let us run with patience the race that is set before us" (Hebrews 12:1). It is so much more difficult for us to carry the cross when our back is already bent with the burdens of bad behavior.

*Second*, the cross is something we cannot shoulder and then stand still with. Of the Savior we read the following: "And he bearing his cross went forth" (John 19:17). The cross is easier to carry *if we keep moving*. Action and service, happily, require enough of our attention that the sagging of self-pity can be avoided.

*Third*, we must realize, finally, that we can only contemplate the cross just so long; rhetoric will not raise it. It must soon either be taken up or turned away from!

*Fourth*, no "natural" resource is more precious and to be used more wisely than time. These mortal moments matter more than we know. There are no idle hours; there are only idle people. In true righteousness there is serenity, but there is an array of reminders that the "sacred present" is packed with possibilities which are slipping by us, which are going away from us each moment.

I have chosen to speak on this topic tonight because of my immense, deep, and high regard for your generation of youth and young adults in the Church. More than you know, and no doubt more than the rest of us know, you have been fashioned for a time in which the Church will be asked to do things we have never done before or done so well. The time you have to prepare yourselves for what will come is shortening with each passing second and moment. I, for one, have such great confidence in you collectively that I find no difficulty at all in believing the utterances of the prophets in this dispensation who have told us (from the beginning of the dispensation) that some of the most choice and special spirits of our Father in heaven will have been reserved for the very last days. If one, therefore, takes that kind of pride in you and has that kind of perspective about you, perhaps he can be pardoned for speaking to you, as I have, about the challenge of lifting and carrying the cross.

Each of us comes to know his cross quite well. We know its con-figurations; we know its weight. We feel its rough edges. It would be so much easier for us to carry it if we could develop the faith which would permit us to cast our cares upon our Father in heaven, because he cares for us, as Peter reminds us. It would be so much easier to carry if we could do as Paul suggests and rid ourselves of the weights that we need not carry. We may think these are a part of carrying the cross when, in fact, they are a function of our own stupidity or our own sin. We can rid ourselves of these so that we may take up the cross and move swiftly and deliberately on to our journey.

## THE ROLE OF YOUTH IN THIS DISPENSATION

At the risk of some repetition for some here, as I close, I should like to suggest to you three different ways of feeling your place in the scheme of things, of sensing your place in this dispensation. Each of the examples I use comes out of an entirely different setting, but I share them with you because each contains an important reality of what lies ahead of you and, in fact, is now upon you, as a generation.

The first comes out of U.S. Marine history. On one of those rare occasions when the U.S. Marines had been driven back and were surrounded, the general commanding that particular unit, instead of sending off a despairing and discouraging communique to the commandant of the corps, sent this interesting message: "At last we have the enemy just where we want him. We are surrounded and we can fire in every direction!" I say to you, at last The Church of Jesus Christ of Latter-day Saints has the world just where we want it—we can serve in every direction! Not only these young men and women present who are now in the Language Training Mission, but each of us. There is always more to be done than we have time to do it in. Rejoice, for though we may seem to be encircled, in fact we are not.

For my second analogy I turn to the prophet Elisha and that episode when a young man (I expect about the age of the young men and women here tonight) awoke one morning and saw that Israel was surrounded by a hostile force. The mountains were compassed about with horses and chariots. In his honest anxiety, the young man went to the prophet and said: "Master, how shall we do?" And Elisha, the matured spiritual leader, said, hoping to comfort the young man: "They that be with us are more than they that be with them." But somehow it was not enough, and the prophet so sensed. The scriptures record that he prayed for the young man and asked that the Lord open his eyes that he, too, might see. The prayer was granted. The scriptures, in words like this, record: "And the Lord opened the eyes of the young man; and he saw: behold, the mountain was full of horses and chariots of fire" (2 Kings 6:15–17). We, too, must have our eyes opened. We must have that perspective which permits us to see that, in fact, insofar as the kingdom of God is concerned, "they that be with us are more than they that be with them." There will be times when it will not be clear to us, but we will be supported by the equivalent of "horses and chariots of fire." Your task is to have your eyes opened.

Third and last, in Shakespeare's *Henry V* are those marvelous lines when the small force face a battle on the morrow. Their leader tried to give them a sense of their place in history by saying to them:

*He that outlives this day, and comes safe home, Will stand a tip-toe when this day is nam'd . . .*
*And gentlemen in England now abed*
*Shall count themselves accurs'd they were not here,*
*And hold their manhoods cheap whiles any speaks*
*That fought with us upon St. Crispin's day.*
[*Henry V,* 4.3.41–42, 64–67]

If we come safely home spiritually, you, in particular, as a generation of young adults, can stand a tip-toe when this part of this dispensation is named, and others will be envious of the special privileges and opportunities which were yours!

Now, these have been my feeble attempts to give you perspective. I have spoken frankly to you about the need to have realistic expectations about the purpose of life, so that when stress comes you will not be taken by surprise or by deepening despondency.

I witness to you that this is the work of our Father in heaven. There is none other! There are many marvelous men and women around this globe who are kept from the truth only because they know not where to find it, but nowhere is there a force of human beings so organized, so authorized, so trained to do what you have been trained to do. Therefore, much of the weight of glory rests upon you prospectively. Therefore, as your friend, as one who has high hopes for what you are clearly capacitated to do, I leave those hopes with you. I am one who sees you, collectively, measuring up to your great mortal moments, a few of which I have attempted to lay before you tonight.

May God bless you to that end. We are prophet-led, and the tempo of that prophet, if we needed any other indication, is so urgent, so selfless, that it is crystal clear that the majestic momentum of the Church in our time will thrust you to your places on the stage even before you feel ready. God grant, however, that you may be ready and that all of us may be ready, is my tender prayer, which I leave in the name of him whose church this is, Jesus Christ. Amen.

# Insights from My Life

———◆———

Neal A. Maxwell

President Oaks, brothers and sisters, it's good to be home. I wasn't sure I qualified for continuing membership in this intellectual community after I read a definition the other day of an intellectual as "any individual who can hear the *William Tell* Overture and not think of the Lone Ranger." I don't pass that test, but I'm glad to be home.

Mention was made by President Oaks in his generous introduction of my duties in connection with priesthood correlation. Correlation is a concept I'm often asked to define. I sometimes respond by citing a story that is told about the Church when a federal army was sent out here to harass the Saints. The Brethren had decided on a policy of irritation without violence. In keeping with that policy Porter Rockwell and Lot Smith were dispatched to a distant army camp where Lot Smith was to secretly and quietly remove the pins from the army's wagon wheels while Porter Rockwell was to drive off all the army's horses. In the dark of night, Lot was busily taking out wagon wheel pins, and Porter war-whooped into the camp and drove off all the horses, including Lot Smith's. Lot later walked

*This devotional address was given at Brigham Young University on 26 October 1976.*

wearily many miles back to Church headquarters and reportedly said, "Brethren, we've just got to get correlated." Today's correlation challenges are different, but the basic need remains.

As I pondered possible topics, some members of my family urged me to use some relevant autobiographical themes. They have had to endure my tales of trudging through snow to school—snow which grew deeper with each parental retelling. They probably saw no reason why you should escape the same punishment. Beware today, therefore, those vertical pronouns and the selectivity of my memory. At other times I have spoken in praise of parents and prophets who have helped me so much, as well as about my renewing and loving wife and family.

Today's episodes involve other people, most of them not known to you. The episodes may seem small, but the lessons were large. We speak and sing in the Church of counting our blessings, and that's a good thing. So is inventorying our insights. My format today will make use of some of the sample experiences I've had, with their resultant or related insights, as a part of my inventory. As you indulge me, remember that there are wheat and chaff in every life. A wise lady once said that what we hope our friends will do is to separate the wheat from the chaff and, with a breath of kindness, blow the chaff away. I am grateful now, as I have been over the years, for friends who have had strong lungs.

## REGRETS AND ASPIRATIONS

My mid-teen years were years when there was a confluence of conditions that tried and vexed me. Those are years when peer approval weighs so heavily, as you know. I found myself contending with shortness of stature, shyness, outdoor plumbing, and a 4-H pig project—each of which had by then become an embarrassment. The periodic pain, can be smiled at now, but it was real enough then. Programmed by doting uncles and by myself in early childhood to love basketball and to aspire to become all-state, I had, until this period in my life, been more adept at basketball than most of my peers. Soon, however, I started not making the first string, and then the second. It was a bitter pill. This failure for the first time to achieve athletically—cruelly combined with other indications that I was, for the first time, outside that hard-to-define but very real inner ring—was a time of long thoughts. Somehow, being at home feeding the pigs was not like working out with the varsity—especially when the boy down the block, whom I had helped some learn to play basketball, was where I wanted to be. He went on to be all-state player, which he deserved.

During this period I noticed that recycling regrets didn't change reality. Pawing through the past is not productive. This period was a time when my aspirations got diverted to the world of words, where there were teachers who would not let me pass without genuine achievement. I honor and sustain them evermore. Thus an insight dawned, although not all at once, showing me that too much attention to what might have been actually gets in the way of what still can be. Those valleys you and I are sometimes in are really the sloping sides of hills to be climbed, with as little muttering as possible.

### DIVINE BLESSINGS AND HUMAN POTENTIAL

In the spring of 1945 I was on Okinawa as a frightened and barely adequate infantry replacement—concerned with victory, to be sure, but very much concerned with selfish survival. Japanese artillery pieces had tried for several days without success to hit the little plateau on which our mortar squad was located. Then one evening they dropped three shells around us. They had finally found the range, and we knew it. Surely they knew it. Since one of those shells fell just several feet from my foxhole, I was stimulated, as you might imagine, to intense prayer, full of promises. Strangely, no more shells fell near us that evening, the very time when more shells should have been fired for effect. Foxhole faith brought some real blessings that evening, causing me to make some covenants which I am still striving to keep. I have often wondered—if the Lord that night not only blessed me and others as he did, so clearly and mercifully, but had also told me to be of good cheer, for not only would I live, but one day, just a few ridges away, I would preach the gospel of Jesus Christ to an LDS chapel full of members—could I have managed that insight. Probably not; yet that is precisely what happened in 1973, twenty-eight years later, as I was privileged to go back to that island and that spot which, for me, is a sacred spot.

Sugar cane has since covered the little plateau, but not my poignant memories of Okinawa, the bloodiest battle in the Pacific. Two insights emerged. First, it is naive to think we can repay God for his blessings. I am more and more in debt to him now than I ever was in 1945, and I will be forever. God blesses according to law, but out of all proportion to the ratios we mortals reckon by. Second, along with believing in the gospel, we need to believe in our own possibilities— not as to status, but as to power to do good. God could surprise—yes, even stun—each of us here today if we could manage such divine disclosures. Such must usually be kept from us (or can only be hinted at) for now. But specific and special opportunities are pending for every person here today, if we can trust God and do each day's duties and bear our present pain. We can't walk a straight and narrow path in the dark; hence, God gives to us the gospel, by which we get *direction*, *motivation*, and *illumination*. But there appears to be no point, I learned, in God's constantly illuminating the trail beyond where my eyes of faith can now see.

## PRAISE AND CRITICISM

Several times in early manhood, friends (who probably did not know then that what they said had such an impact) gave me rather specific and encouraging words, prospective praise. I can remember their specific words today. (Incidentally, I have since told some of those friends who are still living how helpful they were.) You and I listen so well when we are ready to hear. These friends, like good outside auditors, confirmed my net worth and also pointed to possibilities for service in ways that were both timely and tender. Sometimes, in the mutual climb along the straight and narrow path, brothers and sisters, we need friends to shout warnings to us or to give us instructions, but we also need those moments when warm whispers can help us to keep putting one foot in front of the other.

Good friends can give us the gifts of approval and acceptance and of perspective. How many of us have rendered that specific service for someone this month? How long has it been since you have been the recipient of such a gift? Perhaps too long in both instances. "Deserved specific praise" is the ingredient of fellowship, of commending Christians.

Several times in our early marriage I was thrust in a close church or professional association with those of whom I had, for one reason or another, been critical. In one case, less than worthy words had fallen from my lips only a day or two before a call came to work with that individual, a development which turned out to be a rich and happy experience. In such circumstances, one winces for his words, and pride goes first; then comes reluctant reclassification, and finally genuine appreciation. It has happened to me several times in life. It has helped to teach me a recurring lesson: God gives to us the lessons we need most, not the ones we think we need. Also, often that which we resist learning vicariously we must learn the hard way—experientially. There is a learning efficiency that comes with being humble *per se*, because of the word, instead of being compelled to be humble and to be open. I was so grateful I was not too proud in such associations, which will, I trust, be eternal. The Christian receives a customized curriculum in life, which is but one of many signs that we have a loving *and knowing* Father in heaven.

### USES AND DANGERS OF SILENCE

There have been insights for me, too, about the role of silence, its usefulness and its dangers. A few dealings with student dissenters taught me (too late to help them, I'm sorry to say) that my silent disgust did not necessarily teach them. It often created distance. Unexplained indignation is not always communication. True, silence in some circumstances is a powerful reprover, but not in other situations. To withhold deserved reproof, and the reasons therefore, may be to withhold a warning that is urgently needed. Reproof is often a last railing before an erring individual goes over the edge of the cliff.

I've learned, too, that silence can also be productive, even though it makes us very anxious. A fine colleague and friend called my office shortly after I had been sustained as a General Authority to ask for an appointment. I was out, but happily my secretary scheduled an appointment, and it was for more than a mere ten minutes. The friend came. I greeted him warmly, but, contrary to my usual style, I stayed mostly silent. His eyes brimmed with tears as finally he said that, as he had listened to conference, he knew he needed to come and set things right. I resisted the impulse to intervene reassuringly, since I knew of nothing that was wrong. He then continued, saying that he was becoming active in the Church again and knew he needed to repair certain relationships. Happily, again I resisted stemming his flow of feeling. With courage and tenderness, he indicated that at times he had said things about me that were untrue and unkind. He wanted to seek my forgiveness. Only then did I respond by telling him of my regard for him and my unawareness of and unconcern over what he had reportedly said. Most importantly, I told him of my love and admiration and forgiveness. We embraced. I expressed then my admiration also for his courage and for his manhood. He then said how difficult it had been to come that day and how he had almost called to cancel the appointment. We spoke together of the wisdom contained in Matthew 18:15 and Jesus' counsel therein as to what we should do when there are impasses in human relationships: "Moreover if thy brother shall trespass against thee, go and tell him his fault between thee and him alone: if he shall hear thee, thou hast gained thy brother." I love that man and respect him for taking the initiative, since I had been unaware of the matter. He is fully and effectively active in the kingdom today. He needed to say what he said more than I needed to hear it, but I am so grateful I did not rush in to fill the silence that morning in the lesson he taught me so well.

Spiritual silence is a school. We may think we are sitting in that school only waiting, but really we are witnessing those marvelous moments of creative communication and of new commitment.

## CONVERSATION AND SENSATIONAL JOURNALISM

Ten years of interviewing on a television program on KUED increased my respect and appreciation for the lives of individuals whom I got to know a little bit more about, other than in their formal roles of U.S. senators, presidential candidates, U.S. Supreme Court justices, or prophets. The small talk of great men and women is worthwhile. We discover so many wonders when walking carefully through another's garden, not by crashing into it with a Mack truck. Tenderness is usually better than trapping, so far as learning about another is concerned. These insights have given me pause when I see so much of modern journalism searching for sensation—a search which can be addictive to journalists as well as to audiences.

Conversation is a dying art that may go underground—not because it is afraid of light, but because, in certain conversations, confidentiality and mutuality go in tandem. What I call "drop the hanky" reporters, who are still a minority, are too often in the service of accusatory patriotism, which can condition citizens to become eager to believe the worst, whereas "pure charity is never glad," Paul wrote, "when others go wrong" (1 Corinthians, chapter 13, Moffatt translation).

About twenty-two years ago, the late Senator Joseph McCarthy was finally condemned by his colleagues. I was involved in a peripheral way in that episode. I remember, after the votes were taken, that McCarthy went off the Senate floor into a small room with three or four reporters. I went in to watch the final scene. The reporters, who had over the months disagreed with him, in some ways still liked him. In their final exchanges in that room I saw how symbiotic sensationalism can be. McCarthy had been good copy, and now it was over. Some commentators concluded that erring politicians get their just due, that "time wounds all heels." But I saw, too, the realities that crucial causes often fall into the hands of those least able to champion them effectively and also that the media use people—sometimes cruelly.

## WORKHORSES AND SHOW HORSES

While recognition is a basic human need and is important in the public service, there are those who do too many things to be seen of men. I had the privilege of seeing this on a grand scale in the U.S. Senate, where there is normally an imbalance between the show horses and the work horses. I can vividly remember standing next to Lyndon Johnson, then majority leader, one day in a Senate chamber anteroom as we both read the ticker tape with a news story about a major bill coming out of a Senate committee after months of labor. One senator, who had not been attending the sessions while the hearings were being held and the tedious testimony was being taken, had managed, nevertheless, to show up the very day the bill was reported out of committee to take his bows before waiting TV cameras. He was one of those senators who would show up for the opening of an envelope. The man at my side, later to become president, profaned in his disgust for the show horse senator, declaring that the show horse senator was also a lazy liberal who let other liberals do the work while he took the bows.

So often in human affairs I have learned the many depend upon the few to lead, to set the pace, to show the way, to deal with the detail. It was so, even in the inspired sessions of the Constitutional Convention of 1787. I'm grateful to have received, in diverse ways, that insight while yet in my twenties.

Some modest adventures of various kinds into the world of public service have helped me to see, too, that the shaping of choices in the political process is at least as important as choosing among the choices. In electoral ecology, there is a greater impact and influence at the front end of the process than in the voting booth, as sacred and special as the latter is. The voting booth is very democratic, but the shaping of the alternatives is aristocratic; it is work that is done by a few. I've been struck over and over again in my experiences with government and politics, modest as they are, by the Lord's counsel that honest, wise, and good individuals "should be sought for diligently" and that such individuals we should "observe to uphold" (see D&C 98:10). Ponder those words. Seeking out special individuals implies that the special individuals needed may not be those who are first in line as eager volunteers. Along with the search for good candidates is the requirement that we thereafter uphold such while in office. Too many prospective candidates are rightly wary of being abandoned by friends after they have filed or after being elected. It is all so much more than going into the little voting booth and being sixty-second citizens. Lazy citizens who then complain about the choices confronting them are like those who ask not to be disturbed until time for dinner and then sit down to a spare meal and complain about the menu—when they have consistently refused to plant, cultivate, and harvest the garden from which the meal comes.

### FAMILY AND GOVERNMENT

Public service has also helped me to appreciate my many non-LDS friends, whom I have found, on the whole, to be caring and thoughtful individuals. They are able to understand when we must differ without jeopardizing what we have in common, which is so very much. My non-member friends have so often met me more than halfway in our common causes.

I do believe the gospel gives us some insights which are not easy to transmit, such as how vitally appropriate early life experiences are and their impact on society's institutions later on. We know that it is the family wherein all those virtues on which society depends are first and best developed: for instance, self-restraint, the commitment to work, doing one's share, compassion for others. Like it or not, society and the state will mirror our homes. Adolf Hitler's early life experiences may have impacted more on Germany than the Weimar Republic's constitution.

In any event, possessed of such insights, we Latter-day Saints are often responded to a little like John the Baptist. Minus such fundamental insights, I fear that, as conditions worsen, many will react to the failures of too much government by calling for even more government. Then there will be more and more lifeboats launched because fewer and fewer citizens know how to swim. Unlike some pendulums, political pendulums do not swing back automatically;

they must be pushed. History is full of instances when people have waited in vain for pendulums to swing back.

A little experience with federal and state bureaucracies has taught me that such bureaucracies are inhabited by basically good civil servants, onto whom voters have pushed too much power for their good or ours. What we unwittingly court in such circumstances is learning again, painfully, that "almost all" men can't handle authority without abusing it. Whether or not the American people, regardless of party, can tame their governments is yet to be determined, but sunset laws alone will not do it. If citizen appetites, once aroused, merely look to a new agency to do what a disestablished agency once did, it won't be enough. Addicts can always find new pushers.

In one of those illuminating but sad stories that would be funny if it had not involved something terribly important, Peter Druecker tells us that the czar of Russia in 1914 had ordered a general mobilization to fight the Germans, but then he had second thoughts about it. The czar called in his chief of staff and asked him to halt the mobilization. The general answered, "Your Majesty, this is impossible. There is no plan for calling off the mobilization once it is started." Perhaps World War I might not have been any different regardless of what the Russians did, but the sweeping events flowing out of the collapse on the Russian front, paving the way for the rise of Bolshevism, deserve to be pondered in the context of that stupid, bureaucratic rigidity. I remember all too well a brief experience in one federal department when it reached a point in our little shop that the methodology of filing came out by directive and assumed a preeminence over our primary task. This trend was symbolically accompanied by the domesticating appearance of sweet potato foliage on the desk (which was accompanied by my disappearance from that department in search of better tasks).

## THE CHURCH AND PERSONAL RIGHTEOUSNESS

Yet we need some institutionalization, even in the kingdom. Random goodness is, by itself, not enough to resist the march of evil, which takes its victims without pity or remorse. How many of the tens of thousands who went to help victims of the flood would have made their way individually to southeastern Idaho to help without the Church's organization of that concern? I am grateful that God has so organized us and that he has given us specific things to do. Otherwise, we would be like the lonely sharp-shooters trying to slow the advancing army of evil. Sharp-shooters can delay the enemy heroically, but such solitary souls are not the way in which counterattacks are mounted. Counterattacks must be expressed institutionally, as in the case of The Church of Jesus Christ of Latter-day Saints. Concerning this need, the Lord has given us an immense clue in an analogy when he said, "But first let my army become very great, and let it be sanctified before me . . . That the kingdoms of this world may be constrained to acknowledge that the kingdom of Zion is in very deed the kingdom of our God and his Christ" (D&C 105:31, 32). Such remarkable recognition, brothers and sisters, will come in a time of stunning contrasts. It was President Brigham Young who said that it was revealed to him in the commencement of this Church that, as it grew and extended into the nations of the world, so also would the power of the adversary rise—cheek by jowl, wheat by tares.

To wonder if our faith is strong enough for such remarkable developments is natural. The father of Elder Bruce R. McConkie, President Oscar W. McConkie, Sr., in a situation of stress years ago prayed for adequacy. He prayed that he would be able to carry out his heavy assignment and that he could be given the faith of Enoch. The answer to his prayer was Enoch's faith came through personal righteousness. There is a great lesson, brothers and sisters, in that response, which is consistent, of course, with the words in section 121 of the Doctrine and Covenants, in which we are reminded that we cannot control the powers of heaven *except* upon the principles of righteousness. If you and I want to be more effective, we must be more righteous. If we want to have more faith, we must be more righteous, and we might just as well face that reality.

In a time when increasing numbers of our fellowmen are wrongly concluding, but nevertheless concluding, that man is alone in the universe, there is a cosmic chill settling in, an astral aloneness that seems to be about and in the hearts of so many, for which the truths of the gospel are the only real remedy. The hungry of the world are reaching out for these truths, even when you and I present them fumblingly and live them less than perfectly.

### FREEDOM AND VIOLENCE

In addition to this yearning for identity and belonging, we see about us also a yearning for freedom taking its familiar forms—political and economic. But we also see more and more individuals who sense that the freedom they desire involves more than a new constitutional caress. Thoughtful souls see that something even deeper is involved. So many have erred, thinking that freedom, included both freedom to obey or not to obey eternal laws and, wrongly, that it included freedom to change those laws. Not so. Ultimately, freedom involves choice between eternal alternatives, *but not the altering of the alternatives.* We can choose wickedness or happiness, but not wickedness with happiness. A confused Cain, a vain Cain, not only murdered his brother while they conversed together in the field, but also gloried in the murder of Abel, when Cain said (probably shouted), "I am free."

So often violence creates the *illusion* of freedom or possession. So often sin creates a momentary illusion which those involved are taken in by. I've never been able to erase from my mind the boasting words of army buddies following their night of adultery, which I heard while trying to go back to sleep on an army cot no farther away from here than Camp Williams. I saw the shame of several of those same men in the days and weeks that followed. It seemed to me then, as it does now, that the raucousness and the shouting of sin, the Cain-like glorying in it, is also the sound of pain trying to erase itself.

I have found, too, that it is better to trust and sometimes be disappointed than to be forever mistrusting and be right occasionally. This is to endorse empathy, not naivete. Neither is this to suggest that our fellowship be flaccid. The finest of friends must sometimes be stern sentinels, who will insist that we become what we have the power to become. The "no" of such stern sentinels is more to be prized than a "yes" of others. God's seeming sternness is actually a sweetness beyond our comprehension.

Petitioning in prayer has taught me that the vault of heaven, with all its blessings, is to be opened only by a combination lock: one tumbler falls when there is faith, a second when there is personal righteousness, and the third, and final tumbler falls only when what is sought is (in God's judgment, not ours) "right" for us. Sometimes we pound on the vault door for something we want very much, in faith, in reasonable righteousness, and wonder why the door does not open. We would be very spoiled children if that vault door opened any more easily than it does now. I can tell, looking back, that God truly loves me by the petitions that, in his perfect wisdom and love, he has refused to grant me. Our rejected petitions tell us not only much about ourselves, but also much about our flawless Father.

You have been patient with my reminiscences and with this very partial inventory. May I suggest you try not only counting your blessings, but also inventorying your insights from time to time. It "will surprise you what the Lord has done" in teaching you things you so much need to know. Nourish your spirits, brothers and sisters. Your spirit can drive your body and your mind beyond the borders now known to you. I vividly remember first reading the lines that went as follows: "Over a hundred years ago a sailor walked down the streets of Portsmouth, with one arm and one eye and a persistent state of nerves, and unable to tread a ship's deck without being seasick." Indeed, this man would have probably given up except his name was Admiral Lord Nelson.

Now, brothers and sisters, the spirit not only can drive the body beyond where the body first agrees to go; the spirit can enlarge our minds beyond borders we think are fixed, which are not really fixed, but which are movable.

May God bless us to cherish the insights he has given us and to live in such a way that new insights can flow to us. As we count our blessings, let us inventory our insights also, and, in appropriate ways, share with others where they may be helpful. I witness to you, as I have so many times before and which I always do gladly, that The Church of Jesus Christ of Latter-day Saints is *the* Church of Jesus Christ. It is a living Church, not a dying Church. It is built upon, not partial truths, but the wholeness of truth as God has given it to us. May He help us, individually, to rise to that discipleship which is so needed. The time will come in the lifetime of many here when the people of the world will acknowledge that The Church of Jesus Christ of Latter-day Saints is, in fact, the kingdom of our God and His Christ—just what we have said all along it is. What high promises, what soul-stretching experiences await us! May we so live in order that we will not only witness these events, but also accelerate their completion and fulfillment, I pray in the name of Jesus Christ. Amen.

# All Hell Is Moved

———◆———

Neal A. Maxwell

Thank you very much, President Oaks. One of the joys of my life has been the association in recent years with President Oaks. He is, in my opinion, the outstanding university president in America today. He could preside over other universities and render a great service, but I am glad he is here. I am grateful for this beautiful music that has been so well sung, for those anthems of praise, and for the prayer offered in each of our behalfs.

Because President Oaks has been courteous to me many times, I have had this signal honor before; but, as he pointed out, for the first time I feel as though I belong and am one of you. And as a father and an adopted alumnus of this University, may I take this opportunity to thank the faculty of Brigham Young University who have taught and are now teaching so well my four children and two children acquired through marriage. It is a great blessing to have a faculty of such fine men and women and to feel as a father that one's children are being so well taught. With us today also is our first grandchild, Peter, a grandson seven months old, who is checking the campus out.

*This devotional address was given at Brigham Young University on 8 November 1977.*

Hopefully he will come here too, someday, unless today's devotional speaker proves too depressing.

The theme of my address comes from a prophecy in President George Q. Cannon's speech given in the Tabernacle in May of 1866. President Cannon spoke of the generations that had passed before the restoration of the gospel during which the adversary was indifferent and unconcerned with regard to the fractious religious movements among mankind which were not based upon the fulness of truth. However, President Cannon observed that the moment the Holy Priesthood of God and the Church were restored, "then all hell is moved." He catalogued the forms of resistance that can be expected when "all hell is moved."

President Cannon, who knew that the adversary regards this telestial turf as his own, said that Satan will vigorously resist all rezoning efforts because this is his world. President Cannon further observed that the Saints—meaning you and I—must not make the mistake of assuming the existence of any truce between the forces of Satan and God. To believe so, said President Cannon, is "a very great delusion, and a very common one."

President Cannon then warned that the forms of resistance to righteousness will strike us "with wonder and astonishment." This, he said, would occur because "the war" which was waged in heaven has been transferred to the earth," and that this conflict, he said, "will [come to] occupy the thoughts and minds of all the inhabitants of the earth" (*Journal of Discourses* 11:227–29). Brothers and sisters, The Church of Jesus Christ of Latter-day Saints will be at the epicenter of all that.

On the sixth of April, 1845, the Twelve Apostles issued a proclamation which included these words:

> *As this work progresses in its onward course, and becomes more and more an object of political and religious interest and excitement, no king, ruler, or subject, no community or individual, will stand neutral. All will at length be influenced by one spirit or the other; and will take sides either for or against the kingdom of God.* (*Messages of the First Presidency*, p. 257)

Such audacity! Except for apostles. Such presumptuousness! Except for prophets. That prophecy is underway, and it is about that that I wish to speak today.

I stress that I come neither as an alarmist nor as a pessimist, but as one who seeks in his gentle way to remind us of this reality lest we be struck "with wonder and astonishment" and become dismayed and dislocated by difficulties that emerge when "all hell is moved," because the restored kingdom is really rolling now. We may never become accustomed to untrue and unjust criticism of us but we ought not to be immobilized by it. Neither should we be surprised at the proximity of such protagonists and the falsity and the fury of their pronouncements. President Joseph F. Smith said, "there are those— and they abound largely in our midst—who will shut their eyes to every virtue and to every good thing connected with this latter-day work, and will pour out floods of falsehood and misrepresentation against the people of God." President Smith, who endured so much of that proximate persecution, did what we must also do. He said of such detractors, "I forgive them for this. I leave them in the hands of the just Judge" (*Gospel Doctrine*, p. 337).

President Brigham Young observed that it would be at the very time when the Church was reaching out to all the nations of the world, when it was prospering and growing, that there would be in proportion to the spread of the gospel a rise in the power of Satan. We are in that very period of time now, too. The obscurity of the Church has given way to visibility. You who have entered here to learn and who go forth to serve mankind—wafted as you will be from place to place on this planet—are also builders of the kingdom. You must be especially aware of the confluence of events that I am describing. You must still go forth, for you have been sent to this planet at precisely this time because you could cope with the challenges being described.

In the beginning of the Restoration, Joseph Smith quickly became an object of scorn and ridicule. The reaction to him, except by Satan's scale, was all out of proportion. Joseph reflected upon this when he observed:

*How very strange it was that an obscure boy . . . should be thought a character of sufficient importance to attract the attention of the great ones of the most popular sects of the day, and in a manner to create in them a spirit of the most bitter persecution and reviling.*

But as the Prophet observed, "strange or not, so it was " (Joseph Smith 2:23). As with that individual, so with God's institution. When the Saints are spotlighted, it will not always be for us to take curtsies and bows; sometimes the spotlights will be searchlights.

Note, brothers and sisters, that it is the validity which draws the fire of the adversary. Combine validity and visibility, as in our time, and there is even more reaction. The adversary would scarcely pay any attention to a still numerically obscure Church unless he recognized what is underway for just what it is. Jesus declared who he was, and many disbelieved him, but the unclean spirit in Capernaum recognized him and said: "I know thee who thou art" (Mark 1:24). Lucifer and his legions are alert; they know Christ's church is what it is. The adversary is aware.

It should not surprise us, therefore, that as the Church becomes larger and more visible we will sail our rougher waters, and that there will be more "struggling seamen" anxious to be saved and to come on board. Indeed, there are reasons to believe—as the contrasts between the kingdom and the ways of the world become sharper, the choices more obvious, and the issues more irrepressible—that this condition will, in fact, help those who otherwise might delay making a choice or who might make a wrong choice if the issues remained obscured.

It should not puzzle us, if we have studied scriptural history carefully—including what happened to the Savior—that defectors often cause more difficulty than disinterested disbelievers. It should not surprise us either, as Peter observed of those drawn away by false accusers, that it will be they and their followers "by reason of whom the way of truth shall be evil spoken of" (2 Peter 2:2).

There are those who chronically misunderstand the Church because they are busy trying to explain the Church from the outside. They are so busy believing what they want to believe about the Church that they will not take the time to learn what they need to learn about the Church. They prefer any explanation to the real explanation. Some prefer to believe the worst rather than to know the truth. Still others are afraid to part the smokescreen of allegations for fear of what they will see. Yet one cannot see the Louvre by remaining in its lobby. One cannot understand the Church by remaining outside. A non-believing but fair critic of the Church, a friend of mine, once said that the Book of Mormon was the only book some critics felt they did not need to read before reviewing it.

Some dismiss the Church out of hand for not being trendy in its theology and for being authoritarian. To such I say, better a true theocracy with a little democracy than a democracy without any theology. Yes, the kingdom of God is a kingdom; there is no "one many, one vote" rule between its King and its citizens.

Some insist upon studying the Church only through the eyes of its defectors—like interviewing Judas to understand Jesus. Defectors always tell us more about themselves than about that from which they have departed.

Some others patiently feed their pet peeve about the Church without realizing that such a pet will not only bite the hands of him who feeds it, but it will swallow his whole soul. Of course we are a very imperfect people! Remember, however, that while it is possible to have an imperfect people possessed of perfect doctrines (indeed, such is necessary to change their imperfections), you will never, never see the reverse: a perfect people with imperfect doctrines. The more people there are who bear false witness concerning a true movement, the greater the need for us to be true witnesses of the Savior and his way of life. We can be noble even when we are being treated ignobly. We not only can be, but we must be.

It was Peter who warned us about the central cause of so much of this criticism. He said that the days would come when people would deny the Lord who "bought them" (2 Peter 2:1). That scripture of course, is a direct reference to the atonement of Jesus Christ when he ransomed and purchased us, making the resurrection a reality for all. To deny the reality and the validity of his atonement and his resurrection, and therefore the resurrection of mankind, is to deny the very Lord. But such is the case with so much of the existential Christianity. Diluted Christianity is not Christianity, it is a feeble attempt to have Christianity without Christ, for it denies the central service of Jesus' life—the Atonement. Those who call themselves Christians but deny the divinity of Jesus cannot seem to tolerate those of us who accept and proclaim the divinity of Christ. No one, brothers and sisters, would pay us much heed if we were merely non-smoking, nondrinking humanists. Without acknowledging the reality of the Resurrection and the Atonement, believing in the ministry of Jesus would mean slumping into the very Saduceeism which Jesus himself denounced.

Isn't it interesting that the Bible, marvelous and wonderful as it is, has not by itself been able to develop and sustain in so many individuals a deep, clear-cut, lasting, and unvarying commitment to the resurrected Lord Jesus Christ? Paul, who was witness to the resurrected Jesus, warned of such a crippled Christianity when he said : "If in this life only we have hope in Christ, we are of all men most miserable" (1 Corinthians 15:19). If Jesus had not rescued us from death, there would be ultimate misery. If his ministry is viewed as merely mortal, it is robbed of its real relevance. In the midst of such doctrinal disarray stands the church of Jesus Christ, proclaiming the divinity of Jesus of Nazareth. No wonder there is such a sharp reaction from the forces of him who sought the Saviorship for himself.

Jude warned of insidious disbelievers. He said,

> *For there are certain men crept in unawares, who were before of old ordained to this condemnation, ungodly men, turning the grace of our God into lasciviousness, and denying the only Lord God, and our Lord Jesus Christ.* [Jude 4]

Clearly, the Book of Mormon was needed as an added witness in these, the decades of deep doubt. Clearly, the theophany at Palmyra puts to rout all the chatter about the historicity of Jesus; it ended all the theological fuzziness about the nature of the Godhead.

The Lord said of the scriptures and the words of his prophets
something that is so fundamental about the ecology of belief. He
said, "He that will not believe my words will not believe me—that I
am" (Ether 4:12). Thus the Book of Mormon came like a theological thunderbolt on the stage of history—to be a second witness for
the divinity of Jesus Christ "to the *convincing* of the Jew and Gentile
that Jesus is the Christ" (Title page, Book of Mormon; italics added).
Note the word "convincing." The Bible often initiates and helps to
sustain faith in Jesus, but the Book of Mormon is the *convincer* and
the *clarifier*. Isn't it ironical in this regard that there are some who
still wonder if members of The Church of Jesus Christ of Latter-day
Saints are Christians? Was General Douglas MacArthur a West-
Pointer? Was Winston Churchill an Englishman?

We are Christ's kingdom builders. Those who build the heavenly
kingdom have always made nervous the people who are busy building worldly kingdoms. The inspired translation of the Bible gives us
a rendition of Matthew, chapter 6, verse 33, with fourteen additional
words that give us a great clue to our role as kingdom-builders. What
we read in the King James Version is a helpful and motivating, but
still puzzling, verse which says, "But seek ye first the kingdom of
God, and his righteousness; and all these things shall be added unto
you." I shall now read to you that verse (Matthew 6:33; italics added)
as it appears in the inspired translation of Joseph Smith: "Wherefore,
seek not the things of this world; but *seek ye first* to build up *the kingdom of God, and* to establish *this righteousness, and all these things shall
be added unto you.*" This is but one example of how plain and precious things are missing from the King James translation, marvelous
though it is, an inspired book which has survived so much and yet
with such strength and beauty.

Christians who worship a resurrected Jesus Christ (a Jesus who
not only lived but lives) and who believe in the sermon at Capernaum
and the sermon on the Mount are kingdom-builders. When such
individuals, clothed in the purple of the holy priesthood, preach
Christ crucified *and* Christ resurrected, and when such people

become increasingly effective in kingdom-building, indeed "all hell is moved."

It would be so much safer to float with the ebbing theological tides as do so many today who simply regard Jesus as a Galilean Ghandi or as a Socrates who strode in Samaria. But we know Jesus to be divine, the literal Son of the Father. We know that he established his church, and that it is not simply a church built upon doctrinal debris from other dispensations or fragments of the faith from another age. It is a church built upon the fulness of his gospel; it bears his name and is his kingdom in these latter days, a kingdom to which the good men and women of all nations, cultures, and races will be drawn. Knowing this, we are like Joseph Smith—we speak the truth because we can do no other.

How can we expect to be a part of such momentous developments as these and yet expect to pass unnoticed so far as the people of the world are concerned? Surely we will not pass unnoticed in our righteous endeavors so far as the adversary is concerned. In 1820 he noticed an obscure teenage lad going into an obscure grove to pray—of all the prayers offered that day, why bother that boy? But it was sufficiently clear to Satan what was about to transpire. Is it any wonder that those who resist the building of the latter-day kingdom will, from time to time (as described in Ether, chapter 8, or the 38th section of the Doctrine and Covenants), act in "combinations" against the kingdom? Everything in the arsenal of the adversary will eventually be used.

Now, having been briefly descriptive, let me for these closing moments be prescriptive. Let us not be dismayed if the critics of the kingdom exploit our personal errors and work on our individual weaknesses and pounce upon our failures. Let us not forget that the meridian-day saints also knew what it was like when "all hell is moved."

Let us minimize our personal errors which enemies could exploit. Let us conquer the weaknesses which critics could work upon. Let us be harmless, so that we go not forth on ego excursions that damage others, for we are people-builders as well as kingdom-builders. Let our citizenship be spirited but always appropriate and befitting who we are. Let us approach power and authority as the Lord prescribed in the 121st section of the Doctrine and Covenants. Let us be articulate, for while our defense of the kingdom may not stir all hearers, the absence of thoughtful response may cause fledglings among the faithful to falter. What we assert may not be accepted, but unasserted convictions soon become deserted convictions.

The reactions to us will vary: there will be the almost Agrippas, the puzzled Pilates, the timid Van Burens, and the stout Colonel Kanes, and, of course, there will be some scorn and some rage. But deep within the rage and the scorn, if one listens closely, are the sounds of profound pain, hushed hope, and of doubt beginning to doubt itself. Sometimes the chastening that comes to us individually is at least partially deserved. We would not really want a loving Father to stop teaching us and correcting us. Other times the chastening will be underserved; but, said the Prophet Joseph Smith, the Lord will "have a tried people," and "He would purge them as gold" (*Teachings of the Prophet Joseph Smith*, p. 135).

Let your education be emancipating in all the correct ways, but also in another very subtle way, a way clearly related to your role in the tempestuous times before you. I refer to the need to understand the principle of obedience, which has fallen on hard times; obedience is low on the world's scale of values. There are causes for this, of course. Some have done terribly wrong things in obedience to unjust leaders. Some have engaged in senseless subordination to bad causes, becoming mere satellites in mindless orbits. Satan always pretzelizes principles in order to increase human misery.

But obedience is so essential for the gospel journey; it must be rescued from the careless conclusions reached by sloppy intellects. The tests of obedience are always "to whom?" and "to what?" Obedience is not blind faith but following the glimpses we get when seeing with the eye of faith. Obedience is not shrinking from adventure and agency; it is an opening up. Obedience is not being glad to have someone else relieve us of our responsibility. Obedience to correct principles is leaping free of constraints such as fear and ignorance. Obedience will push us into adventures and experiences that free us both from prejudice toward certain people and from prejudice toward certain principles.

Obedience springs from intellectual integrity in that it causes us to be honest and to own up to the validity of precious experiences. Studied closely, the episode involving Adam and his sacrifice will suggest to us that the quality of Adam's previous experiences with the Lord (and probably with angels) was so reliable that when he was asked why he sacrificed, he could reply, "I know not, save the Lord commanded me" (Moses 5:6). For Adam to have excluded his previous experiences from his decision to be obedient would have been dishonest.

Obedience on our part can bring us face to face with new challenges which we need but do not want, challenges from which we may even be running away. Obedience helps us to pioneer beyond the past. Logic may look and tell us that the mountains ahead of us are stern Sierras, but obedience will cause us to press forward anyway over what finally prove to be simply rolling hills.

Therefore, practice emancipating obedience! Do not let your moods maul your faith. Do not allow the absence of social life and dates to color your attitude toward your rendezvous with the resurrection. Do not let a bad day cause you to think that life is bad. Do not let low self-esteem discount your high blessings. In short, do not homogenize your hopes by mixing and treating them as if all hopes and aspirations are equal. They are not. The hope for a resurrection is guaranteed unconditionally by the atonement of the Savior. The hope for a good grade on an exam is quite obviously a hope of a different order; it is of much less significance and it is by no means guaranteed.

Our transitory disappointments are real, but the missing letter from home is not really comparable to the delivered message from heaven, the good news of the gospel. Today's unmet hunger for a few more friends must not be allowed to obscure the marvelous reality of the forever friendship of Jesus for each of us. Do not let uncertainty

about how others seem to feel about you this week get in the way of
how God has always felt about you.

Our intertwining insecurities, the hunger for peer reassurance,
and the tendency to be carried on the tides of today's troubles and
disappointments will diminish as we mature. As our understanding
of the gospel deepens, it becomes ever more clear that proximate
problems need not, and must not, undercut ultimate realities. Thus,
as we confront problems which we might shiveringly sidestep, if we
could, let us realize, as one poet did, that "sometimes the only way
to go is through." We go on that journey with justified hopes to help
our hunger and with realities to reassure us. And, in the midst of our
transitory troubles, we have the knowledge that he is near at hand,
and within us there is even the sense that in the dim past we agreed
to all this and that now we must perform on that pledge.

I salute you as kingdom-builders and as a generation of destiny. A
whole nation can be leavened by a righteous rising generation—or, as
we lamentably read of another group of young adults; "thus . . . the
Lamanites . . . began to decrease as to their faith and righteousness,
because of the wickedness of the rising generation" (3 Nephi 1:30).
You bright spirits could not have chosen a better time to be born,
with more neighbors waiting and needing to be shown the gospel. I
know you have been properly placed because God did it.

How can we remain silent when we know that there will come a
time, as the scriptures have foretold, when there will be a great sign
in heaven and that all flesh shall see Christ together (See D&C 88:93,
D&C 101:23)? No wonder we rejoice! No wonder we reach out!
No wonder we stand all amazed whenever the light of the everlasting gospel lights up a soul, denoting the dawn of a new discipleship.
Hopefully we will never cease to thrill, as did Ammon, when "the
light of everlasting life was lit up" in the soul of Kind Lamoni (Alma
19:6). Meanwhile, it is important that we be as righteous as we can
be, so that no one is deflected from discipleship because of us and our
errors.

As the veil of unbelief thickens around the globe, nothing
can rend "the dark veil of unbelief" (Alma 19:6) that is not sharp,

piercing, bright, and true. Dull disciples will not light the way nor draw people to the kingdom. The philosophies of the world cannot do it, for so far as having some saving and consequential core to them, such philosophies are like peeling an onion. Perhaps that is why we cry when we peel onions. The truths we seek to live and to share are sweet, reassuring, and redeeming. But they are also tough truths; they keep us up against things that really matter. And central to all of these truths is the declaration of the Savior himself in which he said, "Behold, . . . I am the light, and the life, and the truth of the world" (Ether 4:12). These are not the words of some Buddha born in Bethlehem; these are the words of the resurrected Lord Jesus Christ.

We say (without tying it to any sense of personal vindication) what Paul said: that the time will come "at the name of Jesus every knee should bow . . . and that every tongue should confess that Jesus Christ is Lord, to the glory of God the Father" (Philippians 2:10–11).

We know, as a Book of Mormon prophet said, that

*At the last day, when all men shall stand to be judged of him, then shall they confess that he is God; then shall they confess, who live without God in the world, that the judgment of an everlasting punishment is just upon them; and they shall quake, and tremble, and shrink beneath the glance of his all-searching eye.* [Mosiah 27:31]

Yea, even those "who live without God in the world" will also one day kneel in confession of Christ, acknowledging not only the reality of God in the world but also his justice and his love.

The gift of immortality to all mankind through the reality of the Resurrection is so powerful a promise that our rejoicing in these great and generous gifts should drown out any sorrow, assuage any grief, conquer any mood, dissolve any despair, and tame any tragedy. Those who now see life as pointless will one day point with adoration to the performance of the Man of Galilee in those crowded moments of time known as Gethsemane and Calvary. Those who presently say life is meaningless will yet applaud the Atonement which saves us from meaninglessness. Christ's victory over death ended the human predicaments, and from these too we may be rescued by following the teachings of him who rescued us from general extinction.

Our "brightness of hope," therefore, means that at funerals our tears are genuine, but not because of termination—rather because of interruption. Though just as wet, our tears are not of despair but are of appreciation and anticipation. Yes, for disciples, the closing of a grave is but the closing of a door which later will be flung open with rejoicing.

We say, humbly but firmly that it is the garden tomb—not life—that is empty.

That fiery sphere we call the sun, which guides our solar system, will one day burn out, but it provides us with a useful analogy. We may cover our eyes or turn from its light, but its light is still there. We may see it through glass darkly, but it glows on just as brightly. For a few hours we call night it seems to be gone, but it is still shiningly there and will reappear on the morrow. Storms may darken the sky at noonday, but the sun is still there and will soon break through.

So it is with the Son of God, about whom this choir has sung so well today. We may turn from him, but he is still there. We may feel that he is hidden from us because of the cloud cover of our concerns, but he is still close to us. We—not he—let something come between us, but no lasting eclipse need ensue. Our provincialism cannot withstand his universalism. Our disregard of him is no match for his love of us. Yes, Jesus of Nazareth lived! He lives now! He guides his Church!

True, all hell may be moved, but as it moves, the devil's kingdom will be irrevocably shaken, so that many can be shaken loose from his grasp. It is the kingdom of heaven that is coming—triumphant, true, and everlasting! God grant that we may each be faithful to all the assignments given to us during our premortal preparation for these dramatic days, I pray in the name of Jesus Christ. Amen.

# Meeting the Challenges of Today

————◆————

Neal A. Maxwell

Thank you very much, President Oaks; and thank you, sisters, for that lovely music. This is always a great experience for any of us to have.

Often, when speaking to student leaders in higher education, I have used the analogy that—in a university—the faculty, staff, and administration are like the natives, and the students are like the tourists. In many ways, a recurring devotional speaker is more like one of the natives. Even so, I thank President Oaks for once again extending this precious privilege to me. You may conclude today, however, that I am becoming more like a tourist, since I shall try to cover two topics in order to make the most of these fleeting moments.

Discipleship includes good citizenship; and in this connection, if you are careful students of the statements of the modern prophets, you will have noticed that with rare exceptions—especially when the First Presidency has spoken out—the concerns expressed have been over moral issues, not issues between political parties. The declarations are about principles, not people, and causes, not candidates. On

*This devotional address was given at Brigham Young University on 10 October 1978.*

occasions, at other levels in the Church, a few have not been so discreet, so wise, or so inspired.

But make no mistake about it, brothers and sisters; in the months and years ahead, events will require of each member that he or she decide whether or not he or she will follow the First Presidency. Members will find it more difficult to halt longer between two opinions (see 1 Kings 18:21).

President Marion G. Romney said, many years ago, that he had "never hesitated to follow the counsel of the Authorities of the Church even though it crossed my social, professional, or political life" (*CR*, April 1941, p. 123). This is a hard doctrine, but it is a particularly vital doctrine in a society which is becoming more wicked. In short, brothers and sisters, not being ashamed of the gospel of Jesus Christ includes not being ashamed of the prophets of Jesus Christ.

We are now entering a period of incredible ironies. Let us cite but one of these ironies which is yet in its subtle stages: we shall see in our time a maximum if indirect effort made to establish irreligion as the state religion. It is actually a new form of paganism that uses the carefully preserved and cultivated freedoms of Western civilization to shrink freedom even as it rejects the value essence of our rich Judeo-Christian heritage.

M. J. Sobran wrote recently:

*The Framers of the Constitution . . . forbade the Congress to make any law "respecting" the establishment of religion, thus leaving the states free to do so (as several of them did); and they explicitly forbade the Congress to abridge "the free exercise" of religion, thus giving actual religious observance a rhetorical emphasis that fully accords with the special concern we know they had for religion. It takes a special ingenuity to wring out of this a governmental indifference to religion, let alone an aggressive secularism. Yet there are those who insist that the First Amendment actually proscribes governmental partiality not only to any single religion, but to religion as such; so that tax exemption for churches is now thought to be unconstitutional. It is startling* [she continues] *to consider that a clause clearly protecting religion can be construed as requiring that it be denied a status routinely granted to educa-*

*tional and charitable enterprises, which have no overt constitutional protec-*
*tion. Far from* equalizing *unbelief, secularism has succeeded in virtually*
establishing *it.*

[She continues:] *What the secularists are increasingly demanding, in*
*their disingenuous way, is that religious people, when they act politically, act*
*only on secularist grounds. They are trying to equate* acting *on religion with*
establishing *religion. And—I repeat—the consequence of such logic is really*
*to establish secularism. It is in fact, to force the religious to internalize the*
*major premise of secularism: that religion has no proper bearing on public*
*affairs.* [*Human Life Review,* Summer 1978, pp. 51–52, 60–61]

Brothers and sisters, irreligion as the state religion would be the
worst of all combinations. Its orthodoxy would be insistent and its
inquisitors inevitable. Its paid ministry would be numerous beyond
belief. Its Caesars would be insufferably condescending. Its majori-
ties—when faced with clear alternatives—would make the Barabbas
choice, as did a mob centuries ago when Pilate confronted them with
the need to decide.

Your discipleship may see the time come when religious convictions are heavily discounted. M. J. Sobran also observed, "A religious
conviction is now a second-class conviction, expected to step defer-
entially to the back of the secular bus, and not to get uppity about it"
(*Human Life Review,* Summer 1978, p. 58). This new irreligious impe-
rialism seeks to disallow certain of people's opinions simply because
those opinions grow out of religious convictions. Resistance to abortion will soon be seen as primitive. Concern over the institution of
the family will be viewed as untrendy and unenlightened.

In its mildest form, irreligion will merely be condescending
toward those who hold to traditional Judeo-Christian values. In its
more harsh forms, as is always the case with those whose dogmatism
is blinding, the secular church will do what it can to reduce the influence of those who still worry over standards such as those in the Ten
Commandments. It is always such an easy step from dogmatism to
unfair play—especially so when the dogmatists believe themselves to

be dealing with primitive people who do not know what is best for them. It is the secular bureaucrat's burden, you see.

Am I saying that the voting rights of the people of religion are in danger? Of course not! Am I saying, "It's back to the catacombs?" No! But there is occurring a discounting of religiously-based opinions. There may even be a covert and subtle disqualification of some for certain offices in some situations, in an ironic "irreligious test" for office.

However, if people are not permitted to advocate, to assert, and to bring to bear, in every legitimate way, the opinions and views they hold that grow out of their religious convictions, what manner of men and women would they be, anyway? Our founding fathers did not wish to have a state church established nor to have a particular religion favored by government. They wanted religion to be free to make its own way. But neither did they intend to have irreligion made into a favored state church. Notice the terrible irony if this trend were to continue. When the secular church goes after its heretics, where are the sanctuaries? To what landfalls and Plymouth Rocks can future pilgrims go?

If we let come into being a secular church shorn of traditional and divine values, where shall we go for inspiration in the crises of tomorrow? Can we appeal to the rightness of a specific regulation to sustain us in our hours of need? Will we be able to seek shelter under a First Amendment which by then may have been twisted to favor irreligion? Will we be able to rely for counterforce on value education in school systems that are increasingly secularized? And if our governments and schools were to fail us, would we be able to fall back upon the institution of the family, when so many secular movements seek to shred it?

It may well be, as our time comes to "suffer shame for his name" (Acts 5:41), that some of this special stress will grow out of that portion of discipleship which involves citizenship. Remember that, as Nephi and Jacob said, we must learn to endure "the crosses of the world" (2 Nephi 9:18) and yet to despise "the shame of [it]" (Jacob 1:8). To go on clinging to the iron rod in spite of the mockery and scorn that flow at us from the multitudes in that great and spacious building seen by Father Lehi, which is the "pride of the world," is to disregard the shame of the world (1 Nephi 8:26–27, 33; 11:35–36). Parenthetically, why—really why—do the disbelievers who line that spacious building watch so intently what the believers are doing? Surely there must be other things for the scorners to do—unless, deep within their seeming disinterest, there is interest.

If the challenge of the secular church becomes very real, let us, as in all other human relationships, be principled but pleasant. Let us be perceptive without being pompous. Let us have integrity and not write checks with our tongues which our conduct cannot cash.

Before the ultimate victory of the forces of righteousness, some skirmishes will be lost. Even these, however, must leave a record so that the choices before the people are clear and let others do as they will in the face of prophetic counsel. There will also be times, happily, when a minor defeat seems probable, that others will step forward, having been rallied to righteousness by what we do. We will know the joy, on occasion, of having awakened a slumbering majority of the decent people of all races and creeds—a majority which was, till then, unconscious of itself.

Jesus said that when the fig trees put forth their leaves "summer is nigh" (Matthew 24:32). Thus warned that summer is upon us, let us not then complain of the heat.

Have I come today only to add one more to the already long list of special challenges faced by you and me? Not really. I have also come to say to you that God, who foresaw all challenges, has given to us a precious doctrine which can encourage us in meeting this and all other challenges.

The combined doctrine of God's foreknowledge and of fore-ordination is one of the doctrinal roads least traveled by, yet these clearly underline how very long and how perfectly God has loved us and known us with our individual needs and capacities. Isolated from other doctrines or mishandled, though, these truths can stoke the fires of fatalism, impact adversely upon our agency, cause us to focus on status rather than service, and carry us over into predestination. President Joseph Fielding Smith once warned:

*It is very evident from a thorough study of the gospel and the plan of salva-*
*tion that a conclusion that those who accepted the Savior were predestined*
*to be saved no matter what the nature of their lives must be an error. . . .*
*Surely Paul never intended to convey such a thought.* [*The Improvement*
*Era*, May 1963, pp. 350–51]

Paul, you will recall, brothers and sisters, stressed running the life's
race the full distance; he did *not* intend a casual Christianity in which
some had won the race even before the race had started.

Yet, though foreordination is a difficult doctrine, it has been given
to us by the living God, through living prophets, for a purpose. It
can actually increase our understanding of how crucial this mortal
estate is and it can encourage us in further good works. This precious
doctrine can also help us to go the second mile because we are doubly
called.

In some ways, our second estate, in relationship to our first estate,
is like agreeing in advance to surgery. Then the anesthetic of forgetfulness settles in upon us. Just as doctors do not de-anesthetize a
patient in the midst of authorized surgery to ask him again if the surgery should be continued, so, after divine tutoring, we agreed once to
come here and to submit ourselves to certain experiences and have no
occasion to revoke that decision.

Of course, when we mortals try to comprehend, rather than
merely accept, foreordination, the result is one in which finite minds
futilely try to comprehend omniscience. A full understanding is
impossible; we simply have to trust in what the Lord has told us,
knowing enough, however, to realize that we are not dealing with
*guarantees* from God but extra *opportunities*—and heavier responsibilities. If those responsibilities are in some ways linked to past performance or to past capabilities, it should not surprise us.

The Lord has said,

*There is a law, irrevocably decreed in heaven before the foundations of this*
*world, upon which all blessings are predicated—*

*And when we obtain any blessing from God, it is by obedience to that law upon which it is predicated.* [D&C 130:20–21]

This is an eternal law, brothers and sisters—it prevailed in the first estate as well as in the second. It should not disconcert us, therefore, that the Lord has indicated that he chose some individuals before they came here to carry out certain assignments and, hence, these individuals have been foreordained to those assignments. "Every man who has a calling to minister to the inhabitants of the world was ordained to that very purpose in the Grand Council of Heaven before the world was. I suppose that I was ordained to this very office in that Grand Council" (Joseph Fielding Smith, comp., *Teachings of the Prophet Joseph Smith*, p. 365).

Foreordination is like any other blessing—it is a conditional bestowal subject to our faithfulness. Prophesies foreshadow events without determining the outcomes, because of a divine foreseeing of outcomes. So foreordination is a conditional bestowal of a role, a responsibility, or a blessing which, likewise, foresees but does not fix the outcome.

There have been those who have failed or who have been treasonous to their trust such as David, Solomon, Judas. God foresaw the fall of David, but was not the cause of it. It was David who saw Bathsheba from the balcony and sent for her. But neither was God surprised by such a sad development. God foresaw, but did not cause, Martin Harris's loss of certain pages of the translated Book of Mormon; God made plans to cope with that failure over fifteen hundred years before it was to occur (see D&C 10 and Words of Mormon).

Thus foreordination is clearly no excuse for fatalism or arrogance or the abuse of agency. It is not, however, a doctrine that can simply be ignored because it is difficult. Indeed, deep inside the hardest doctrines are some of the pearls of greatest price. The doctrine pertains not only to the foreordination of the prophets, but to each of us. God—in his precise assessment, beforehand, as to those who will respond to the words of the Savior and the prophets—is a part of the plan. From the Savior's own lips came these words: "I am the good

shepherd, and know my sheep, and am known of mine" (John 10:14).
Similarly the Savior said, "My sheep hear my voice, and I know them,
and they follow me" (John 10:27). And further in this dispensation,
he declared, "And ye are called to bring to pass the gathering of
mine elect; for mine elect hear my voice and harden not their hearts"
(D&C 29:7).

This responsiveness could not have been gauged without divine
foreknowledge concerning all of us mortals and our response, one
way or another, to the gospel. God's foreknowledge is so perfect it
leaves the realm of prediction and enters the realm of prophecy.

The foreseeing of those who would accept the gospel in mortality, gladly and with alacrity, is based upon their parallel responsiveness in the premortal world. No wonder the Lord could say as he
did to Jeremiah, "Before I formed thee in the belly I knew thee; . . .
and I ordained thee a prophet unto the nations" (Jeremiah 1:5). Paul,
when writing to the saints in Rome, said, "God hath not cast away
his people which he foreknew" (Romans 11:2). Paul also said of God
that "he hath chosen us in him before the foundation of the world"
(Ephesians 1:4).

The Lord, who was able to say to his disciples, "Cast the net on
the right side of the ship," knew beforehand there was a multitude of
fishes there (John 21:6). If he knew beforehand the movements and
whereabout of fishes in the little Sea of Tiberias, should it offend us
that he knows beforehand which mortals will come into the gospel
net?

It does no violence even to our frail human logic to observe that
there cannot be a grand plan of salvation for all mankind, unless there
is also a plan for each individual. The salvational sum will reflect
all its parts. Once the believer acknowledges that the past, present,
and future are before God simultaneously—even though we do not
understand how—then the doctrine of foreordination may be seen
somewhat more clearly. For instance, it was necessary for God to
know how the economic difficulties and crop failures of the Joseph
Smith, Senior, family in New England would move this special family
to Cumorah country where the Book of Mormon plates were buried.

God's plans could scarcely have so unfolded if—willy-nilly—the Smiths had been born Manchurians and if, meanwhile, the plates had been buried in Belgium!

The Lord would need to have perfect comprehension of all the military and political developments, including those now underway in the Middle East—which, when they unfold, will combine to bring to pass a latter-day condition in which "all nations" will be gathered against Jerusalem to battle (Zechariah 14:2–4). It should not surprise us that the Lord who notices the fall of each sparrow and the hair from every head would know centuries before how much money Judas would receive—thirty pieces of silver—at the time he betrayed the Savior (Matthew 26:15; 27:3; Zechariah 11:12).

Quite understandably, the manner in which things unfold seems to us mortals to be so natural. Our not knowing what is to come (in the perfect way that God knows) thus preserves our free agency completely. When, through a process we call inspiration and revelation, we are permitted at times to tap that divine databank, we are accessing, for the narrow purposes at hand, the knowledge of God. No wonder that experience is so unforgettable!

There are clearly special cases of individuals in mortality who have special limitations in life, which conditions we mortals cannot now fully fathom. For all we now know, the seeming limitations may have been an agreed-upon spur to achievement—a "thorn in the flesh." Like him who was blind from birth, some come to bring glory to God (John 9:1–3). We must be exceedingly careful about imputing either wrong causes or wrong rewards to all in such circumstances. They are in the Lord's hands, and he loves them perfectly. Indeed, some of those who have required much waiting upon in this life may be waited upon again by the rest of us in the next world—but for the highest of reasons.

Thus, when we are elected to certain mortal chores, we are elected "according to the foreknowledge of God the Father" (1 Peter 1:2). When Abraham was advised that he "was chosen before he was born," and that he was among the "noble and great ones" (Abraham 3:22–23), we received a marvelous insight. Through the revelation given to us by the prophet Joseph F. Smith we read that "The Prophet Joseph Smith, . . . Hyrum Smith, Brigham Young, John Taylor, Wilford Woodruff, and other choice spirits" were also reserved by God "to come forth in the fullness of times to take part in laying the foundations of the great latter-day work" (JFS Vision 53). These individuals are among the rulers whom Abraham had described to him centuries earlier by God. They were to be "rulers in the Church of God" (JFS Vision 55), not necessarily rulers in secular kingdoms. Thus those seen by Abraham were the Pauls, not the Caesars; the Spencer W. Kimballs, not the Churchills. Wise secular leaders do much lasting and commendable good; but as Paul observed to the saints in Corinth, as the world measured greatness and wisdom "not many wise men after the flesh, not many mighty, not many noble, are called" (1 Corinthians 1:26).

President Joseph Fielding Smith wrote: "In regard to the holding of the priesthood in preexistence, I will say that there was an organization there just as well as an organization here, and men there held authority. Men chosen to positions of trust in the spirit world held priesthood" (*Doctrines of Salvation* 3:81). Alma speaks about foreordination with great effectiveness and links it to the foreknowledge of God and, perhaps, even to our previous performance (Alma 13:3–5). The omniscience of God made it possible, therefore, for him to determine the boundaries and times of nations (Acts 17:26; Deuteronomy 32:8).

Elder Orson Hyde said of our life in the premortal world, "We understood things better there than we do in this lower world." Elder Hyde also surmised as to the agreements we made there as follows: "It is not impossible that we signed the articles thereof with our own hands,—which articles may be retained in the archives above, to be presented to us when we rise from the dead, and be judged out of our own mouths, according to that which is written in the books." Just because we have forgotten, said Elder Hyde, "our forgetfulness cannot alter the facts" (Brigham Young, *Journal of Discourses* 7:314–15). Brothers and sisters, the degree of detail involved in the covenants and promises we participated in at that time may be a much more highly customized thing than many of us surmise. Yet, on occasion even with our forgetting, there may be inklings. President Joseph F. Smith wrote:

*But in coming here, we forget all, that our agency might be free indeed, to choose good or evil, that we might merit the reward of our own choice and conduct. But by the power of the Spirit, in the redemption of Christ* through obedience, we often catch a spark from the awakened memories of the immortal soul, *which lights up our whole being as with the glory of our former home.* [*Gospel Doctrines,* pp. 13–14; emphasis added]

As indicated earlier, this powerful teaching of foreordination is bound to be a puzzlement in some respects, especially if we do not have faith and trust in the Lord. Yet if we think about it, even within our finite framework of experience, it should not startle us. Mortal parents are reasonably good at predicting the behavior of their children in certain circumstances. Of this Elder James E. Talmage wrote:

*Our Heavenly Father has a full knowledge of the nature and disposition of each of His children, a knowledge gained by long observation and experience in the past eternity of our primeval childhood; a knowledge compared with which that gained by earthly parents through mortal experience with their children is infinitesimally small. By reason of that surpassing knowledge, God reads the future of child and children, of men individually and of men collectively as communities and nations; He knows what each will do under given conditions, and sees the end from the beginning. His foreknowledge is based on intelligence and reason. He foresees the future as a state which naturally and surely will be; not as one which must be because He has arbitrarily willed that it shall be.—From the author's* Great Apostasy, *pp. 19, 20.* [*Jesus the Christ,* p. 29]

Another helpful analogy for students is the reality that universities, including this one, can and do predict with a high degree of accuracy the grades entering students will receive in their college careers based upon certain tests, past performances, and so forth. If mortals can do this with reasonable accuracy (and even with a short span of familiarity and finite data), God, the Father, who knows us perfectly, surely can foresee how we will respond to various challenges. While we often do not rise to our opportunities, God is neither pleased nor surprised. But we cannot say to him later on that we could have achieved if we had just been given the chance! This is all part of the justice of God.

One of the most helpful—indeed very necessary—parallel truths to be pondered when studying this powerful doctrine of foreordination is given in the revelation of the Lord to Moses in which the Lord says, "And all things are present with me, for I know them all" (Moses 1:6). God does not live in the dimension of time as do we. Moreover, since "all things are present with" God, his is not simply a predicting based solely upon the past. In ways which are not clear to us, he actually *sees*, rather than *foresees*, the future—because all things are, at once, present before him.

In a revelation given to the Prophet Joseph Smith, the Lord described himself as "The same which knoweth all things, for all things are present before mine eyes" (D&C 38:2). From the prophet Nephi we receive the same basic insight in which we, likewise, must trust: "But the Lord knoweth all things from the beginning; wherefore, he prepareth a way to accomplish all his works among the children of men" (1 Nephi 9:6). It was by divine design that Mary became the mother of Jesus. Further, Lucy Mack Smith, who played such a crucial role in the rearing of Joseph Smith, did not come to that assignment by chance.

One of the dimensions of worshipping a living God is to know that he is alive and living in the sense of seeing and acting. He is not a retired God whose best years are past, to whom we should pay a retroactive obeisance, worshipping him for what he has already done. He is the living God who is, at once, in all the dimensions of time— the past and present and future—while we labor constrained by the limitations of time itself.

It is imperative, brothers and sisters, that we always keep in mind the caveats noted earlier, so that we do not indulge ourselves or our whims, simply because of the presence of this powerful doctrine of foreordination, for with special opportunities come special responsibilities and much greater risks. But the doctrine of foreordination properly understood and humbly pursued can help us immensely in coping with the vicissitudes of life. Otherwise, time can tug at us and play so many tricks upon us. We should always understand that while God is never surprised, we often are.

Life episodes can take on a new meaning. For instance, Simon, the Cyrenian, wandered into Jerusalem that very day and was pressed into service by Roman soldiers to help carry the cross of Christ (see Mark 15:21). Simon's son, Rufus, joined the Church, and was so well thought of by the apostle Paul that the latter mentioned Rufus in his epistle to the Romans, describing him as "chosen in the Lord" (Romans 16:13). Was it, therefore, a mere accident that Simon "who passed by, coming out of the country" (Mark 15:21), was asked to bear the cross of Jesus?

Properly humbled and instructed concerning the great privileges that are ours, we can cope with what seem to be very dark days and difficult developments, because we will have a true perspective about "things as they really are," and we can see in them a great chance to contribute. Churchill, in trying to rally his countrymen in an address at Harrow School in October of 1941, said to them:

*Do not let us speak of darker days; let us speak rather of sterner days. These are not dark days: these are great days—the greatest days our country has ever lived; and we must all thank God that we have been allowed, each of us according to our stations, to play a part in making these days memorable in the history of our race.* [Bartlett's Familiar Quotations, p. 923]

Brothers and sisters, so we should regard the dispensation of the fullness of times—even when we face stern challenges and circumstances, "these are great days"! Our hearts need not fail us. We can be equal to our challenges, including the aforementioned challenge of the secular church.

The truth about foreordination also helps us to taste the deep wisdom of Alma, when he said we ought to be content with things that God hath allotted to each of us (Alma 29:3, 4). If, indeed, the things allotted to each of us have been divinely customized according to our ability and capacity, then for us to seek to wrench ourselves free of our schooling circumstances could be to tear ourselves away from carefully matched opportunities. To rant and to rail could be to go against divine wisdom, wisdom in which we may have once concurred before we came here. God knew beforehand each of our coefficients for coping and contributing and has so ordered our lives.

The late President Henry D. Moyle said,

> *I believe that we, as fellow workers in the priesthood, might well take to heart the admonition of Alma and be content with that which God hath allotted us. We might well be assured that we had something to do with our "allotment" in our preexistent state. This would be an additional reason for us to accept our present condition and make the best of it. It is what we agreed to do.* [CR, October 1952, p. 71]

By the way, brothers and sisters, I hasten to add that among the things "allotted" are not included things like a bad temper. The deficiencies of a developmental variety are those we are expected to overcome.

Now, as I prepare to conclude, may I point out what a vastly different view of life the doctrine of foreordination gives to us. Shorn of this perspective, others are puzzled or bitter about life. Without gospel perspective life would be a punishment, not a joy—like trying to play a game of billiards on a table with a rumpled cloth, with a crooked cue and an elliptical billiard ball (from Sir William S. Gilbert's libretto of *The Mikado*). (Perhaps the moral of that analogy is that we should stay out of pool halls.) In any event, pessimism does not really reckon with life and the universe as these things "really are." The disciple will be puzzled at times, too. But he persists. Later he rejoices over how wonderfully things fit together, realizing only then that, with God, things never were apart.

Jacob said that the Spirit teaches us the truth "of things as they really are, and of things as they really will be" (Jacob 4:13). Centuries later Paul said that the "Spirit searcheth . . . the deep things of God" (1 Corinthians 2:10). Of some of these deep things we have spoken today, and of how things really are. Brothers and sisters, in some of those precious and personal moments of deep discovery, there will be a sudden surge of recognition of an immortal insight, a doctrinal déjà vu. We will sometimes experience a flash from the mirror of memory that beckons us forward toward a far horizon.

When in situations of stress we wonder if there is any more in us to give, we can be comforted to know that God, who knows our capacity perfectly, placed us here to succeed. No one was foreordained to fail or to be wicked. When we have been weighed and found wanting, let us remember that we were measured before and we were found equal to our tasks; and, therefore, let us continue, but with a more determined discipleship. When we feel overwhelmed, let us recall the assurance that God will not overprogram us; he will not press upon us more than we can bear (D&C 50:40).

The doctrine of foreordination, therefore, is not a doctrine of repose; it is a doctrine for the second-milers; it can draw out of us the last full measure of devotion. It is a doctrine of perspiration, not aspiration. Moreover, it discourages aspiring, lest we covet, like two early disciples, that which has already been given to another (Matthew 20:20–23). Foreordination is a doctrine for the deep believer and will only bring scorn from the skeptic.

When, as Joseph F. Smith said, we "catch a spark from the awakened memories of the immortal soul," let us be quietly grateful. And when of great truths we can come to say "I know," that powerful spiritual witness may also carry with it the sense of our having known before. With rediscovery, what we are really saying is, "I know— again!" No wonder that, so often, real teaching is mere reminding.

God bless you and keep you, my special friends, to the end that you will each carry out all of the assignments given to you so very long ago. You have been measured and found adequate for the challenges that will face you as citizens of the kingdom of God; of that you should have a deep inner assurance. Be true to that trust, as all of us must, I pray in the name of Jesus Christ. Amen.

# Patience

Neal A. Maxwell

Thank you very much, Bob. I appreciate this great privilege each time that it is mine, my brothers and sisters. I am grateful to the choral group today for that last number, the lyrics of which I hope will linger with you somewhat, because I will turn to them as I close my speech.

I have chosen to speak today about a very pedestrian principle: patience; I hope that I do not empty the Marriott Center by that selection. Perhaps the topic was selfishly selected because of my clear and continuing need to develop further this very important attribute. But my interest in patience is not solely personal; for the necessity of having this intriguing attribute is cited several times in the scriptures, including once by King Benjamin who, when clustering the attributes of sainthood, named patience as a charter member of that cluster (Mosiah 3:19; see also Alma 7:23).

Patience is not indifference. Actually, it means caring very much but being willing, nevertheless, to submit to the Lord and to what the scriptures call the "process of time."

*This devotional address was given at Brigham Young University on 27 November 1979.*

Patience is tied very closely to faith in our Heavenly Father. Actually, when we are unduly impatient we are suggesting that we know what is best—better than does God. Or, at least, we are asserting that our timetable is better than His. Either way we are questioning the reality of God's omniscience as if, as some seem to believe, God were on some sort of postdoctoral fellowship and were not quite in charge of everything.

Saint Teresa of Avila said that unless we come to know the reality of God, including his omniscience, our mortal existence "will be no more than a night in a second-class hotel" (quoted by Malcolm Muggerridge in "The Great Liberal Death Wish," *Imprimis* [Hillsdale College, Michigan], May 1979.) Our second estate can be a first-class experience only if you and I develop a patient faith in God and in his unfolding purposes.

We read in Mosiah about how the Lord simultaneously tries the patience of His people even as He tries their faith (Mosiah 23:21). One is not only to endure, but to endure well and gracefully those things which the Lord "seeth fit to inflict upon [us]" (Mosiah 3:19), just as did a group of ancient American saints who were bearing unusual burdens but who submitted "cheerfully and with patience to all the will of the Lord" (Mosiah 24:15).

Paul, speaking to the Hebrews, brings us up short by writing that, even after faithful disciples had "done the will of God," they "[had] need of patience" (Hebrews 10:36). How many times have good individuals done the right thing only to break or wear away under subsequent stress, canceling out much of the value of what they had already so painstakingly done? Sometimes that which we are doing is correct enough but simply needs to be persisted in patiently, not for a minute or a moment but sometimes for years. Paul speaks of the marathon of life and of how we must "run with patience the race that is set before us" (Hebrews 12:1). Paul did not select the hundred-meter dash for his analogy!

The Lord has twice said: "And seek the face of the Lord always, that *in patience ye may possess your souls*, and ye shall have eternal life" (D&C 101:38, emphasis added; see also Luke 21:19). Could it be, brothers and sisters, that only when our self-control becomes total do we come into the true possession of our souls?

Patience is not only a companion of faith but is also a friend to free agency. Inside our impatience there is sometimes an ugly reality: We are plainly irritated and inconvenienced by the need to make allowance for the free agency of others. In our impatience—which is not the same thing as divine discontent—we would override others, even though it is obvious that our individual differences and preferences are so irretrievably enmeshed with each other that the only resolution which preserves free agency is our patience and longsuffering with each other.

The passage of time is not, by itself, an automatic cure for bad choices; but often individuals like the prodigal son can "in process of time" come to their senses. The touching reunion of Jacob and Esau in the desert, so many years after their youthful rivalry, is a classic example of how generosity can replace animosity when truth is mixed with time. When we are unduly impatient, we are, in effect, trying to hasten an outcome when this kind of acceleration would be to abuse agency. Enoch—brilliant, submissive, and spiritual—knew what it meant to see a whole city-culture advance in "process of time." He could tell us much about so many things, including patience. Patience makes possible a personal spiritual symmetry which arises only, brothers and sisters, from prolonged obedience within free agency.

There is also a dimension of patience which links it to a special reverence for life. Patience is a willingness, in a sense, to watch the unfolding purposes of God with a sense of wonder and awe, rather than pacing up and down within the cell of our circumstance. Put another way, too much anxious opening of the oven door and the cake falls instead of rising. So it is with us. If we are always selfishly taking our temperature to see if we are happy, we will not be.

When we are impatient, we are neither reverential nor reflective because we are too self-centered. Whereas faith and patience are companions, so are selfishness and impatience. It is so easy to be confrontive without being informative; so easy to be indignant without being intelligent; so easy to be impulsive without being insightful.

It is so easy to command others when we are not in control of ourselves.

I remember as a child going eagerly to the corner store for what we then called an "all-day sucker." It would not have lasted all day under the best usage, but it could last quite awhile. The trick was to resist the temptation to bite into it, to learn to savor rather than to crunch and chew. The same savoring was needed with a precious square of Hershey milk chocolate to make the treat last, especially in depression times.

In life, however, even patiently stretching out sweetness is sometimes not enough; in certain situations, enjoyment must actually be deferred. A patient willingness to defer dividends is a hallmark of individual maturity. It is, parenthetically, a hallmark of free nations that their citizens can discipline themselves today for a better tomorrow. Yet America is in trouble (as are other nations) precisely because a patient persistence in a wise course of public policy is so difficult to attain. Too many impatient politicians buy today's votes with tomorrow's inflation.

But back to the personal relevance of patience which, among many things, permits us to deal more effectively with the unevenness of life's experiences. I recorded the substance of this speech about three months ago while driving to a stake conference in Elko, Nevada, across that rather barren, but beautiful in its own way, stretch of desert. (Incidentally, as soon as most of this speech on patience was dictated my car threw two fan belts!) During that drive, it was brought forcibly to me that the seeming flat periods of life give us a blessed chance to reflect upon what is past as well as to be readied for some rather stirring climbs ahead. Instead of grumbling and murmuring, we should be consolidating and reflecting, which would not be possible if life were an uninterrupted sequence of fantastic scenery, confrontive events, and exhilarating conversation.

Patience helps us to use, rather than to protest, these seeming flat periods of life, becoming filled with quiet wonder over the past and with anticipation for that which may lie ahead, instead of demeaning the particular flatness through which we may be passing at the time.

We should savor even the seemingly ordinary times, for life cannot be made up all of kettledrums and crashing cymbals. There must be some flutes and violins. Living cannot be all crescendo; there must be some dynamic contrast.

Clearly, without patience we will learn less in life. We will see less; we will feel less; we will hear less. Ironically, "rush" and "more" usually mean "less." The pressure of "now," time and time again, go against the grain of the gospel with its eternalism.

There is also in patience a greater opportunity for that discernment which sorts out the things that matter most from the things that matter least. The mealtime episode of the Savior in the home of Mary and Martha is an example. Anxious, impatient Martha focused on getting food on the table while Mary wisely chose "the good part"—companionship and conversation instead of calories—a good choice, the Savior said, which would not be taken from her.

In our approach to life, patience also helps us to realize that while we may be ready to move on, having had enough of a particular learning experience, our continued presence is often needed as a part of the learning environment of others. Patience is thus closely connected with two other central attributes of Christianity—love and humility. Paul said to the saints at Thessalonica, "Be patient toward all men"—clearly a part of keeping the second great commandment (1 Thessalonians 5:14).

The patient person assumes that what others have to say is worth listening to. A patient person is not so chronically eager to put forth his or her own ideas. In true humility, we do some waiting upon others. We value them for what they say and what they have to contribute. Patience and humility are special friends.

Since our competition in life, as Elder Boyd K. Packer has perceptively said, is solely with our old self, we ought to be free, you and I, as members of the Church, from the jealousies and anxieties of the world which go with interpersonal competition. Very importantly, it is patience, when combined with love, which permits us "in process of time" to detoxify our disappointments. Patience and love take the

radioactivity out of our resentments. These are neither small nor
occasional needs in most of our lives.

Further, the patient person can better understand how there are
circumstances when, if our hearts are set too much upon the things of
this world, they must be broken—but for our sakes, and not merely
as a demonstration of divine power. But it takes real patience in such
circumstances to wait for the later vindication of our trust in the
Lord.

Therefore, if we use the process of time well, it can cradle us
as we develop patient humility. Keats tenderly observed: "Time,
that aged nurse, /Rock'd me to patience" (John Bartlett, *Familiar
Quotations*, 14th ed. [Boston: Little, Brown and Company, 1968],
p. 580). Clearly, patience so cradles us when we are in the midst of
suffering. Paul, who suffered much, observed in his epistle to the
Hebrews: "Now no chastening for the present seemeth to be joyous,
but grievous: nevertheless afterward it yieldeth the peaceable fruit
of righteousness unto them which are exercised thereby" (Hebrews
12:11).

Patience permits us to cling to our faith in the Lord when we are
tossed about by suffering as if by surf. When the undertow grasps us,
we will realize that even as we tumble we are somehow being carried
forward; we are actually being helped even as we cry for help.

One of the functions of the tribulations of the righteous is that
"tribulation worketh patience" (Romans 5:3). What a vital attribute
patience is if tribulation is worth enduring to bring about its development! Patience in turn brings about the needed experience, as
noted in the stunning insight the Lord gave to the Prophet Joseph
Smith: "All these things shall give thee experience, and shall be for
thy good" (D&C 122:7). Perhaps one can be forgiven if, in response
to this sobering insight, his soul shivers just a bit. James also stressed
the importance of patience when our faith is being tried, because
those grueling experiences "[work] patience," and said, in what was
almost a sigh of the soul, "Let patience have her perfect work . . ."
(James 1:3-4).

To Joseph Smith, the Lord described patience as having a special finishing and concluding quality, for "These things remain to overcome through patience, that such may receive a more exceeding and eternal weight of glory" (D&C 63:66). A patient disciple, for instance, will not be surprised nor undone when the Church is misrepresented. Peter, being toughminded as well as tender, made the test of our patience even more precise and demanding when he said, "For what glory is it, if, when ye be buffeted for your faults, ye shall take it patiently? but if, when ye do well, and suffer for it, ye take it patiently, this is acceptable with God" (1 Peter 2:20). The dues of discipleship are high indeed, and how much we can take so often determines how much we can then give. I believe it was George MacDonald who observed that, in the process of life, we are not always the already-tempered and helpful hammer which is shaping and pounding another. Sometimes we are merely the anvil.

Thus, as already indicated, patience is a vital mortal virtue in relation to our faith, our free agency, our attitude toward life, our humility, and our suffering. Moreover, patience will not be an obsolete attribute in the next world.

My brothers and sisters, the longer I examine the gospel of Jesus Christ, the more I understand that the Lord's commitment to free agency is very deep—indeed, much deeper than is our own. The more I live, the more I also sense how exquisite is His perfect love of us. It is, in fact, the very interplay of God's everlasting commitment to free agency and His everlasting and perfect love for us which inevitably places a high premium upon the virtue of patience. There is simply no other way for true growth to occur.

God's attributes of omniscience and omnipotence no doubt made the plan of salvation feasible. But it was His perfect love which made the plan inevitable. And it is His perfect patience which makes it sustainable. Do we not, again and again, get breathtaking glimpses of God's perfect patience in the execution of the plan of salvation, concerning which He has said that his "course is one eternal round" (D&C 3:2)?

Thus it is that patience is to human nature what photosynthesis is to nature. Photosynthesis, the most important single chemical reaction we know, brings together water, light, chlorophyll, and carbon dioxide, processing annually the hundreds of trillions of tons of carbon dioxide and converting them to oxygen as part of the process of making food and fuel. The marvelous process of photosynthesis is crucial to life on this planet, and it is a very constant and patient process. So, too, is an individual's spiritual growth. Neither patience nor photosynthesis are conspicuous processes.

Patience is always involved in the spiritual chemistry of the soul, not only when we try to turn the trials and tribulations—the carbon dioxide, as it were—into joy and growth, but also when we use it to build upon the seemingly ordinary experiences to bring about happy and spiritual outcomes.

Patience is, therefore, clearly not fatalistic, shoulder-shrugging resignation. It is the acceptance of a divine rhythm to life; it is obedience prolonged. Patience stoutly resists pulling up the daisies to see how the roots are doing. Patience is never condescending or exclusive—it is never glad when others are left out. Patience never preens itself; it prefers keeping the window of the soul open.

I have struggled to find adequate words to express these concluding feelings and these thoughts about our need to be patient with ourselves and with our circumstances in this second estate.

Some of us have been momentarily wrenched by the sound of a train whistle spilling into the night air, and we have been inexplicably subdued by the mix of feelings that this evokes. Or perhaps we have been beckoned by a lighted cottage across a snow-covered meadow at dusk. Or we have heard the warm and drawing laughter of children at a nearby playground. Or we have been tugged at by the strains of congregational singing from a nearby church. Or we have encountered a particular fragrance which has awakened memories deep within us of things which once were. In such moments, we have felt a deep yearning, as if we were temporarily outside of something to which we actually belonged and of which we so much wanted again to be a part.

There are spiritual equivalents of these moments. Such seem to occur most often when time touches eternity. In these moments we feel a longing closeness—but we are still separate. The partition which produces this paradox is something we call the veil—a partition the presence of which requires our patience. We define the veil as the border between mortality and eternity; it is also a film of forgetting which covers the memories of earlier experiences. This forgetfulness will be lifted one day, and on that day we will see forever—rather than "through a glass, darkly" (1 Corinthians 13:12).

There are poignant and frequent reminders of the veil, adding to our sense of being close but still outside. In our deepest prayers, when the agency of man encounters the omniscience of God, we sometimes sense, if only momentarily, how very provincial our petitions are; we perceive that there are more good answers than we have good questions; and we realize that we have been taught more than we can tell, for the language used is not that which the tongue can transmit.

We experience this same close separateness when a baby is born, but also as we wait with those who are dying—for then we brush against the veil, as goodbyes and greetings are said almost within earshot of each other. In such moments, this resonance with realities on the other side of the veil is so obvious that it can be explained in only one way!

No wonder the Savior said that His doctrines would be recognized by His sheep, that we would know His voice, that we would follow Him (John 10:14). We do not, therefore, follow strangers. Deep within us, His doctrines do strike the promised chord of familiarity and underscore our true identity. Our sense of belonging grows in spite of our sense of separateness; for His teachings stir our souls, awakening feelings within us which have somehow survived underneath the encrusting experiences of mortality.

This inner serenity which the believer knows as he brushes against the veil is cousin to certitude. The peace it brings surpasses our understanding and certainly our capacity to explain. But it requires a patience which stands in stark contrast to the restlessness of the world in which, said Isaiah, the wicked are like the pounding and troubled sea which cannot rest (Isaiah 57:20).

But mercifully the veil is there. It is fixed by the wisdom of God for our good. It is no use being impatient with the Lord over that reality, for it is clearly a condition to which we agreed so long ago. Even when the veil is parted briefly, it will be on His terms, not ours. Without the veil, we would lose that precious insulation which would constantly interfere with our mortal probation and maturation. Without the veil, our brief mortal walk in a darkening world would lose its meaning—for one would scarcely carry the flashlight of faith at noonday and in the presence of the Light of the World. Without the veil, we could not experience the gospel of work and the sweat of our brow. If we had the security of having already entered into God's rest, certain things would be unneeded; Adam and Eve did not clutch social security cards in the Garden of Eden.

And how could we learn about obedience if we were shielded from the consequences of our disobedience? And how could we learn patience under pressure if we did not experience pressure and waiting? Nor could we choose for ourselves if we were already in His holy presence, for some alternatives do not there exist. Besides, God's Court is filled with those who have patiently overcome—whose company we do not yet deserve.

Fortunately, the veil keeps the first, second, and third estates separate—hence our sense of separateness. The veil avoids having things "compound in one" to our everlasting detriment (2 Nephi 2:11). We are cocooned, as it were, in order that we might truly choose. Once, long ago, we chose to come to this very setting where we could choose. It was an irrevocable choice. And the veil is the guarantor that our ancient choice will be honored.

When the veil which encloses us is no more, time will also be no more (D&C 84:100). Even now, time is clearly not our natural dimension. Thus it is that we are never really at home in time. Alternately, we find ourselves impatiently wishing to hasten the passage of time or to hold back the dawn. We can do neither, of course. Whereas the bird is at home in the air, we are clearly not at home in time—because we belong to eternity. Time, as much as any one thing, whispers to us that we are strangers here. If time were natural to us, why is it that we have so many clocks and wear wristwatches?

Thus the veil stands—not to shut us out forever, but to remind us of God's tutoring and patient love for us. Any brush against the veil produces a feeling of "not yet," but also faint whispers of anticipation of that moment when, in the words of today's choral hymn, "Come, Let Us Anew," those who have prevailed "by the patience and hope and the labor of love" will hear the glorious words," 'Well and faithfully done; / Enter into my joy and sit down on my throne' " (*Hymns*, number 17).

May each of us live for that special moment patiently and righteously, I pray in the name of Him who is so patient with me as I strive to be an "especial witness" for him in all the world, even Jesus Christ. Amen.

# True Believers in Christ

—◆—

Neal A. Maxwell

I am delighted to be with you brothers and sisters today. It is not difficult for those of us who have admired President Holland for so long to anticipate joyfully the things he will bring to this new assignment. Among them will be his personal, small-town warmth, which will shrink the size of this big campus, and I foresee that his literacy will prove to be as contagious as is his laughter. If Mark Twain, one focus of Jeffrey Holland's graduate work, could have experienced Jeffrey's effective teaching of the Book of Mormon, Twain would not have made his uninformed and unkind remark about that book. At least Jeff would not have let him start reading in the book of Ether. And perhaps Jeff could even have put Twain "under," but not in the sense Twain meant, rather in the best missionary meaning of those words.

In our time, the words "true believer" have come to mean the manipulable and mindless who are part of political mass movements, seeking to escape from the burdens of freedom. Many years ago, a similar phrase was used, but with major definitional distinctions. The

*This devotional address was given at Brigham Young University on 7 October 1980.*

Apostle Nephi, and, even earlier, Alma, wrote of the "true believers in Christ." (see Alma 46:14 and 4 Ne. 1:36.) It is a concept too precious not to bring to the fore simply because of the current connotations of those two words. Someday, perhaps, we can rescue still other words even more sadly abused and inverted, such as "gay" and "welfare."

There are some sobering parallels between our times and these earlier groups of "true believers" in Christ who were "faithful" members of the Church, including the Three Nephites, and who had "gladly" taken upon themselves the name of Christ (see Alma 46:15). They were persecuted by the disbelievers and irreligionists of their time, but they did not retaliate because of their commitment to Christ and because of their humility (see 4 Ne. 1:29–37). Theirs, too, was a time of polarities, for there was a "great division among the people" (4 Ne. 1:35).

So much for the background of today's theme. The "true believers in Christ" will be spoken of for the sake of convenience throughout my discussion in terms of "he," but, of course, this group includes both women and men.

Jesus, of course, knows who His true believers are. Others may know who His disciples are by the central characteristic of love, as we were so well taught by today's lovely choral hymn, "Love One Another."

To begin with, the true believer, notwithstanding his weaknesses, is settled in his basic spirituality. He is settled, to use another of Alma's phrases, in his "views of Christ" (Alma 27:28), so his views of everything else are put in that precious perspective.

There are, of course, other kinds of believers who are not "true believers." In the parable of the seeds, one outcome was when the seed had no root, typifying those who "for a while believe" but who "in time of temptation fall away" (Luke 8:13). Alma warned us (in his own seed analogy) about the withering effect when the "heat of the sun cometh and scorcheth" the undernourished tree of shallow root (Alma 32). Other observations of Jesus add the insight about how tribulation and persecution cause the weak to be offended and to fall away (Matt. 13:6, 21).

Most of us here have had the sad experience of seeing some wither because they cannot stand the heat. They are not likely to acknowledge that as the real reason for their failures but will conveniently choose an issue over which they can become offended. Another dynamic operates, too. In racing marathons, one does not see the dropouts make fun of those who continue; failed runners actually cheer on those who continue the race, wishing they were still in it. Not so with the marathon of discipleship in which some dropouts then make fun of the spiritual enterprise of which they were so recently a part!

In the Joseph Smith translation of the Bible, Jesus comments about bearing one's cross and the demands of discipleship and then adds, "Wherefore, settle this in your hearts, that ye will do the things which I shall teach, and command you" (Inspired Version, Luke 14:28). Being so settled is a part of becoming a true believer.

The need for such deep determination fits well with other scriptural descriptions in which words like these are used: "stablished," "settled," "grounded," "rooted." When we are so situated, then let the heat of the sun come. (see, Col. 2:7; Col. 1:23; 1 Pet. 5:10.)

Getting settled also includes achieving a comfortableness with the behavioral standards of the Savior. When we do this, said Paul in an intriguing verse, we will then know the love of Christ "which passeth knowledge" (Phil. 4:7), and we can truly "comprehend . . . the breadth, and length, and depth, and height" of things (Eph. 3:17, 18). We can size things up spiritually because added perceptivity actually comes to us when we live righteously. Should it surprise us that behaving leads to further knowing? Could the scripture about particular blessings coming from particular obedience to laws be any more plain?

Those, however, who "for a while believe" never have these adventures which are reserved for the "true believers of Christ." Those who "almost" believe will never know these joys, for they are far too easily satisfied. Those who believe for a while make only a brief tour in the kingdom, though, thereafter, they often feel qualified to inform those who know even less about the Church; but the fact is they were really only tourists—not natives who really knew the kingdom's countryside.

The true believers are helped in keeping the basic commandments by gladly performing their specific duties in the kingdom. These duties, brothers and sisters, are usually measurable and straightforward. They include: partaking of the sacrament, receiving the gospel ordinances, attending meetings and the temple, praying, fasting, studying the scriptures, rendering Christian service, attending to all family duties, being involved in missionary work and reactivation, doing genealogical work, paying tithes and offerings, and being temporally prepared. The true believer willing does these things because he sees their clear connection to keeping the commandments. For instance, proper participation in the Lord's welfare program carries with it this significant blessing: *"For the sake of retaining a remission of your sins from day to day,* . . . I would that ye should *impart of your substance to the poor"* (Mos. 4:26; italics added).

These duties are practical and specific expressions of keeping the first two great commandments—the love of God and the love of neighbor. Clearly, we cannot become true believers in Christ merely by keeping the sixth commandment—"Thou shalt not kill."

Discipleship, therefore, means being drawn by seemingly small and routine duties toward the fulfillment of the two great and most challenging commandments.

Of the Ten Commandments, *as originally given*, eight were stated as "thou shalt nots" and two were required affirmations. (See Ex. 20, Deut. 5, but also Lev. 19:18.) Jesus' later statement cast the two great commandments as grand affirmatives (see Matt. 22:34–40). Brothers and sisters, our duties involve implementing ways of keeping the two great commandments because they require us to "do" rather than to merely "abstain." Abstentions do not necessarily move us on to affirmative actions, and our duties constitute the "thou shalts" in the gospel of Jesus Christ.

True enough, the highly developed disciple will have no difficulty translating his devotion to the Savior into loving his neighbor; he will find a hundred quality ways to implement the truths in today's choral hymn, "Love One Another," but most of us need specific steppingstones.

While we resist being driven by quotas into doing temple work or scolded into achieving convert baptisms, at the same time, reminders are relevant. As we grow and develop, a particular reminder may become necessary—but only "in that thing."

Moreover, the duty least enjoyed by us, like the doctrine least understood, may be the one we need the most. Furthermore, our reminders to do these specific duties are often a call to an unkept rendezvous, to an experience we would not want to miss. The true believer understands this; he does his duties even though they are seemingly repetitious, but he is never surprised if duty develops into a new adventure.

Great care must be exercised, however, so that in all of this, we do not pass off our personal preferences as the Lord's program; we must not confuse our personal religious hobbies with His orthodoxy. Nor must we ever pass off a personal obsession as a spiritual impression.

Because true believers are "meek and lowly of heart," they are ready to be taught things they "never had supposed" as was Moses, the most meek man upon the earth (see Moses 1:7–11; Num. 12:3). Let the intellectually proud pace up and down in their tight conceptual cells if they choose, but the humble find such too confining.

Two other virtues of the meek are that they are not easily offended and they do not resist counsel. Nor are these lowly in heart inclined to see themselves as being "above" all the seemingly routine duties of discipleship. Duties are not to be rejected on the basis of "I've done all that before," as if God were required to supply us with new thrills. Mortality has been described by the Lord as being like working in a vineyard—never as an afternoon at a carnival. Besides, how could we pretend to be true believers of Christ, if we shunned the chores of the kingdom!

Furthermore, brothers and sisters, we will find that when we have personal spiritual experiences—which keep us close to the Lord—these will almost always occur in the course of our carrying out the specific duties named earlier, since it is not enough for us to have once been close to the Savior. (So was Sidney Rigdon.) Alma said, if we have once "felt to sing the song of redeeming love," can we "feel so now?" (Alma 5:26). Dutiful discipleship creates many happy memories, but it does not make nostalgia a substitute for fresh achievement.

Instead of having a "woeful countenance," the true believer in Christ has a *disciplined enthusiasm* to work righteousness. As, week after week, he tries to help people who "droop in sin" (see 2 Ne. 4:28), the electricity of his enthusiasm for righteousness helps to brace and to straighten the sad.

Becoming a true believer, however, means trusting not only in the Lord's plan for all of mankind but especially trusting in His unfolding and particularized plan for each of us. This means much more than merely acknowledging that God is in charge. Alma's warning that living without God in the world is "contrary to the nature of happiness" (Alma 41:11) was not just for agnostics but also for passive believers. Putting first things first is vital, as these eloquent words of Malcolm Muggeridge attest:

> *When I look back on my life nowadays, which I sometimes do, what strikes me most forcibly about it is that what seemed at the time most significant and seductive, seems now futile and absurd. For instance, success in all of its various guises; being known and being praised, ostensible pleasures, like acquiring money or seducing women, or traveling, going to and fro in the world and up and down in it like Satan, exploring and experiencing whatever Vanity Fair has to offer. In retrospect all these exercises in self-gratification seem pure fantasy, what Pascal called "licking the earth." They are diversions designed to distract in this world, which is, quite simply, to look for God, and, in looking, to find Him, and, having found Him, to love Him, thereby establishing a harmonious relationship with His purposes for His creation.* [Thomas Nelson, *A Twentieth Century Testimony* (New York, 1978)]

Our fully "harmonious relationship" with God must also reckon, however, with the episode of the young man who told the Savior that he had kept all the commandments from his youth. Jesus then gave him a very customized challenge: to go and sell all that he had, giving the proceeds to the poor and then taking up the cross and following the Savior. Doing so, indicated the Savior to the young man, would take care of the "one thing thou lackest" (Mark 10:21). The good and decent young man went away sorrowing because he could not meet that customized challenge; he was clearly an admirer of Jesus, but not a true believer in Christ. Nor are we, if we shrink from our customized challenges.

Indeed, would that some of us, like the young man, lacked just one thing. But having a healthy awareness of that which we yet "lack" can be a needed spur. We may have proved, for instance, that we can play checkers, but are we now ready to play chess? Are we willing to let the Lord lead us into further developmental experiences? Or do we shrink back? The things which "greatly enlarge the soul" inevitably involve stretching.

Tactical tests to help us measure how we are doing in developing the spirituality that characterizes the true believers in Christ might include the following:

1. The true believer has struck a balance between being too content with himself and being caught up in the equally dangerous human tendency of wishing for an enlarged and more important role. Alma said, "I ought to be content with the things which the Lord hath allotted unto me" (Alma 29:3). Often ignored is the tutoring sixth verse which follows: "Now, seeing that I know these things, why should I desire more than to perform the work to which I have been called?" To develop careful contentment by using our existing opportunities is obviously one of our great challenges, particularly so when we seem to be in a "flat" period of life. We may feel underused, underwhelmed, and underappreciated, even as we ironically ignore unused opportunities for service which are all about us.

2. The true believer has some Jethros in his life to give him needed and sometimes hard counsel.

*And Moses' father in law said unto him, The thing that thou doest is not good.*

*Thou wilt surely wear away, both thou, and this people that is with thee: for this thing is too heavy for thee; thou are not able to perform it thyself alone.* [Ex. 18:17–18]

Do we have Jethros who can speak to us with that kind of directness and yet be humbly received by us?

Furthermore, since a Jethro may be anywhere, do we listen "down" and "sideways" as well as "up"?

*And* [Naaman's] *servants came near, and spake unto him, and said, My father, if the prophet had bid thee do some great thing, wouldest thou not have done it? How much rather then, when he saith to thee, Wash, and be clean?* [2 Kings 5:13]

Naaman, fortunately, decided not to overlook "underlings." Notably, though Naaman expected a dramatic display of healing, he was cleansed by doing a seemingly routine thing.

3. The true believer has a sense of proportion so that Martha-like anxieties do not crowd out the Mary-like choices.

*And Jesus answered and said unto her, Martha, Martha, thou are careful and troubled about many things:*

*But one thing is needful: and Mary hath chosen that good part, which shall not be taken away from her.* [Luke 10:41–42; see also verses 38–40]

Martha was not the last conscientious Church member who was confused about priorities.

4. His personal prayers are not the easy, casual petitions—like the one of which the Lord said, "Behold, you have not understood; you have supposed that I would give it unto you, when you took no thought save it was to ask me" (D&C 9:7). The true believer's prayers, at least some of the time, are *inspired* petitions.

*But know this, it shall be given you what you shall ask.* [D&C 50:30]
*He that asketh in the Spirit asketh according to the will of God; wherefore it is done even as he asketh.* [D&C 46:30]

The Lord said commandingly to a true believer in another age:

*And now, because thou hast done this with such unwearyingness, behold, I will bless thee forever; and I will make thee mighty in word and in deed, in faith and in works; yea, even that all things shall be done unto thee* according to thy word, *for thou shalt not ask that which is contrary to my will.* [Hel. 10:5; emphasis added]

5. The true believer has both right conduct *and* right reasons for that conduct. He is so secure in his relationship with the Lord that his goodness would continue even if he were not seen of men. He would fill his role in the Church even if there were no mortal taking of the roll:

*Take heed that ye do not alms before men,* to be seen of them. [*Matt. 6:1;* emphasis added]
*We then that are strong ought to bear the infirmities of the weak,* and not to please ourselves. [Rom. 15:1; emphasis added]
*Not with eyeservice,* as men-pleasers, but as the servants of Christ, doing the will of God from the heart. [Eph. 6:6; emphasis added]

6. When professionally, associationally, or even in Church service, he may seem to have been "put out to pasture," the true believer can still say of the Lord (and mean it), "He maketh me to lie down in green pasture" (Ps. 23:2).

7. When he is misrepresented, misquoted, or misused, he still loves and prays sincerely for those who despitefully use him.

8. When someone seems to surpass him spiritually and does his "thing" even better than he, he genuinely rejoices and gives them heartfelt and sincere praise. He never regards colleagues as competitors.

9. The true believer remembers that forgetting is a dimension of forgiving. It is Lordlike: "I [will] remember [their sins] no more" (D&C 58:42). He really helps others to get deservingly reclassified, and, like the Lord, does not "mention" their past mistakes to them (Ex. 18:22).

His generosity reassures the repentant and also beckons the almost-repentant who warily probe the possibility of both fellowship and forgiveness.

He can, to use Alma's phrase, "give place" for the spiritual growth of others. He is truly ready to receive not only the repentant but to recognize the frail who have, happily, grown strong. He knows that in the City of Zion there will be many "new kids on the block."

10. The true believer is careful about giving offense or causing others to stumble.

In writing about the City of Enoch a few years ago a true believer was used to say these things about how shortcomings beget shortcomings:

*How often the weakness in one man becomes a temptation to another man! My desire for wealth and gems can cause another man's envy; my temper has at time, dissolved your patience. One man's incontinence destroys what little is left of a righteous woman's resolve. One person's lust becomes another's way to wealth. A man's drunkenness becomes another man's excuse for Sabbath-breaking to enlarge his vineyards.* [Neal A. Maxwell, *Of One Heart* (Salt Lake City: Deseret Book Co., 1975), p. 28]

11. The true believer insists that within deprivation there may be opportunity. He can wait for the unfolding of opportunity hidden within tragedy, as did Joseph anciently. When in their later Egyptian rendezvous, Joseph lovingly reassured his anxious brothers, "But as for you, ye thought evil against me, but God meant it unto good, to bring to pass, as it is this day, to save much people alive" (Gen. 50:20). So often, before we can save others, however, we must first be shaped and refined.

12. The true believer is growing in his patience, including being patient in following the living prophets. He knows that trying to get ahead of the Brethren is a sure way of falling behind.

13. He is ready to follow the Lord into soul-stretching experiences even if it means enrolling the schooling of suffering and paying his tuition.

These words from a sobering, sweet letter written to me by a gallant, but modest, student now at BYU attest to a significant spirituality in one so young—one who rejoices in the many blessings he now has without brooding over those that are temporarily withheld from him.

*I have now had leukemia diagnosed for fifteen months, although few people even know about it. My goal has been to lead as normal a life as is possible; hence, the subject rarely gets mentioned because most people I have encountered, doctors, included, tend to treat it as a tragedy rather than as an incentive to get one's affairs in order promptly.*

*My parents took the news quite hard, perhaps because my brother died unexpectedly eleven years ago of undiagnosed causes. Most people are pessimistic; however, I have failed to see how pessimism would help me make the best use of my time which is of unknown length, not only for me, but for everyone.*

*Against medical and parental advice, I have since been married and am at BYU and we're expecting a baby in July. I feel great and am truly enjoying the blessings that are coming from being married in the temple, studying the scriptures, working hard in school, and living each day rather than simply waiting to die.*

*Fifteen months ago, my then fiancée and I thought that if I could live long enough for us to be sealed, that would be all we would ask for. Therefore, we consider everything since then as a great gift from the Lord. We still dream and plan for a long family life together, and it gives us a certain comfort to know that our situation is in the Lord's hands and is not bound by man's limitations.*

Like Job, this remarkable young man has avoided the usual human tendency when under stress to charge God foolishly (see Job 1:22).

Along with the attributes already noted in the tests cited, the true believer in Christ may be further characterized.

He is innocent as to sin, but he is not naïve about worldly things. He is kind but he is candid. He is harmless because he keeps the second commandment. But he is powerful because his righteousness permits him access to the powers of heaven, which cannot be handled in any other way.

The true believer is serious about the living of his life, but he is of good cheer. His humor is the humor of hope and his mirth is the mirth of modesty—not the hollow laughter or the cutting cleverness of despair. Unlike those of a celebrated "devil-*may*-care" lifestyle, his is the quiet "heaven-*does*-care" attitude.

He understands the difference between ends and means and sees that some Church aids are, in a sense, scaffolding for the soul, which scaffolding one day will be removed—like waterwings or training wheels.

He is humble enough to "serve tables" but is sensible enough to share his time and talents on the basis of priorities—doing the "things of most worth."

Like his Master, the true believer loves his life but is willing to lay it down or to see it slip slowly away through affliction. If he is given a "thorn in the flesh," he does not demand to see the rose garden.

Let the kaleidoscope of life's circumstances be shaken, again and again, and the "true believer of Christ" will still see "with the eye of faith" divine design and purpose in his life.

There is a quiet regalness about the true believer in Christ, however humble in appearance he may be. Hence, the true believer's light has become more than a little one; however, he is apt to be quite innocent of his growing incandescence. The true believer's "*cris de coeur*," or "cry of the heart," is heard—not always over tragedy as the world measures tragedy—but when observing the tragedy of sin; for in seeing "things as they really are," he also sees what might have been.

Being settled in his soul, he has a serenity even in the midst of war and tumult. If he lives, he lives unto the Lord, if he dies, he dies unto the Lord, just as President Brigham Young said:

> *I say to the brethren who are leaving home . . . when you pray for your families . . . you must feel—if they live, all right; if they die, all right; if I die, all right; if I live, all right; for we are the Lords' and we shall soon meet again.* [*Journal of Discourses* 6:273]

The true believer can read the depressing signs of the times without being depressed because he has a particularized and "perfect brightness of hope" (2 Ne. 31:20). He knows that "Christ will lift [us] up" (Mor. 9:25). He does not naively depend on mortal rulers, assemblies, congresses, or parliaments to lift him up, though he is genuinely grateful for any true success by these. Rather, he has the precious perspective of Joseph Smith who observed:

> *The laws of men may guarantee to a people protection in the honorable pursuits of this life, and the temporal happiness arising from a protection against unjust insults and injuries; and when this is said, all is said, that can be in truth, of the power, extent, and influence of the laws of men, exclusive of the laws of God.* [*Teachings of the Prophet Joseph Smith*, (Salt Lake City: Deseret Book Co., 1972) p. 50]

Besides, the true believer knows that in the awful winding-up scenes human deterioration will be finally and decisively and mercifully met by divine intervention. He understands, therefore, that in such conditions the sooner he renounces the world, the sooner he can help to save some souls in it.

Let us, brothers and sisters, seek to become such true believers in Christ. Let us make our way, righteously and resolutely, notwithstanding our weaknesses, to the beckoning City of God. There, the sole and self-assigned gatekeeper is Jesus Christ. He awaits us at the gate not only to *certify* us—but because His deep, divine desire brings Him there to *welcome* us. "He employeth no servant there" (2 Ne. 9:41). If we acknowledge Him now, He will lovingly acknowledge us then.

May God bless you as a generation with a continuing sense of impending rendezvous with tasks you know not of yet, but for which you must be prepared. I see you, frankly, as a generation further along the path than your parents' generation was at your same age, settling in sooner on the way to becoming "true believers in Christ." I see you as a generation fitted before you came here, measured for the challenge to be given to you, and as adequate for all that you will be asked to do. I plead with you, therefore, with some sense of trembling and awe for you collectively, in anticipation of that which you will be called upon to do. My pleading is that you determine to settle in spiritually—even more so by moving along in the pathway to becoming "true believers in Christ." Then as the heat comes, having been stablished, settled, grounded, and rooted in Christ, you can withstand the heat of the sun when it comes to scorch; you can be of good cheer and lift others up. Such can be your blessings, such are surely your promises, for the fulfillment of which I pray in love as I once again bear my witness to you as to the validity of the work in which we are engaged.

Nothing else is even in the same solar system of significance. God bless you to keep your rendezvous, to be true believers in Christ, and to be so settled that others can look to you for constancy amid turmoil and for truth amid falsehood. And in the powers of my office I bless you so that you shall be accelerated in this quest and do so, knowing of my accountability for that which I have said to you this day, but knowing also of your accountability for what has been said to you. All of which I say humbly, but most importantly, in the holy name of Jesus Christ. Amen.

# Grounded, Rooted, Established, and Settled (Ephesians 3:17, 1 Peter 5:10)

Neal A. Maxwell

P resident and Sister Holland, brothers and sisters all, even more fervently than you, I wish President Kimball were here today to be appropriately honored as was planned. However, what was postponed, as President Holland indicated, can now be anticipated, and I join with you in prayerful anticipation.

## GROWTH OF THE CHURCH

Since President Kimball is not here today and since we are out of the immediate range of his modesty, it is perhaps appropriate to share several statistical indicators about the Church growth in this vibrant era. Thus far in President Kimball's not-quite-eight years as president, the Church has grown from a membership of about 3.3 million to a membership of nearly 5 million.

As a better indicator of true growth, the total number of stakes has grown from 630 to 1,293—663 additional stakes as of today, more than doubling in less than eight years. The 109 missions have grown by 85 to a total of 194. Nineteen more countries outside the United

---

*This devotional address was given at Brigham Young University on 15 September 1981.*

States have been added to the 47 where the Church is established, opening the work for a total of 66 countries wherein units of the Church operate. The language areas in which the Church now functions have grown by 27, from 31 to 58, so that, as the scriptures foreshadow, people can hear the gospel in their own languages (see D&C 90:11). A symbolic statistic is this one: There are now more stakes and members of the Church in Chile than in Canada, with 28 stakes and approximately 100,000 members in Chile!

The indicators just recited do not have even a close parallel in Church history. Beyond the dramatic demographics, however, there is something much more significant. We are blessed, all of us, by the personal impact of President Kimball on our lives. As such a beloved leader, his personal influence is impossible to measure, but it is even more pervasive and remarkable than the numbers recited.

## GROUNDED, ROOTED, ESTABLISHED, SETTLED

Indeed it is in the context of such pleasing but challenging growth that the theme for today will be addressed—from the words of Paul and Peter, "grounded, rooted, established, and settled." This is a vital objective for all members of the Church, but especially for your generation because of the special circumstances which will confront you. In fact, you may be the first generation in Church history, because of lamentably changing conditions in the world, who will be asked to believe and to behave "because of the word" and not circumstances. In varying degrees, you will not have the same affirmative influence of societal institutions which once strongly supported the family and principles such as chastity and fidelity. Those supporting influences, in many respects, will, unfortunately fall away like so much scaffolding. Then we will see who stands, both on holy ground and on holy principles!

Jesus described some of these realities and the casualties of conversion and retention thusly:

*Some* [seeds] *fell upon stony places, where they had not much earth: and forthwith they sprung up, because they had no deepness of earth:*

*And when the sun was up, they were scorched; and because they had no root, they withered away.* [Matthew 13:5–6]

Happily, Alma elaborated concerning how that gospel seed can grow, nourished by "faith with great diligence, and with patience" (Alma 32:41). Properly nourished, it will develop a good root system, and even when the heat of the sun comes and scorches, it will not wither (see Alma 32:28–38). By using a word as graphic as *scorched* to describe the heat which believers will feel, the Lord, who is not given to hyperbole, tells us something about the heat that will come, not alone in the rigors of individual life, but also in the special summer of circumstances which Jesus said would come when the leaves of the fig tree sprouted (see Matthew 24:32). That summer is upon us, and only those who are grounded, rooted, established, and settled will survive spiritually.

I do not, therefore, worry about your generation's lack of adventure. Before you are through, you are likely to appreciate, in those lines from *Fiddler on the Roof*, what Tevye said when he wished aloud that the Lord would choose someone else for a change. You will become very conscious of who you are. However, today I will not stress the extraordinariness of your times but the immense possibilities which lie within the seeming ordinariness of your lives.

Since you are part of the Lord's unfolding purposes, remember how deep the divine determination is.

*There is nothing that the Lord thy God shall take in his heart to do but what he will do it.* [Abraham 3:17]

You are a part of that unfolding process. But he will not revise the structure of this second estate just because you and I have had a bad day.

## ATTRIBUTES AND SKILLS NEVER OBSOLETE

It is especially helpful to remember also that the temptations and challenges we face are common to man (see 1 Corinthians 10:13), yet we must respond uncommonly. It is also useful to ponder the fact that, along with even the Savior himself, we are to experience certain things "according to the flesh" (Alma 7:12) and to learn "in process of time" (Moses 7:21). Built, therefore, into the seemingly ordinary experiences of life are opportunities for us to acquire such eternal attributes as love, mercy, meekness, patience, and submissiveness and to develop and sharpen such skills as how to communicate, motivate, delegate, and manage our time and talents and our thoughts in accordance with eternal priorities. These attributes and skills are portable; they are never obsolete and will be much needed in the next world.

How often have you and I really pondered just what it is, therefore, that will rise with us in the resurrection? Our intelligence will rise with us, meaning not simply our I.Q., but our capacity to receive and to apply truth. Our talents, attributes, and skills will rise with us, certainly also our capacity to learn, our degree of self-discipline, and our capacity to work. Note that I said "our capacity to work" because the precise form of our work here may have no counterpart there, but the capacity to work will never be obsolete. To be sure, we cannot, while here, entirely avoid contact with the obsolescent and the irrelevant. It is all around us. But one can be around irrelevancy without becoming attached to it, and certainly we should not become preoccupied with obsolete things.

By these remarks I do not intend to create discontent with the paraphernalia of this probationary estate, but it is a grave error to mistake the scenery and the props for the real drama which is underway. Nor do I wish to bear down too much on the fact that certain mortal vocations will be irrelevant in the next world. A mortician does useful work here, especially if it is done with excellence, compassion, and reverence for life. Whatever our vocation, we should be sweetened, not hardened. Keeping our sense of proportion *whatever* we do, keeping our precious perspective *wherever* we are, and keeping the commandments *however* we are tested reflect being settled, rooted, and grounded in our discipleship.

## A PRECIOUS PERSPECTIVE

Remaining settled and established is not easy, for we are crowded by the cares of the world. We are diverted by the praise of the world; we are buffeted by the trials of the world, drawn by the appetites and temptations of the world, and bruised by the hardness of the world. But when we are grounded, rooted, established, and settled, we can have a precious perspective which puts other things in their proper place. This is no small blessing, for it lifts us above our immediate circumstances and concerns, giving us a larger view of things, as this secular episode illustrates:

> In 1918, Ernest Rutherford, a physicist, missed a meeting of experts advising the British government on anti-submarine warfare. When criticized for missing the meeting, he replied, "I had been engaged in experiments which suggest that the atom can be artificially disintegrated. If it is true, it is of far greater importance than a war." [George F. Will, The Pursuit of Happiness, and Other Sobering Thoughts (New York: Harper and Row, 1978), p. 228]

The precious perspective of the gospel also helps to keep before us the reality of what lies ahead. Malcolm Muggeridge put it so very well:

> Now, the prospect of death overshadows all others for me. I am like a man on a sea voyage nearing his destination. When I embarked, I worried about having a cabin with a porthole, whether I should be asked to sit at the captain's table, who were the more attractive and important passengers. All such considerations become pointless, however, when I shall soon be disembarking. [Ian Hunter, ed., Things Past (New York: Morrow, 1979), p. 166]

## GUIDANCE OF THE HOLY SPIRIT

So it is, brothers and sisters, that neither a sense of impending cataclysm nor of our eventual death should keep us from proceeding with our mortal chores. It is very desirable, for instance, that you go forward with your education even in the midst of the gathering

storm. I cherish these lines from C. S. Lewis given over 40 years ago
to students and scholars at Oxford in the midst of another gathering
storm. He said:

*If men had postponed the search for knowledge and beauty until they were
secure, the search would never have begun. . . . Life has never been normal.
. . . Humanity . . . wanted knowledge and beauty now, and would not wait
for the suitable moment that never comes. . . . The insects have chosen a
different line: they have sought first the material welfare and security of
the hive, and presumably they have their reward. Men are different. They
propound mathematical theorems in beleaguered cities, conduct metaphysi-
cal arguments in condemned cells, make jokes on scaffolds, discuss the last
new poem while advancing to the walls of Quebec, and comb their hair
at Thermophylae. This is not a* panache; *it is our nature.* ["Learning
in War-Time," *The Weight of Glory and Other Addresses* (New York:
Macmillan, 1980), pp. 21–22]

Be true, therefore, to the buoyancy in your nature which responds
to your innate cravings for truth and beauty in spite of circumstance.
Besides, in a very real sense, given the purpose of the mortal experience, your university education is an education within an education.
You will wonder sometimes about life—if mortality consists only of
large classes. In fact, life is designed to be quite tutorial in nature so far
as how the lessons are usually taught and learned. Each of us will surely
need to take the Holy Spirit as our Teacher, Guide, and Comforter
throughout this stretching experience (see D&C 45:57). He can reassure us that the president of the Church is a prophet of God. There
will be times when you will need that reinforcement. After all, prophets are not just for following in the Sinai or on a westward journey.
President Brigham Young told of one man who, instead of going west,
wanted to wait in the East for the impending redemption of Zion and
who was told by George A. Smith that the nearest way to Missouri
was through Salt Lake City (*JD* 8:198). There will be some equivalent
counsel given to you in your lifetime.

Moses, an inspired leader, desired an inspired people. On one occasion reports reached him that certain members of the camp were prophesying, and when Joshua wanted it forbidden, Moses said unto him:

*Enviest thou for my sake? would God that all the Lord's people were prophets, and that the Lord would put his spirit upon them!* [Numbers 11:27–29]

It is not merely a matter of lessening the burden of the few, but of enlarging the perspectives of the many.

With the Holy Spirit as our guide, our conscience stays vibrant and alive. Things which we had never supposed come into view. Seeming routine turns out to be resplendent. Ordinary people seem quite the opposite. What we once thought to be the mere humdrum of life gives way to symphonic strains. Circumstances or a mere conversation which look quite pedestrian nevertheless cause a quiet moment of personal resolve, and a decision affecting all eternity is made. Sometimes you and I even sense it as it happens, but there are no bands playing, and there are no headlines. Therefore, a very significant part of getting settled in one's discipleship consists of coming to terms with the realities around us that seem so routine. Routine, like trials, can bring us closer to God or move us away from him. What seems commonplace seldom is.

### DANGER IN LACK OF LOVE

Occasionally I see individuals who are meeting life's challenges reasonably well but who unfortunately fail to appreciate the general adequacy of their response. They let the seeming ordinariness of life dampen their spirits. Though actually coping and growing, some lack the quiet inner-soul satisfaction which can steady them. Instead they seem to experience a lingering sense that there is something more important they should be doing or that their chores are somehow not quite what was expected, as if what is quietly achieved in righteous individual living or in parenthood is not sufficiently spectacular.

Feeling unrequited as to role and feeling underwhelmed do not occur, however, because of a structural failure in this divinely designed second estate. Rather they occur because of a lack of love, for love helps us to see and to respond to those opportunities which have been allotted to us and which lie unused all about us. Before we complain about the curriculum in mortality, or more particularly our current class schedules, we would do well to remember who designed the curriculum and to allow for however many other places it has been successfully used.

True, there are more things to be done than we do, more opportunities for service than are used. True we make mistakes. Even some of our achievements are flawed by a lack of finesse. True there are seeming flat periods in life when we may feel underwhelmed. In such situations, however, we had best get back to the basics of why we are here. In the terse communiqué from the Gods about our being placed on this planet, the basic objective of life on this planet was stated:

*And we will prove them herewith, to see if they will do all things whatsoever the Lord their God shall command them.* [Abraham 3:25]

This is a pithy but sweeping declaration of divine intent. The second estate has been carefully structured so as to carry out that intent. To misunderstand this straightforward and tutorial purpose of life as a proving process is to make a fundamental error which ensure that thousands of additional errors will naturally follow. If our focus on the fundamental purpose of life is blurred, we will not see "things as they really are" (Jacob 4:13).

### SOME LESSONS THE HARD WAY

Hence there should be no surprise about the second estate when it features lessons to be learned the hard way "according to the flesh." There should be no resentment or mystery regarding the patient personal development which must occur "in process of time." God's purposes are plain!

Since we are here to thus be proved, how can that occur except we are tested? If we are here to learn to choose wisely, how can that occur except there be alternatives? If our soul is to be stretched, how can that happen without growing pains? How can personal development really occur amid routine unless we have authentic challenges on which to practice? Therefore, those who wait for some other insight about the purpose of this life heretofore inscrutably withheld from us will wait in vain. A sense of surprise, if there is one, is far more likely to occur, therefore, when some plain truth which we have known all along intellectually is suddenly or dramatically confirmed experientially. They err who, instead of concentrating on commandment keeping and personal spiritual progress, desire sweeping significance and high visibility in the second estate.

Is it really numbers of people touched at the moment which measure the impact of an individual? Did tens of thousands hear the Sermon on the Mount? Did it make the six-o'clock news? Is Abraham to be measured by the volume of his trade with nomadic caravans in the desert or by living quietly and righteously so as one day to see fulfilled the promise that his posterity would be as numberless as the stars in the heavens? Was Ruth's eloquent and touching entreaty to Naomi to be assessed by the size of her audience? Demographics are not a complete measure.

Or is it the terrain one traverses which is the true test of his life? If so, should those of us who travel in the jet age view with condescension the mileage logged by Jesus during his mortal ministry? In those days, "from Dan to Beersheba" seemed so sweeping, yet it involved only a little over a hundred miles. One day our travels about his planet will seem quite provincial too when we are wafted from planet to planet. Distance, therefore, is not much of a determinant either.

Actually if it is sweeping insight we desire, and surprise, let us save room for surprise as the moment arrives when the eternal family's eventual itinerary is fully unveiled. But family life seems so ordinary now. Even so, some may still say, "Should I not be doing something else?" Ah, but that is not the real question! The real question is: "Why should I desire more than to perform the work to which I have been called?" (Alma 29:6). That is the question.

## PATIENCE AND ENDURING WELL

One's task is to do more and to perform well within his callings, but it is not something else or another work he should seek. God will not judge us according to the calling of another. Therefore, how we utilize the seemingly ordinary experiences of our life and how well we keep the commandments are true tests of our performance in this second estate. One can, while in the employ of a railroad company, learn something of patience while struggling to keep the train schedule meticulously up to date. But the patience will long outlast the printed train schedule. A discovering scientist may augment his awe and meekness before his Creator because of the breathtaking order in the universe even if his new discoveries erelong are swallowed up in even more immense discoveries.

But it is also true that routine may cause a gravedigger to become indifferent to the sorrows of the bereaved gathered about those fresh mounds of earth. The gravedigger may even become cynical about the resurrection which one day will empty all those graves. A marriage counselor can become encrusted with a protective layer of clinical indifference brought on by the routine and incessant nature of his chores. If so, his techniques will never compensate for his lack of caring. A civil servant who has forgotten how to be civil may have some sway now in the procurement division of a vast governmental direction, but he is headed in just the opposite developmental direction needed for sway in the next world.

On the other hand, one who listens more and more effectively to others with a genuine desire to understand and to help, if not always to agree, will have no regrets later on. Such an individual may occasionally run out of time here, but he is fitting himself for eternity. Love and patience are never wasted; they only appear to be. The devoted wife and mother who is a quiet but effective neighbor but whose obituary is noticed by a comparative few may well have laid up precious little here in the current coin-of-the-realm, recognition, yet rising with her in the resurrection will be relevant attributes and skills honed and refined in family and neighborhood life. Contrariwise, the civic leader whose thirst for recognition causes him to do things to be seen of men has his reward. He too will receive the gift of immortality during which expanse he can work on meekness and humility.

## LOOK BEYOND APPEARANCES

Thus when life is viewed superficially, it seems routine and even pedestrian. However, what appears on the surface can be a thin cover for developments of great spiritual significance. Those who passed by the football stadium at the University of Chicago several decades ago did not know what was underway below those empty seats. The atom was being split, after which the world was never again to be the same. Such a quiet stadium too. It is left to us, therefore, in our varied circumstances but with common challenges to make the interplay of our time and talent bring about the development of the key eternal attributes and the everlasting skills. A botched performance here means less chance to serve there. Any resulting advantage we have in the world to come clearly will result from taking advantage of the opportunities this life affords us. Hence those who are grounded, rooted, established, and settled will be serious about the eternal objectives on which this life should focus.

Brothers and sisters, when anciently we shouted for joy in anticipation of this mortal experience, we did not then think it would be ordinary and pedestrian at all. We sensed the impending high adventure. Let us be true to that first and more realistic reaction.

## PERSPECTIVE MUCH NEEDED

May I note in closing how much needed the perspective is which goes with being established and settled as we contemplate our varied circumstances. Some in the Church are divorced; some are unmarried but yearn to be and are worthy to be married. Some are widowers, and some are widows; others are blessed to be in traditional intact families. Some are healthy; others are ill, some seriously and terminally ill. Some members are struggling economically, but a few are quite comfortable economically. Some are lonely, and others have almost more friends than they can manage. Our immediate circumstances surely differ, but these circumstances will pass away soon enough, though at times it may seem otherwise.

Notice in contrast how our basic circumstances and eternal opportunities are strikingly similar. Each of us is a child of God. Each of us agreed to pass through this mortal experience with its common temptations and seeming ordinariness. Eventually each of us can have the privilege of receiving all the gospel ordinances. Each of us is accountable for our thoughts and actions. Each of us is loved perfectly by a Heavenly Father who knows us and our needs perfectly. Each of us has the same commandments to keep and must walk the same straight and narrow path in order to have happiness here and there. Each of us has the same eternal attributes to develop. So our fundamental circumstances are the same.

A hundred years from now, today's seeming deprivations and tribulations will not matter then unless we let them matter too much now. A hundred years from now, today's serious physical ailment will be but a fleeting memory. A thousand years from now, those who now worry and are anguished because they are unmarried will, if they are faithful, have smiles of satisfaction on their faces in the midst of a vast convocation of their posterity. The seeming deprivation which occurs in the life of a single woman who feels she has no prospects of marriage and motherhood properly endured is but a delayed blessing, the readying of a reservoir into which a generous God will pour all that he hath. Indeed, it will be the Malachi measure: "there shall not be room enough to receive it" (Malachi 3:10).

In eternity, the insensitivities and injustices of today's grumpy boss will not matter when we then live in the presence of a God who is perfect in his justice and his mercy. A thousand years from now, today's soul pain inflicted by a betraying or deserting spouse will be gone. A thousand years from now, if one has been misrepresented or misunderstood, the resentment will be gone. So much depends, therefore, upon our maintaining gospel perspective in the midst of ordinariness and the pressures of temptation, tribulation, and deprivation. As we come to love the Lord more and more, we can understand, rather than resent, his purposes. He who should know has said that there is no other way. Besides, when the Savior urged even his closest disciples to "settle this in your hearts, that ye will do the things which I shall teach, and command you" (JST Luke 14:28), he spoke of the high cost of discipleship, "signifying there should not any man follow him, unless he was able to continue" (JST Luke 14:31). Clearly Jesus was underscoring the importance of having his followers become thoroughly grounded in the gospel, rooted in resolve, established in their expectations about life, and settled in their devotion to the Savior. May we so become I pray in the name of Jesus Christ. Amen.

# Meekly Drenched in Destiny

Neal A. Maxwell

I welcome you to a Christian campus where discipleship and scholarship are uniquely blended. I salute your ecclesiastical and academic leaders, so many of whom are with us tonight. They will serve you exceedingly well.

My brothers and sisters, as on another occasion at this pulpit, I will speak out of my own strugglings about another unglamorous but very crucial gospel objective. Then, the subject was *patience*, a virtue which is regarded by some as quite pedestrian but which is essential to our development and happiness.

## A COMPANION VIRTUE TO PATIENCE

Our focus tonight will be on *meekness*, a companion virtue to patience. Meekness, too, is one of the attributes of Deity. Instructively, Jesus, our Lord and Exemplar, called attention to Himself as being "meek and lowly in heart" (Matthew 11:29). Paul extolled the "meekness and gentleness of Christ" (2 Corinthians 10:1).

---

*This fireside address was given at Brigham Young University on 5 September 1982.*

The Greek rendition of the word *meek* in the New Testament, by the way, is *gentle* and *humble*.

Actually, meekness is not only an attribute essential for itself; Moroni declared that it is also vital because one simply cannot develop those other crucial virtues—faith, hope, and charity—without meekness. In the ecology of the eternal attributes these cardinal characteristics are inextricably bound up together. Among them, meekness is often the initiator, the facilitator, and the consolidator.

Moreover, if one needs any further persuasion as to how vital this virtue is, Moroni warned, "none is acceptable before God save the meek and the lowly in heart" (Moroni 7:44). If we could but believe, really believe, in the reality of that bold but accurate declaration, you and I would then find ourselves focusing on the crucial rather than the marginal tasks in life! We would then cease pursuing life-styles which, inevitably and irrevocably, are going out of style!

There would be little reason for speaking to you of meekness if you were not serious candidates for the celestial kingdom. You live in coarsening times, times in which meekness is misunderstood and even despised. Yet meekness has been, is, and will remain a non-negotiable dimension of true discipleship. Its development is a remarkable achievement in any age, but especially in this age.

Furthermore, whether you realize it or not, you are a generation drenched in destiny. If you are faithful, you will prove to be a part of the winding-up scenes for this world, and as participants, not merely as spectators, though on later occasions you might understandably prefer to be the latter.

### WHY SO IMPORTANT?

Even so, why the stress on meekness? Merely because it is nice to be nice? The reasons are far more deeply imbedded in the "plan of happiness" (Alma 42:8) than that!

God, who has seen billions of spirits pass through His plan of salvation, has told us to be meek in order to enhance our enjoyment of life and our mortal education. Will we be meek and listen to Him and learn from Him? Or will we be like the Gadarene swine, that pathetic example of *totus porcus*—going whole hog—after the trends of the moment?

Perhaps, brothers and sisters, what we brought with us as intelligences into our creation as spirit children constitutes a "given" within which even God must work. Add to that possibility the clear reality of God's deep commitment to our free agency—and we begin to see how essential meekness is! We need to learn so much, and yet we are free to choose (see 2 Nephi 2:27)! How crucial it is to be teachable! There "is no other way" in which God could do what He has declared it is His intent to do. No wonder He and His prophets emphasize meekness time and time again!

Since God desired to have us become like Himself, He first had to make us free, to learn, to choose, and to experience; hence our humility and teachability are premiere determinants of our progress and our happiness. Agency is essential to perfectibility, and meekness is essential to the wise use of agency—and to our recovery when we have misused our agency.

Let us not brush by this developmental premise. The scriptures concerning life's purposes do make it clear that we *are* to become like the Father and His Son, Jesus Christ: "Be ye therefore perfect, even as your Father which is in heaven is perfect" (Matthew 5:48). "Therefore I would that ye should be perfect even as I, or your Father who is in heaven is perfect" (3 Nephi 12:48). "Therefore, what manner of men [and women] ought ye to be? Verily I say unto you, even as I am" (3 Nephi 27:27). It is an awesome objective—impossible of attainment without meekness.

The Father and our Savior desire to lead us through love, for if we were merely driven where They wish us to go, we would not be worthy to be there, and, surely, we could not stay there. They are Shepherds, not sheepherders.

In that premortal council, wherein Jesus *meekly* volunteered to aid the Father's plan, He said, "Here am I, send me" (Abraham 3:27). It was one of those special moments when a few words are preferred to many. Never has one individual offered, in so few words, to do so much for so many as did Jesus when He *meekly* proffered Himself as ransom for us, billions and billions of us!

In contrast, we see in ourselves, brothers and sisters, the unnecessary multiplication of words—not only a lack of clarity, but vanity. Our verbosity is often a cover for insincerity or uncertainty. Meekness, the subtraction of self, reduces the multiplication of words.

Without meekness, the conversational point we insist on making often takes the form of *I*, that spearlike, vertical pronoun. Meekness, however, is more than self-restraint; it is the presentation of self in a posture of *kindness* and *gentleness*. It reflects certitude, strength, serenity; it reflects a healthy self-esteem and a genuine self-control.

So in matters little or large, if our emulation of the Lord is to be serious, we must do more than note and admire Jesus' meekness. He passed through "all of these things" which gave Him, too, needed experiences.

### DEVELOPMENT GRADUAL, SOMETIMES PAINFUL

However, meekness is one of those attributes acquired only by experience, some of it painful, for it is developed "according to the flesh" (Alma 7:11, 12). It is not an attribute achieved overnight, nor is it certified to in but one exam; rather, it is certified to "in process of time" (Moses 7:21, 68, 69). The Savior said we are to "take up [the] cross daily" (Luke 9:23)—not just once or occasionally—and taking up the cross daily surely requires meekness.

There is, of course, much accumulated stereo-typing surrounding this virtue. We even make nervous jokes about meekness, such as, "If the meek intend to inherit the earth, they are going to have to be more aggressive about it!" We even tend to think of a meek individual as being used and abused—as being a doormat for others. However, Moses was once described as being the most meek man on the face of the earth (see Numbers 12:3), and we recall his impressive boldness in the courts of Pharaoh and his scalding indignation following his descent from Sinai.

President Brigham Young, who was tested in many ways and on many occasions, was once tried in a way that required him to "take it"—even from one he adored and admired. Brigham "took it" because he was meek. Yet, surely, none of us sitting here would think of Brigham Young as lacking in boldness or firmness. However, even President Young, in the closing and prestigious days of his life, spent some time in courtrooms being unjustifiably abused. When he might have chosen to assert himself politically, he "took it"—meekly.

Fortunately, you and I have had a chance to see, at rather close range, the remarkable meekness which operates in the life of President Spencer W. Kimball. His, too, is an impressive meekness which has combined with sweet boldness, producing signal achievments in the Kingdom.

Granted, none of us like, or should like, to be disregarded, to be silenced, to see a flawed argument prevail, or to endure a gratuitous discourtesy. But such circumstances as these seldom constitute that field of action from which meekness calls upon us to retire gracefully. We usually do battle unmeekly over far less justifiable issues, such as "turf."

Just what is this "turf" we insist on defending at almost the slightest provocation? If it is real estate, it will not rise with us in the resurrection. If it is concern over the opinions of us held by others, there is only one opinion of us that really matters. Besides, the opinions of others will only be lowered if we go on and ego tantrum. If "turf" is status, we should not be overly concerned with today's organizational charts. Who cares now about the peck order in the Sanhedrin of A.D. 31 which meant so much to some at the time?

Granted, there are some things worth being aroused about, as the Book of Mormon says, such as our families, our homes, our liberties, and our sacred religion (see Alma 43:45). But, if all our anxiety amounts to is our so-called image, it's an image that needs to be displaced anyway, so that we can receive His image in our countenances (see Alma 5:14).

## FURTHER CONSIDERATION

Let us consider meekness further.

The meek are filled with awe and wonder with regard to God and His purposes in the universe. At the same time, the meek are not awe-struck by the many frustrations of life; they are more easily mobilized for eternal causes and less easily immobilized by the disappointments of the day.

Because they make fewer demands of life, the meek are less easily disappointed. They are less concerned with their entitlements than with their assignments.

When we are truly meek, we are not concerned with being pushed around but are grateful to be pushed along. When we are truly meek, we do not engage in shoulder-shrugging acceptance but shoulder-squaring—in order that we might better bear the burdens of life and others.

Meekness can also help us in coping with the injustices of life—of which there are quite a few. By the way, our experiences with mortal injustices will generate within us even more adoration of the perfect justice of God—another of His attributes. Besides, there can be dignity even in silence, as was the case when Jesus meekly stood, unjustly accused, before Pilate. Silence can be an expression of strength. Holding back and holding on can be signs of great personal discipline, especially when everyone else is letting go.

Furthermore, not only are the meek less easily offended, but they are less likely to give offense to others. In contrast, there are some in life who seem to be waiting to be offended. Their pride covers them like boils which will inevitably be bumped.

Meekness also cultivates in us a generosity in viewing the mistakes and imperfections of others:

> *Condemn me not because of mine imperfection, neither my father, because of his imperfection . . . but rather give thanks unto God that he hath made manifest unto you our imperfections, that ye may learn to be more wise than we have been.* [Mormon 9:31]

Those of us who are too concerned about status or being last in line or losing our place need to reread those words about how the "last shall be first" and the "first shall be last" (Matthew 19:30). Assertiveness is not automatically bad, of course, but if we fully understood the motives which underlie some of our acts of assertion, we would be embarrassed. Frankly, when others perceive such motivations, they are sometimes embarrassed for us.

Granted, the meek go on fewer ego trips, but they have far greater adventures. Ego trips, those "travel now and pay later" indulgences, are always detours. The straight and narrow path is the only path which takes us to new and breathtaking places.

Meekness means less concern over being taken for granted and more concern over being taken by the hand. Less concern over revising our own plans for us and more concern about adopting His plans for us are other sure signs of meekness.

When you and I sing that Church hymn with the words, "More used would I be" (P. P. Bliss, "More Holiness Give Me," *Hymns*, no. 114), one condition which keeps us from being "more used" is our lack of meekness. Sometimes, too, brothers and sisters, in our prayers we ask for the Lord to take the lead of our minds and hearts, but as soon as we say "Amen," we go unmeekly in our predetermined directions.

Meekness does not mean tentativeness, but thoughtfulness. Meekness makes room for others: "Let nothing be done through strife or vainglory; but in lowliness of mind let each esteem other better than themselves" (Philippians 2:3).

### EXAMPLES, GOOD AND BAD

There are, brothers and sisters, ever so many human situations in which the only additional time and recognition and space to be made available must come from the meek who will yield—in order to make time and recognition and space available for others. There could be no magnanimity without humility. Meekness is not a display of humility; it is the real thing. True meekness is never proud of itself, never conscious of itself.

It was said of one able, but comparatively meek, member of a nineteenth-century British cabinet, serving in Parliament:

*If it was his duty to speak, he spoke, but he did not want to speak
when it was not his duty—silence was no pain and oratory no pleasure to
him.* [Forrest Morgan, ed., *The Works of Walter Bagehot* (Hartford,
Connecticut: travelers Insurance, 1889)]

The meek think of more clever things to say than are said. And
it's just as well, for there is so much more cleverness in the world than
wisdom, so much more sarcasm than idealism.

It is quite understandable, brothers and sisters, that we admire
boldness and genius as we see these qualities convinced in some of
the great figures in history. A merciful God has let such individuals
make their significant contributions to humanity, such as in the political and economic realms. I cannot help but wonder, however, what
more God might have done with such individuals if they had been
sufficiently and consistently meek.

I think, for instance, of the towering and courageous Winston
Churchill, admired in so many ways, including by me, but who had
serious difficulty containing his ego which sometimes tarnished his
otherwise remarkable contributions. One winces, even at this late
date, as he reads Balfour's rebuke, in 1905, of a pressing and eager
young Churchill in Parliament. Just after Winston had been exces-
sive, Balfour rose in dignity and said:

*As for the junior member of Oldham . . . I think I may give him some
advice which may be useful to him in the course of what I hope may be a
long and distinguished career. It is not, on the whole, desirable to come down
to this House with invective which is both prepared and violent. The House
will tolerate, and very rightly tolerate, almost anything within the rule
of order which evidently springs from genuine indignation aroused by the
collision of debate. But to come down with these prepared phrases is not usually successful, and at all events, I do not think it was very successful on the
present occasion. If there is preparation, there should be more finish, and if
there is so much violence, there should certainly be more veracity of feeling.*

NEAL A. MAXWELL **131**

[Ted Morgan, *Churchill: Young Man in a Hurry* (New York: Simon and Schuster, 1982), p. 175.]

I think, too, of the remarkable General of the Army Douglas MacArthur whose place in history will also be rightfully generous. His mistakes, too, usually occurred as a result of a lack of meekness; his bravery was, on occasion, matched by his vanity. The brilliant and victorious sealord, Admiral Nelson, both achieved and suffered similarly.

I am not trying to fault these individuals, for each has significantly added to the measure of freedom so many mortals have enjoyed. Rather, I am suggesting how important to genuine and lasting greatness the virtue of meekness is, for its absence constitutes a limitation—even upon those whom we judge to be great by worldly criteria.

Granted, we admire boldness and dash, but boldness and dash can so easily slip into pomp and panache.

### PROPER USE OF POWER AND AUTHORITY

By contrast, the meek are able with regularity to peel off the encrustations of ego that form on one's soul like barnacles on a ship. They are thus able to avoid the abuse of authority and power—a tendency to which, the Lord declared, "almost all" succumb. Except the meek. The meek use power and authority properly, no doubt because their gentleness and meekness reflect a love unfeigned, a genuine caring. The influence they exercise flows from a deep concern:

*No power or influence can or ought to be maintained by virtue of the priesthood, only by persuasion, by long-suffering, by gentleness and meekness, and by love unfeigned.* [D&C 121:41]

How anxious we ought to be to emulate the manner in which God wields power! And this in a world of push and shove and shout. If we become too efficient at pushing, shoving, and shouting, then we are too adapted to this world—too busy polishing skills which will ere-long become obsolete.

Meekness rests on trust and courage. It is reflected in Nephi's meek acceptance of an assignment when he said, "I will go and do" (1 Nephi 3:7), without knowing beforehand all the implications of what he was undertaking.

Meekness permits us to be confident, as was Nephi, of that which we do know—even when we do not yet know the meaning of all other things (1 Nephi 11:17). Meekness constitutes a continuing invitation to continuing education. No wonder the Lord reveals His secrets to the meek, for they are "easy to be entreated" (Alma 7:23). Not only are the meek more teachable, but they continuously receive, with special appreciation, "the engrafted word" (James 1:21), as the apostle James said—and, as Joseph Smith described it, the pure flow of intelligence (see *Teachings*, p. 151)—all from the divine databank.

If we are meek, we will also handle our critics more wisely than did these predecessors:

> *Now there was a strict law among the people of the church, that there should not any man, belonging to the church, arise and persecute those that did not belong to the church, and that there should be no persecution among themselves.*
>
> *Nevertheless, there were many among them who began to be proud, and began to contend warmly with their adversaries, even unto blows; yea, they would smite one another with their fists.* [Alma 1:21–22]

Meekness will permit us to endure more graciously the cruel caricaturing and misrepresentation that accompany discipleship, especially in the rugged last days of this dispensation. Remember the fingers of scorn in Lehi's vision which pointed and mocked at those who clung to the iron rod (see 1 Nephi 8:26–33)? The mockers were not a small minority. And they were persistent and preoccupied in their scorn of the saints. You will come to see that preoccupation.

Meekness permits us to be prompted as to whether to speak out or, as Jesus once did, be silent. But even when the meek speak up, they do so without speaking down.

I stress again that meekness does not mean we are bereft of boldness. A meek, imprisoned Joseph Smith displayed remarkable boldness in rebuking the grossness of the guards in Richmond jail:

*Silence, ye fiends of the infernal pit! In the name of Jesus Christ I rebuke you and command you to be still; I will not live another minute and hear such language. Cease such talk, or you or I die this instant!* [HC 3:208, note]

Isn't it interesting, in a world wrongly impressed with *machismo*, that we see more and more coarseness which is mistaken for manliness, more and more selfishness masquerading as individuality?

Meekness can make another very significant contribution as it aids us in bearing up under our personal afflictions (see Mosiah 3:19). Since the Lord has said he will have a "tried people," how can we possibly endure without meekness, the factoring experiences of this mortal probation?

### THE WORLD TAKES A DIFFERENT VIEW OF MEEKNESS

Illustratively, I turn now to an excerpt from President Brigham Young's secretary's journal for a choice insight brought to my attention by Professor Ronald Esplin. When asked in conversation, "Why are men left alone and often sad? Why is not God always at man's side promoting universal happiness at least for His Saints? Why does not God do everything for man?" President Young responded concerning how man's divine destiny requires individual experience and practice in learning "to act as an independent being"—to see what we will do, whether we will be "for God or not"—and in developing our own resources. Such experiences will teach us to be "righteous in the dark—to be a friend of God" (Brigham Young Office Journal, 28 January 1857). This is a sobering and revealing insight about God's plans for us here, and it underlines with urgency the need for

the attribute of meekness, especially when one feels forsaken and forgotten and alone "amid th' encircling gloom" (J. H. Newman, "Lead,
Kindly Light," *Hymns*, no. 112).

In spite of all these advantages of meekness, will the world mistake meekness, however, for something else? Yes. But we must not let
the world call the cadence for our march through life any more than
we would let the world set the direction of that march.

Brothers and sisters, this mortal experience through which we are
passing is one in which beauties abound; subtleties and delicacies are
all about us, waiting to be noticed. Wonders are everywhere to be
seen. It is, however, the observing meek, who will contemplate the
lilies of the field, will ponder the galaxies and see God moving in His
majesty and power. It is also the meek who will notice, and then lift
up, those whose hands hang down (see D&C 81:5).

Peter waxed poetic when he urged "the Ornament of a meek and
quiet spirit" (1 Peter 3:4). The meek and quiet spirit, which Peter
recommended, is essential to our happiness here and hereafter, men
and women alike.

Besides, even if our being meek results in our being abused in this
world, we need to remember that we are being fitted for chores in
another and better world—one which will be everlasting, not fleeting.

Some may still say, however, "Does not meekness invite abuse
and dominance by the unmeek?" It may. But life's experiences suggest
that sufficient unto every circumstance are the counterbalancing egos
thereof; force tends to produce counterforce.

Please do not think of meekness, therefore, in the stereotyped
ways. You will see far more examples of those in desperate need of
meekness than you will ever see of the truly meek being abused.

### DEVELOPMENT OF MEEKNESS DIFFICULT

I do not say that the development of meekness is easy. There are
strivings and struggles and setbacks, inching forward when we would
prefer to run. Even when we make some progress, there is the sober
realization that our very best meekness is but a pale copy to Jesus'
meekness. But it is "a type and shadow of things which are to come"

(Mosiah 13:10). None of the divine virtues is easy to develop. But each is possible and portable. None of them will ever be obsolete. Besides, what are the alternatives? Genius unmodified by meekness? History amply attests that such is both a blessing and a curse! Expertise wrapped in overmuch ego? It is so difficult to utilize. Boldness and swiftness unrestrained by gentleness? Such traits are as likely to trample on people as to lift them!

It is meekness, therefore, that helps us to step gratefully forward to place on the altar the talents and time and self with which we are blessed—to be at God and His children's disposal. The offering is of a gentled self, a self concerned with charity—not parity.

Yes, there are real costs associated with meekness. A significant down payment must be made. But it can come from our sufficient supply of pride. We must also be willing to endure the subsequent erosion of unbecoming ego. Furthermore, our hearts will be broken in order that they might be rebuilt. As Ezekiel said, one's task is to "make you a new heart and a new spirit" (Ezekiel 18:31). There is no way that such dismantling, such erosion, such rebuilding can occur without real cost in pain, pride, adjustments, and even some dismay. Yet since we cannot be "acceptable before God save [we are] meek and lowly in heart" (Moroni 7:44), the reality of that awesome requirement must be heeded. Better to save one's soul than to save one's face.

## CONCLUSION

I have spoken to you of this fundamental attribute because you truly are a generation drenched in destiny. May it prove to be meekly drenched in destiny. The attainment of your full possibilities will depend, as with all of us, on your developing adequately the eternal and cardinal attributes, including meekness.

God bless you and those like you the world over. Depend, meekly, upon God, for each of you—in ways yet to be experienced—will be depended upon by ever so many others.

I love you; I bless you, in apostolic authority, that you will not fail your individual rendezvous with those who await your touch and your ministry. Do not fail them! Prepare yourself in meekness to serve them, and God will bless you. I so bless you in that authority and in the name of Jesus Christ. Amen.

# "A Choice Seer"

Neal A. Maxwell

I am aware that my wise and gentle friend Elder David B. Haight spoke about the Prophet Joseph a month ago. Please bear with me, therefore, as I seek to place the spotlight on the Seer in yet a different way on this Easter Sunday, during which our rejoicing is made more resplendent by the revelations and translations concerning Jesus that came to us through Joseph.

My appreciation is expressed to President Jeffrey Holland, Dean Robert Matthews, Professors Hugh Nibley, Jack Welch, Truman Madsen, Richard Anderson, Dean Jessee, and others for sharing knowledge with me that has been so helpful. These men do their part to slow the process of my becoming intellectually arthritic.

## THE PROPHET JOSEPH SMITH

Whenever we talk about the Prophet Joseph Smith, it is important to remember what he said of himself: "I never told you I was perfect; but there is no error in the revelations which I have taught" (*Teachings*, p. 368). He was a good man, but he was called by a perfect

*This fireside address was given at Brigham Young University on 30 March 1986.*

Lord, Jesus of Nazareth! Joseph received his first counsel from God the Father, "This is My Beloved Son. Hear Him!" (JS—H 1:17). Joseph Smith listened carefully to Jesus then and ever after.

Ages ago in the Great Council, Jesus was the prepared but meek volunteer. As the Father described the plan of salvation and the need for a Savior, it was Jesus who stepped forward and said humbly but courageously, "Here am I, send me" (Abraham 3:27; see also Moses 4:2). Never has anyone offered to do so much for so many with so few words!

It is through the Prophet Joseph Smith, whom the resurrected Jesus called, that we learn these things, and so much more, about Jesus—long before Bethlehem and well beyond Calvary. Whenever we speak of the Prophet Joseph Smith, therefore, it should be in reverent appreciation of the Lord who called him and whom Joseph served so well.

From Joseph Smith, one unlearned and untrained in theology, more printed pages of scripture have come down to us than from any other mortal—in fact, as President Holland has pointed out, more than the combined pages, as available at present, from Moses, Paul, Luke, and Mormon.

But it is not only a matter of impressive quantity, it is also a qualitative matter, since dazzling doctrines came through the Prophet, including key doctrines previously lost from the face of the earth, a loss that caused people to "stumble exceedingly" (1 Nephi 13:34). "Plain and precious" things, because of faulty transmission, were "kept back" or "taken away" (see 1 Nephi 13:34, 39–40), and thus do not appear in our treasured Holy Bible.

What came *through* Joseph Smith was *beyond* Joseph Smith, and it *stretched* him! In fact, the doctrines that came through that "choice seer" (2 Nephi 3:6–7) by translation or revelation, are often so light-intensive that, like radioactive materials, they must be handled with great care!

By the way, it appears that in the process of translating the Book of Mormon in the spring of 1829, Joseph was moving along at the rate of seven to ten current printed pages a day. This is but one illustration of how blessed that "choice seer" was. Although Joseph could translate the words of the Book of Mormon, "The learned shall not read them, for they have rejected them" refers to a mind-set that is with us to this day, belonging to more than Professor Anthon (see 2 Nephi 27:20 and JS—H 1:64–65). In contrast, among an increasing number of mortals, Joseph is, as foreseen, "esteemed highly" (2 Nephi 3:7).

In 1833 Joseph was told not only that Jesus was with God premortally, but that:

> *Man was also in the beginning with God. Intelligence, or the light of truth, was not created or made, neither indeed can be.* [D&C 93:29]

What a stunning parting of the curtains so that man could have a correct view of himself! The silence of centuries was officially broken. As the morning of the Restoration began to break, the shadows of false doctrines began to flee. Man's view of himself could become clearer, unimpeded by the overhanging of "original sin." We are accountable to a just God for our actual and individual sins—not for Adam's original transgression.

> *And the Lord said unto Adam: Behold I have forgiven thee thy transgression in the Garden of Eden.*
>
> *Hence came the saying abroad among the people, that the Son of God hath atoned for original guilt, wherein the sins of the parents cannot be answered upon the heads of the children, for they are whole from the foundation of the world.* [Moses 6:53–54; see also D&C 93:38 and Articles of Faith 1:2]

A stretching view of the universe was also made possible. Note what accompanied a wondrous witnessing of the resurrected Jesus:

> *For we saw him, even on the right hand of God; and we heard the voice bearing record that he is the Only Begotten of the Father—*

*That by him, and through him, and of him, the worlds are and were created, and the inhabitants thereof are begotten sons and daughters unto God.* [D&C 76:23–24]

In June 1830 came "this precious morsel," which expands our perspective about this planet, described by Maimonides as "a speck among the worlds" (see Hugh Nibley, *Old Testament and Related Studies* [Salt Lake City: Deseret Book, 1986], p.139).

*And worlds without number have I created; and I also created them for mine own purpose; and by the Son I created them, which is mine Only Begotten. . . .*
*For behold, this is my work and my glory—to bring to pass the immortality and eternal life of man.* [Moses 1:33, 39]

Even as our view of the universe was greatly enlarged, our view of human history was made much more intimate and familial:

*Three years previous to the death of Adam, he called . . . the residue of his posterity who were righteous, into the valley of Adam-ondi-Ahman, and there bestowed upon them his last blessing.*
*And the Lord appeared unto them, and they rose up and blessed Adam, and called him Michael, the prince, the archangel.*
*And the Lord administered comfort unto Adam, and said unto him: I have set thee to be at the head; a multitude of nations shall come of thee, and thou art a prince over them forever.*
*And Adam stood up in the midst of the congregation; and, notwithstanding he was bowed down with age, being full of the Holy Ghost, predicted whatsoever should befall his posterity unto the latest generation.*
*These things were all written in the book of Enoch, and are to be testified of in due time.* [D&C 107:53–57]

This startling and informing revelation came, by the way, in the midst of verses otherwise concerned with chronologies, genealogies, and duties.

Let others, if they choose, make jokes about our first parents, Adam and Eve, or regard them as mere myths. As a result of the Prophet Joseph Smith's revelations, we are blessed to know much more about "things as they really were, are, and will be" (see Jacob 4:13 and D&C 93:24)!

Latter-day Saints expectantly await the book of Enoch as being among the "many great and important things pertaining to the Kingdom of God" that God "will yet reveal" (Articles of Faith 1:9). As Professor Robert Matthews has observed, through Joseph Smith we received eighteen times as much as is in the Bible concerning Enoch. Without the Restoration, we would not even know there was a City of Enoch!

While others wonder if their mortal existence is absurd and pointless, we know otherwise about God's purposes, which he described before declaring, "This is the plan of salvation unto all men" (Moses 6:57–63). The process is a stern test:

*And we will prove them herewith, to see if they will do all things whatsoever the Lord their God shall command them.* [Abraham 3:25]

*Nevertheless the Lord seeth fit to chasten his people; yea, he trieth their patience and their faith.* [Mosiah 23:21]

How marvelous it is that these and so many other precious truths, just as prophesied, are "had again" among the children of men (Moses 1:41). No wonder there can and should be times for openly *enjoying* the faith as well as *defending* the faith.

These restored truths came fully formed. Joseph Smith did not receive such truths through Solomon Spaulding, Ethan Smith, Sidney Rigdon, Oliver Cowdery, or any others to be advanced by those desperate for any explanation other than the correct one. In 1850 Joseph's devoted helper, Phineas Young, wrote to Brigham Young in praise of Oliver Cowdery. Phineas wrote that the rebaptized Oliver Cowdery was now dead, but no one should forget his last testimony in which he said of Church headquarters in the West, "There was no salvation but in the valley and through the priesthood there." Oliver knew the source of the truths and priesthood which were restored through Joseph and the later *locus* of the presiding priesthood power. (see Phineas Young to Brigham Young, April 25, 1850, Brigham Young Collection, Historical Department, The Church of Jesus Christ of Latter-day Saints)

There is a legal doctrine meaning "the thing speaks for itself." The Everest of ecclesiastical truth built from the translations and revelations of the Prophet Joseph Smith speaks for itself as it towers above the foothills of philosophy. Even so, most will ignore it. Still others will reject the Restoration, supplying their own alternative explanations, just as some did who once heard thunder instead of the voice of God (see John 12:27–30). However, in a happy day ahead, "They that murmured shall learn doctrine" (Isaiah 29:24; 2 Nephi 27:35). This suggests that doctrinal illiteracy is a significant cause of murmuring among Church members.

The Restoration responds resoundingly and reassuringly to the key human questions and provides the firm framework of our faith. Do we actually live in an unexplained and unexplainable universe? Is there really purpose and meaning to human existence? Why such unevenness in the human condition? Why so much human suffering?

The marvelous truths of the Restoration respond to these questions and are highly global, highly personal, and even galactic in their dimensions! Identity exists amid immensity. We are enclosed in divine purposes! There is no need for despair! No wonder the restored gospel is such "good news."

These and other revelations came to us through an inspired prophet, Joseph Smith. His spelling left something to be desired, but how he provided us with the essential grammar of the gospel!

## THE RESTORATION

Our present appreciation of the restored gospel lags embarrassingly far behind the stretching significance of its doctrines and theology. So far as our exploring the terrain of truth opened up to us by the Prophet Joseph is concerned, we have barely reached the Platte River, and it is time for us as a people to move on!

The Prophet is that "choice seer" of whom ancient Joseph spoke (2 Nephi 3:6–11), a major spiritual benefactor of the world. His salvational impact ultimately will be enormous, as the demographics of this dispensation alone assure (see D&C 135:3).

Like another prophet, Joseph served "notwithstanding [his] weakness" (2 Nephi 33:11). "Out of [Joseph's] weakness he [was] made strong" (2 Nephi 3:13). At one point, when he was translating the fourth chapter of 1 Nephi, Emma was acting as his scribe. Joseph reportedly encountered the words about the wall around Jerusalem (see 1 Nephi 4:5). He apparently paused and asked Emma if, in fact, there was a wall around Jerusalem. She replied in the affirmative. Joseph hadn't known (see *The History of the Reorganized Church of Jesus Christ of Latter Day Saints,* 1896, reprint [Independence, Missouri: Board of Publication, 1967], 4:447). According to Emma, when she and Joseph were interrupted during his translating, Joseph would later resume on the very sentence from which he had left off (see *Saints Herald,* 1 October 1879, pp. 289–90; see also Parley P. Pratt, *Autobiography of Parley P. Pratt* [Salt Lake City: Deseret Book Co., 1938], p. 62).

We naturally would like to know about that process of translation. In October 1831, Joseph Smith was asked by his brother Hyrum, at a conference held in Orange, Ohio, to give a firsthand account concerning the coming forth of the Book of Mormon. The Prophet replied "that it was not intended to tell the world all the particulars of the coming forth of the Book of Mormon; and . . . it was not expedient for him to relate these things" (*HC* 1:220). Since Joseph, who knew the "particulars," chose not to describe them in detail then, we cannot presently be definitive about methodology. But we can and should savor the supernal substance of the revelations and translations, which combine to prove to the world "that the holy scriptures are true" (D&C 20: 11; see also 1 Nephi 13:39–40).

Joseph Smith's time and place was one of religious fervor: "Lo, here!" and "Lo, there!" is Christ (JS—H 1:5). Ours is an age when, instead, the historicity of Christ is increasingly questioned. This condition only increases the relevance of the Restoration with its affirmation of Jesus' reality and his resurrection.

While Jesus declared that the scriptures "testify" of him (John 5:39), he neither expected nor received much coverage in secular history. Therefore, it is no surprise for studious Christians to learn that the secular history of that meridian period is nearly silent about the ministry of Jesus. Three secular writers, each writing after Jesus' crucifixion, touched slightly upon Christ. Tacitus (about A.D. 55–117), thought by many to be the greatest Roman historian, wrote only this: "Christus . . . had undergone the death penalty in the reign of Tiberius, by sentence of the procurator Pontius Pilatus" (*Annals of Tacitus* 15:44).

Suetonius (about A.D. 70–140), a Roman who wrote about the lives of various Caesars, called Jesus "Chrestus" and provided a sentence linking Chrestus to civil disturbance. Yet even this brief mention may contain a possible chronological error. (see *The Lives of the Caesars*, trans. J. C. Rolfe [Cambridge, Massachusetts: Harvard University Press, 1914], 5:51–52).

Josephus (about A.D. 37–95), in his *Antiquities*, wrote a few lines about the founder of Christianity, but later interpolations may cloud his meager lines (see, for example, 18:3). How important it is, given these conditions, that the New Testament not stand alone as evidence for Christ!

Joseph Smith was also an eyewitness of the resurrected Christ. Yet, as with all true disciples, Joseph went through a process of *proving, reproving,* and *improving,* while simultaneously serving as the human conduit through whom God chose to give his word to this generation (D&C 5:10).

The period of adversity commencing in Richmond Jail and continuing in Liberty Jail from 1 December 1838 until the first week in April 1839 provides a special window through which we can see the process of revelation and personal consolidation under way. Elder B. H. Roberts called the jail the "prison temple" (B. H. Roberts, *A Comprehensive History of the Church* [Salt Lake City, Utah: The Church of Jesus Christ of Latter-day Saints, 1930], 1:526). Ironically, this period of enforced idleness, grim though the conditions were, was perhaps the only time in the Prophet's often hectic adult life when there was much time for reflection.

The dungeon at Liberty Jail had inner and outer walls which, combined, were four feet thick. Loose rocks were placed between the walls to thwart any attempt at burrowing through. Unjustly arrested and unjustly confined, Joseph and his companions tried twice to escape but failed. As thick as those walls and that door were, and as securely as they kept the Prophet and his fellow prisoners in, the walls were not thick enough to keep revelation out!

During his stay in Liberty Jail, the Prophet Joseph Smith received some of the most sublime revelations ever received by any prophet in any dispensation, known now as sections 121 and 122 of the Doctrine and Covenants. Therein are divine tutorials by which the Lord schooled his latter-day prophet—probably the most tender tutorials in all of holy writ now available.

### A SPECIAL RELATIONSHIP

Joseph Smith was probably first made intellectually aware of the special relationship he had with ancient Joseph, whom we commonly refer to as Joseph in Egypt, when the Prophet Joseph translated the third chapter of 2 Nephi. It was not until Liberty Jail, however, that the record indicates any public affirmation of this unusual relationship. In one of his last letters from Liberty Jail, Joseph wrote, "I feel like Joseph in Egypt" (*The Personal Writings of Joseph Smith*, comp. Dean C. Jessee [Salt Lake City: Deseret Book, 1984], p. 409). It was not an idle comparison, for it reflected an important verse in the third chapter of 2 Nephi. Ancient Joseph spoke of the latter-day seer, saying, "And he shall be like unto me" (2 Nephi 3:15).

When Joseph Smith, Jr., was given a blessing by Father Smith in December 1834, an extensive portion of that blessing informed modern Joseph of his special relationship to ancient Joseph (see Joseph Smith, Sr., blessing, 9 Dec. 1934, Church Historical Department, 1:3–4).

The comparisons between the two Josephs, of course, reflect varying degrees of exactitude, but they are, nevertheless, quite striking. Some similarities are situational, others are dispositional. Some are strategic, such as ancient Joseph's making stored grain available in time of famine (see Genesis 41:56), while modern Joseph opened the granary of the gospel after years of famine.

First, both Josephs had inauspicious beginnings. Initially, they were unlikely candidates to have had the impact they did on Egyptian history and American history, respectively.

Both had visions at a young and tender age (see Genesis 37:2–5 and JS—H 1). The visions brought to both men hate from their fellowmen (see Genesis 37:5–8 and JS—H 1:21–26). Both knew sibling jealousy. Modern Joseph had to contend with a mercurial brother, William, whom Joseph forgave many times (see HC 2:353–54).

Both Josephs were generous to those who betrayed them. Ancient Joseph was generous to his once-betraying brothers whom he later saved from starvation (see Genesis 45:1–15).

Both prophesied remarkably of the future of their nations and the challenges their governments would face (see Genesis 41:29–31 and D&C 87).

They both knew what it was to be falsely accused, and they both were jailed.

Both, in their extremities, helped others who shared their imprisonment, but who later forgot their benefactors. In the case of ancient Joseph, it was the chief butler (see Genesis 40:20–23). Joseph Smith worried over an ill cell mate, Sidney Rigdon, who was freed in January 1839. The Prophet rejoiced. Three months later, the Prophet inquired "after Elder Rigdon if he has not forgotten us" (*Writings*, p. 399).

Both Josephs were torn from their families, although ancient Joseph suffered through this for a much, much longer time.

Very significantly, both were "like unto" each other in being amazingly resilient in the midst of adversity. This, in each man, is a truly striking quality.

Both were understandably anxious about their loved ones and friends. Ancient Joseph, when his true identity became known, inquired tenderly of his brothers, "Doth my father yet live?" (Genesis 45:3). From Liberty Jail, the Prophet Joseph Smith, with comparative awareness, wrote, "Doth my friends yet live if they live do they remember me?" (*Writings*, p. 409).

Indeed, these two uncommon men had much in common, being truly "like unto" each other!

## IN THE PRISON TEMPLE

The "prison temple" involved a time of obscurity, adversity, irony, and testimony. W. W. Phelps had briefly faltered, being part of the betrayals that had placed Joseph Smith in Liberty Jail. Joseph was, at the time, indignant over Brother Phelps' failures. Yet later on, Joseph was generous. The next year, 1840, when W. W. Phelps pled for readmission into the Church, Joseph Smith, who pledged from jail to act later "in the spirit of generosity," wrote a powerful and redemptive letter, the closing lines of which were, "Come on, dear brother, since the war is past, For friends at first, are friends again at last" (*HC* 4:164; see also pp. 162–63).

No wonder a grateful Brother Phelps, soon after Joseph's June 1844 martyrdom, wrote the text "Praise to the man who communed with Jehovah" (*Hymns*, 1985, no. 27).

The ironies in Liberty Jail are many. Though deprived of his constitutional rights, Joseph Smith therein praised the glorious U.S. Constitution. Then, after the misery of Missouri, Joseph declared with inspired anticipation:

*I am will to be sacrificed . . . maintaining the laws & Constitution of the United States if need be for the general good of mankind.* [Andrew F. Ehat and Lyndon W. Cook, comps. and eds., *The Words of Joseph Smith* (Provo, Utah: Religious Studies Center, Brigham Young University, 1980), p. 320]

While being grossly abused by some biased political, judicial, and military leaders who wrongly used their powers Joseph received a glorious revelation. A sizable portion of that revelation, D&C 121, contrastingly sets forth the style and substance the Lord wants from his leaders that diverges so sharply from the ways of the world (see D&C 121:34–46).

Though Joseph was jailed nearly five months, more than four of these in Liberty Jail, he was told by the tutoring Lord that these things shall be "but for a small moment" (D&C 122:4; see also D&C 121:7). Though Joseph was suffering, the Lord reminded him that he was, not suffering as much as Job had (see D&C 121:7–11). Only the Lord can compare crosses, and on that particular occasion he did (D&C 122:8).

The conditions in Liberty Jail were grim. The food was scanty and often consisted of leftovers from the jailer's table brought to them in a basket where chickens slept at night and which was often not cleaned. When the prisoners were permitted to cook, they had to endure smoke. It was also a particularly cold winter. The constant darkness bothered the prisoners' eyes. Joseph wrote about how his hand actually trembled as he penned his next-to-last letter to Emma (see *Writings*, p. 409).

In the midst of this stark obscurity and incessant difficulty, and with twelve thousand of Joseph's followers driven from the state of Missouri, the enemies of the Church probably felt that they had destroyed Joseph's work. Yet in the midst of all this deprivation, affliction, and obscurity, Joseph received the Lord's stunning assurance that "the ends of the earth shall inquire after thy name" (D&C 122:1).

How inspired and audacious a prophecy for any religious leader, let alone one on the obscure nineteenth-century American frontier. Meanwhile, Joseph's contemporary frontier and religious leaders have since become mere footnotes to history. But not Joseph!

Joseph, earlier in his imprisonment, had special assurances of which he later wrote,

*Death stared me in the face, and . . . my destruction was determined upon, as far as man was concerned; yet, from my first entrance into the camp, . . . that still small voice, which has so often whispered consolation to my soul, in the depth of sorrow and distress, bade me be of good cheer, and promised deliverance, which gave me great comfort. [Writings* (November 1839), p. 443]

However, Joseph was not unmindful or unaware of how grim things looked. With unusual empathy he observed from his prison temple: "Those who have persecuted us and smitten us and borne false witness against us . . . do seem to have a great triumph over us for the present"; then, "[But] Zion shall yet live though she seemeth to be dead" (*Writings*, pp. 375, 382).

It was from Liberty Jail that Joseph, more than once, testified that through God "we received the Book of Mormon" (*Writings*, p. 399), "that the Book of Mormon is true," and "that the ministering angels sent forth from God are true" (*Writings*, p. 407).

It was soon after his release from Liberty Jail that the Prophet Joseph Smith spoke about how the Book of Mormon was "the keystone of our religion" (*HC* 4:461).

After the Liberty Jail experience, the Prophet gave fervent public testimony about the Book of Mormon to a congregation of about three thousand in Philadelphia. When Sidney Rigdon, in his remarks on that same occasion, seemed to neglect the Book of Mormon in favor of citing the Bible, Joseph took the pulpit and declared, "If nobody else had the courage to testify of so glorious a message from Heaven, and of the finding of so glorious a record, he felt to do it" (*Words*, p. 45). The atmosphere, according to one present, was electric.

This is not to say that Joseph had not earlier been clear and declarative regarding the Book of Mormon. For instance, in an 1834 sermon, Joseph observed, "Take away the Book of Mormon and the revelations, and where is our religion?" (*Teachings*, p. 71).

Sharing the jail with Joseph was his brother Hyrum, ever faithful at Joseph's side. We have yet to pay Hyrum his due. Alas, we have little from his pen, but his actions spoke for him. However, on 16 March 1839, he wrote from Liberty Jail to a Sister Grinnal who was nursing Hyrum's wife, Mary Fielding, to his daughter, Lovina, and to a girl, Clarrinda. To Clarrinda he wrote:

> *Let mother give you one of the Books of Mormon & write your name in it. I want you to seek every opportunity to read it through. Remember me both night and morning in your prayers.*

To Lovina he wrote:

> *You may have my small Book of Mormon. You must try to read it through. Pray for your father that the Lord may help him to come home.* [Letter used with permission of Elder Eldred G. Smith, in whose possession it is.]

In the extremity of jail, Hyrum, so much at the center of things, joined Joseph in stressing the Book of Mormon.

Significantly, Joseph was released from the bondage of Liberty Jail 6 April 1839, and a few days later was allowed to escape from his captors. As you know, April 6 is the date of Jesus' birth. It is also the date of birth of his latter-day church (D&C 20:1). Additionally, the time of Joseph's release from the bondage of jail is often part of the season of Passover when our Jewish friends celebrate ancient Israel's deliverance and subsequent release from bondage in Egypt.

By the way, after Jesus' ascension when Herod "stretched forth his hands to vex certain of the church," he killed James, the brother of John, with a sword. When Herod saw the people's approval, he had Peter imprisoned, thinking to bring him to the people after Easter. But Peter was helped by the Lord to escape from prison during this same spring season (see Acts 12:1–5). Easter time is filled with rich remembrances.

The day the Prophet Joseph ended his bondage in Liberty Jail, 6 April 1839, involved yet another significant event. Heber C. Kimball recorded in his journal that on that day

*the following words came to my mind, and the Spirit said unto me, "write,"*
*which I did by taking a piece of paper and writing on my knee as follows: . . .*
*"Verily I say unto my servant Heber, thou art my son, in whom I am well*
*pleased for thou art careful to hearken to my words, and not transgress my*
*law, nor rebel against my servant Joseph Smith, for thou has a respect to the*
*words of mine anointed, even from the least to the greatest of them; therefore*
*thy name is written in heaven, no more to be blotted out for ever, because of*
*these things." [Words, p. 18]*

Note how much importance the Lord attached to our being loyal
to his servants! It is no different now.

With regard to the ministry of Joseph Smith, there are significant expressions of divine determination. In each of these examples,
the Lord issued his declarations using the word "shall." The books
of scripture that were to come through the "choice seer" *"shall* grow
together" (2 Nephi 3:11–12; emphasis added). The books of scripture
that came through Joseph Smith are joined with the Holy Bible, especially now with the new recent publication of the four standard works.

Another promise was given in the same chapter: those who would
try to destroy the work of the latter-day seer *"shall* be confounded"
(2 Nephi 3:14; emphasis added). This promise continues to be kept.

Joseph also received another *shall* promise, which likewise has
never been revoked: "Thy people *shall* never be turned against thee by
the testimony of traitors" (D&C 122:3; emphasis added). This continues to be true today.

Furthermore, the central tutorial theme in Liberty Jail was also a
promise: "All these things *shall* give thee experience, and *shall* be for
thy good" (D&C 122:7; emphasis added).

Joseph Smith, Jr., was that "choice seer!" All the "shall" promises
about him shall be fulfilled, as the "ends of the earth shall inquire
after [his] name" (D&C 122:1).

### A CHOICE SEER

Brigham Young, who was not easily impressed by anyone, observed that before he met Joseph Smith, he was searching for just such a seer:

*The secret feeling of my heart was that I would be willing to crawl around the earth on my hands and knees, to see such a man as was Peter, Jeremiah, Moses, or any man that could tell me anything about God and heaven. . . .*

*. . . When I saw Joseph Smith, he took heaven, figuratively speaking, and brought it down to earth; and he took the earth, brought it up, and opened up, in plainness and simplicity, the things of God; and that is the beauty of his mission.* [*JD* 8:228, 5:332]

On another occasion, Brigham said, "I feel like shouting hallelujah, all the time, when I think that I ever knew Joseph Smith" (*JD* 3:51). Significantly, Brigham's last mortal words were, "Joseph! Joseph! Joseph!" (Leonard J. Arrington, *Brigham Young: American Moses* [New York: Alfred A. Knopf, 1985], p. 399).

We have obligations to the Lord's prophets, past and present, which include being fair, posthumously or presently, concerning their words. The "choice seer," Joseph, reminded the Church in an epistle (December 1838) from jail that, "our light speeches from time to time . . . have nothing to do with the fixed principle of our hearts" (*Writings*, p. 376). Should we not distinguish between the utterances of the moment and considered opinions? Do not all of us wish for that same understanding on the part of our friends, hoping they, "with the breath of kindness," will "blow the chaff away"?

We are wise to follow, therefore, the example of Lorenzo Snow rather than that of Thomas B. Marsh. Marsh let himself become so preoccupied with the imperfections in the Prophet Joseph Smith that he found himself disaffected and out of the Church for a season. Lorenzo Snow said he had observed some imperfections in the Prophet Joseph Smith, but his reaction was that it was marvelous to see how the Lord could still use Joseph. Seeing this, Lorenzo Snow—

later President Snow—concluded that there might even be some hope for him!

One of the great messages that flows from the Lord's use of Joseph Smith as a "choice seer" in the latter days is that there is indeed hope for each of us! The Lord can call us in our weaknesses and yet magnify us for his purposes.

In the 1834 blessing, Father Smith promised Joseph, "Thou shalt fill up the measure of thy days" (Joseph Smith, Sr., blessing, pp. 3–4). The Lord likewise reassured the Prophet in Liberty Jail, "Thy days are known, and thy years shall not be numbered less" (D&C 122:9). It proved to be so. However, the Prophet was conscious of the pressures of time upon him. President Brigham Young, who visited Joseph in the prison temple, noted that Joseph told him, more than once, that he, Joseph, would not live to see his fortieth year *(Wilford Woodruff's Journal,* July 28, 1844 [Salt Lake City: Kraut's Pioneer Press, 1982]).

In the 1834 blessing, Joseph was promised that during his ministry, "Thy heart shall be enlarged" (Joseph Smith, Sr., blessing, pp. 3–4). An enlarged Joseph wrote from Liberty Jail,

*It seems to me my heart will always be more tender after this than ever it was before . . . for my part I think I never could have felt as I now do if I had not suffered the wrongs that I have suffered. [Writings, pp. 386, 387]*

In the 1834 blessing, the Prophet Joseph was promised, "Thou shalt like to do the work the Lord thy God shall command thee" (Joseph Smith, Sr., blessing, pp. 3–4). How often that intrinsic satisfaction sustained the Seer, when extrinsic conditions were so unsatisfactory!

On 4 April 1839, Joseph wrote his last letter to Emma from Liberty Jail "just as the sun [was] going down" while peeking through the "grates of this lonesome prison . . . with emotions known only to God" *(Writings,* p. 425). Such was Joseph's view of a temporal sunset that evening. But what a view of eternity he had and gave to us!

Joseph, as B. H. Roberts wrote, lived "in crescendo!" Looking back upon his busy, task-filled years, the Prophet said near the end,

"No man knows my history. I cannot tell it: I shall never undertake it. I don't blame anyone for not believing my history. If I had not experienced what I have, I would not have believed it myself" (*HC* 6:317). Thus, even in his adversity, Joseph had unusual empathy for those who lacked his special perspective.

This empathy extended beyond Joseph's own time and circumstances. He actually saw his prison sufferings as helping and expanding him "to understand the minds of the Ancients" *(Writings,* p. 387). A linkage was felt with their "afflictions," so that, said Joseph, "in the day of judgment . . . we may hold an even weight in the balances with them" (*Writings,* p. 395). How else could Joseph take his rightful place, "crowned in the midst of the prophets of old" (*Hymns;* 1985, no. 27)?

I gladly and gratefully testify that Joseph was and is a "choice seer," a prophet of God!

### THE LORD AND HIS SERVANTS

Now may I close my message by bringing to the fore again, Jesus of Nazareth, who as the resurrected Lord and Savior called Joseph Smith. Let us focus on a particular part of the Atonement that makes the celebration of Easter possible.

A short while before Gethsemane and Calvary, Jesus prayed, "Now is my soul troubled; and what shall I say? Father, save me from this hour." Then, as if in soliloquy, he said, "But for this cause came I unto this hour" (John 12:27). The awful weight of the Atonement had begun to descend upon him. We next find him in Gethsemane.

*And they came to a place which was named Gethsemane: and he saith to his disciples, Sit ye here, while I shall pray.*

*And he taketh with him Peter and James and John, and began to be sore amazed, and to be very heavy.* [Mark 14:32–33]

The Greek for "very heavy" is "depressed, dejected, in anguish." Just as the Psalmist had foreseen, the Savior was "full of heaviness"

(Psalms 69:20). The heavy weight of the sins of all mankind were falling upon him.

He had been intellectually and otherwise prepared from ages past for this task. He is the creator of this and other worlds. He knew the plan of salvation. He knew this is what it would come to. But when it happened, it was so much worse than even he had imagined!

Now, brothers and sisters, this was not theater; it was the real thing. "And he went forward a little, and fell on the ground, and prayed that, if it were possible, the hour might pass from him" (Mark 14:35). Only in the Gospel of Mark do we get this next special pleading, "And he said, Abba, Father, all things are possible unto thee; take away this cup from me" (Mark 14:36). When Jesus used the word "Abba," it was a most personal and intimate familiar reference—the cry of a child in deepest distress for his father to help him in the midst of this agony.

Did Jesus hope there might be, as with Abraham, a ram in the thicket? We do not know, but the agony and the extremity were great. The sins and the grossness of all mankind were falling upon someone who was perfectly sinless, perfectly sensitive. This pleading to the Father included the doctrine he had taught in his ministry as Jehovah to Abraham and Sarah. "Is anything too hard for the Lord?" (Genesis 18:14). He had taught it in his mortal messiahship: "All things are possible to him that believeth" (Mark 9:23). Hence, this resounding plea. And then came that marvelous spiritual submissiveness: "Nevertheless not what I will, but what thou wilt" (Mark 14:36).

Luke wrote that at a particular point, an angel appeared to strengthen him. I do not know who that angel was, but what a great privilege to be at the side of the Son of God as he worked out the Atonement for the whole human family!

Jesus bled at every pore, and the bleeding started in Gethsemane. He was stretched to the limits. Later, when Jesus was on the cross, the Father, for reasons that are not completely apparent, withdrew his immediate presence from his son. The full weight fell upon him one last time, and there came the great soul cry, "My God, my God, why hast thou forsaken me?" (Mark 15:34).

Through that marvelous Prophet Joseph, in the book of Alma, we learned that Jesus not only suffered for our sins, but, in order to perfect his capacity of mercy and empathy, he also bore our sicknesses and infirmities that he might know "according to the flesh" (see Alma 7:11–12) what we pass through and thus become the perfect shepherd, which he is.

This is Jesus' church, and Joseph was his prophet, and all the prophecies pertaining to his second coming will be fulfilled just as surely as all pertaining to his birth and early ministry were fulfilled.

He is our Lord, he is our God, and the day will come, brothers and sisters, when the veil will be stripped away, and you and I will see the incredible, spiritual intimacy that prevails between the Lord and his servants. Moses in the Sinai before the Exodus was on an exceedingly high mountain with Jesus—Jehovah. Not many centuries later, on the Mount of Transfiguration, Moses was again with his Lord and Savior, Jesus Christ. Someday we will see the interlacings of the lives of the Lord, his prophets, and our own. It is all part of Father in Heaven's glorious and wondrous plan of salvation—about which we know so much that matters through that remarkable Prophet Joseph Smith.

Praise to the man who communed with Jehovah! Praise to Jehovah for loving us and leading us and atoning for us. Praise to God the Father. Whenever we learn finally to love him, we must remember that he loved us first. Out of his love he has given to us this remarkable plan of salvation.

May God send us on our way with hearts brimming with joy for what we know. May we search the scriptures, follow their commandments, and rejoice in them. This is my prayer for myself and for you on this Easter evening, in the name of Jesus Christ. Amen.

# "*Meek and Lowly*"

Neal A. Maxwell

## WEARING HIS YOKE

Meekness ranks so low on the mortal scale of things, yet so high on God's: "For none is acceptable before God, save the meek and lowly in heart" (Moroni 7:44). The rigorous requirements of Christian discipleship cannot be met without the tutoring facilitated by meekness: "Take my yoke upon you, and learn of me; for I am meek and lowly" (Matthew 11:29). Jesus, the carpenter, "undoubtedly had experience making yokes" with Joseph (*Interpreter's Dictionary of the Bible*, vol. 4 [New York: Abingdon Press, 1962], p. 925), and thus the Savior gave us that marvelous metaphor (see Matthew 11:20). Unlike servitude to sin, by wearing his yoke, we truly learn of the Yoke Master in what is an education for eternity as well as for mortality.

Meekness is needed, therefore, in order for us to be spiritually successful—whether in matters of the intellect, in the management of power, in the dissolution of personal pride, or in coping with the

*This devotional address was given at Brigham Young University on 21 October 1986.*

challenges and routine of life. With meekness, living in "thanksgiving daily" is actually possible even in life's stern seasons (Alma 34:38).

Meanwhile, the world regards the meek as nice but quaint people, as those to be stepped over or stepped on. Nevertheless, the development of this virtue is a stunning thing just to contemplate, especially in a world in which so many others are headed in opposite directions. These next requirements clearly show the unarguable relevance as well as the stern substance of this sweet virtue.

Serious disciples are not only urged to do good but also to avoid growing weary of doing good (see Galatians 6:9 and Helaman 10:5).

They are not only urged to speak the truth but also to speak the truth in love (see Ephesians 4:15).

They are not only urged to endure all things but also to endure them well (see D&C 121:8).

They are not only urged to be devoted to God's cause but also to be prepared to sacrifice all things, giving, if necessary, the last full measure of devotion (see *Lectures on Faith* 6:7).

They are not only to do many things of worth but are also to focus on the weightier matters, the things of most worth (see Matthew 23:23).

They are not only urged to forgive but also to forgive seventy times seven (see Matthew 18:21–22).

They are not only to be engaged in good causes, but also they are to be "anxiously engaged" (see D&C 58:27).

They are not only to do right but also to do right for the right reasons.

They are told to get on the strait and narrow path, but then are told that this is only the beginning, not the end (see 2 Nephi 31:19–20).

They are not only to endure enemies but also to pray for them and to love them (see Matthew 5:44).

They are urged not only to worship God but, astoundingly, they are instructed to strive to become like him! (See Matthew 5:48; 3 Nephi 12:48, 27:27.)

In the midst of "all these things," they are given a Sabbath day for rest, during which they do the sweetest but often the hardest work of all. Who else but the truly meek would even consider such a stretching journey? The preceding enumeration is certainly a verification of the crucial role meekness plays in the lives of serious disciples. Thus, if we really learn of the Savior, it will be by taking the yoke of such experiences upon us. This is a high-yield, but very severe form of learning. However, there is "no other way." Moreover, when so yoked, we may then get much more learning than we bargained for. Furthermore, to be spiritually successful, Jesus' yoke cannot be removed part way down life's furrow, even after a good showing up to that point; we are to endure well to the end.

### THE KEY TO DEEPENING DISCIPLESHIP

Did Paul not speak knowingly of the "fellowship of [Christ's] sufferings" (Philippians 3:10)? Are we not told that meekness is so vital that God actually gives us certain challenges in order to keep us humble (Ether 12:27)? Did not Peter write regarding how Christians should expect to be familiar with fiery trials (1 Peter 4:12)? Furthermore, as the disciple enriches his relationship with the Lord, he is apt to have periodic "public relations" problems with others, being misrepresented and misunderstood. He or she will have to "take it" at times. Meekness, therefore, is a key to deepening discipleship.

In the exchange between Jesus and a righteous young man, we see how one missing quality cannot be fully compensated for, even by other qualities, however praiseworthy.

*The young man saith unto him, All these things have I kept from my youth up: what lack I yet?*

*Jesus said unto him, If thou wilt be perfect, go and sell that thou hast, and give to the poor, and thou shalt have treasure in heaven: and come and follow me.*

*But when the young man heard that saying, he went away sorrowful: for he had great possessions.* [Matthew 19:20–22]

In this instance the missing meekness prevented a submissive response by the young man; this deficiency altered his decision and the consequences flowing there from.

There appears to be "no other way" to learn certain things except through the relevant, clinical experiences. Happily, the commandment "Take my yoke upon you, and learn of me; for I am meek and lowly in heart" (Matthew 11:29) carries an accompanying and compensating promise from Jesus—"and ye shall find rest unto your souls." This is a very special form of rest. It surely includes the rest resulting from the shedding of certain needless burdens: fatiguing insincerity, exhausting hypocrisy, and the strength-sapping quest for recognition, praise, and power. Those of us who fall short, in one way or another, often do so because we carry such unnecessary and heavy baggage. Being thus overloaded, we sometimes stumble and then feel sorry for ourselves.

We need not carry such baggage. However, when we're not meek, we resist the informing voice of conscience and feedback from family, leaders, and friends. Whether from preoccupation or pride, the warning signals go unnoticed or unheeded. However, if sufficient meekness is in us, it will not only help us to jettison unneeded burdens, but will also keep us from becoming mired in the ooze of self-pity. Furthermore, true meekness has a metabolism that actually requires very little praise or recognition—of which there is usually such a shortage anyway. Most of the time, the sponge of selfishness quickly soaks up everything in sight, including praise intended for others.

Disciples are to make for themselves "a new heart" by undergoing a "mighty change" of heart (Ezekiel 18:31; Alma 5:12–14). Yet we cannot make such "a new heart" while nursing old grievances. Just as civil wars lend themselves to the passionate preservation of ancient grievances, so civil wars within the individual soul—between the natural and the potential man—keep alive old slights and perceived injustices, except in the meek.

Is there not deep humility in the omnicompetent Christ, the majestic Miracle Worker, who acknowledged, "I can of mine own self do nothing" (John 5:30)? Jesus neither misused nor doubted his power, but he was never confused about its source, either. Instead, we mortals—perhaps even when otherwise modest—are sometimes quite willing to display our accumulated accomplishments, as if we had done it all by ourselves. Hence this sobering reminder:

*And thou say in thine heart, My power and the might of mine hand hath gotten me this wealth.*

*But thou shalt remember the Lord thy God: for it is he that giveth thee power to get wealth, that he may establish his covenant which he sware unto thy fathers, as it is this day.* [Deuteronomy 8:17–18]

Meekness is especially needed to labor in the Lord's vineyard, which involves such lowly work—as the world measures worth. No wonder, as one prophet wrote, the laborers in the Lord's vineyard are comparatively "few." Moreover, the Lord's work is not usually performed on a luxuriant landscape, but, said Jacob, in "the poorest spot in all the land of [the] vineyard" (see Jacob 5:21, 70). The world's Caesars pay little heed to such workers.

Had Jesus not been meek and lowly when "a great multitude with swords and staves" (Mark 14:43) came to take him, he could have resisted his destiny. Led by Judas, there came "thither" that band of men "with lanterns and torches" (John 18:3). So spiritually blind was the multitude, they actually needed lanterns to see and capture the "Light of the World"!

Though he was actually the Creator of this world, the earth being his footstool, Jesus' willingness to become from birth a person of "no reputation" provides one of the great lessons in human history. He, the leader-servant, who remained of "no reputation" mortally, will one day be he before whom every knee will bow and whose name every tongue will confess (see Philippians 2:10–11). Jesus meekly stayed his unparalleled course.

Brigham Young, who stayed his lesser but very impressive course, knew both the fatigue of leadership and the rest Jesus promised. He counseled those less spiritually secure and more anxious about the outcome:

*It is the Lord's work. I know enough to let the kingdom alone, and do my duty. It carries me, I do not carry the kingdom. I sail in the old ship Zion, and it bears me safely above the raging elements.* [*JD* 11:252]

In our own time, the late Elder LeGrand Richards was heard by some of us to declare that he did not fret about the Church, because it is the Lord's Church, "so I let him worry about it!"

Wise secular leaders are not strangers to meekness either. The following episode in the life of George Washington involved potential mutiny:

*Washington called together the grumbling officers on March 15, 1783. . . . He began to speak—carefully and from a written manuscript, referring to the proposal of "either deserting our Country in the extremest hour of her distress, or turning our Arms against it. . . ." Washington appealed simply and honestly for reason, restraint, patience, and duty—all the good and unexciting virtues.*

*And then Washington stumbled as he read. He squinted, paused, and out of his pocket he drew some new spectacles.*

*"Gentlemen, you must pardon me," he said in apology. "I have grown gray in your service and now find myself growing blind."*

*Most of his men had never seen the general wear glasses. Yes, men said to themselves, eight hard years. They recalled the ruddy, full-blooded planter of 1775; now they saw . . . a big, good, fatherly man grown old. They wept, many of those warriors. And the Newburgh plot dissolved.* [Bart McDowell, *The Revolutionary War: America's Fight for Freedom* (Washington, D.C.: National Geographic Society, 1967), pp. 190–91]

The meek leader, having "humbleness of mind" (Colossians 3:12), is not only more easily taught, but he is also freer. Even in routine he is relieved, for instance, of the pressure to be the single or even the chief source of ideas for the group. Nor need he be the sole source of his group's memory. He lets others, too, report what they see by the light of what Samuel Coleridge called experience and history's "lantern on the stern." The meek individual is more concerned with the light on the bow, which shines ahead.

He need not be afraid to praise, lest someone gain on him. He follows the pattern of rejoicing in the achievements of others as shown so effulgently by the Father and the Son. After all, the meek and lowly Leader did not need advance men or paid demonstrators with bands and banners: "Behold, thy King cometh unto thee, meek, and sitting upon . . . a colt" (Matthew 21:5).

## TRUE EDUCATION

Meekness of mind is not only essential salvationally. It is also vital, of course, if one is to experience true intellectual growth, especially that which heightens his understanding of the great realities of the universe. Such meekness is a friend, not a foe, of true education. Stephen spoke of Moses: "And Moses was learned in all the wisdom of the Egyptians, and was mighty in words and in deeds" (Acts 7:22). Though Moses was a learned man, he was the most meek man "upon the face of the earth" (Numbers 12:3). So it was that he could and did learn things he "never had supposed" (Moses 1:10).

As the well-educated Paul warned, the indiscriminate or arrogant approach to learning fails to distinguish between chaff and kernels. Therefore, some are proudly "Ever learning, and never able to come to the knowledge of the truth" (2 Timothy 3:7). Unsurprisingly, therefore, great stress is deservedly placed upon the need for intellectual meekness—"humbleness of mind."

Meekness is thus so much more than a passive attribute that merely deflects discourtesy. Instead, it involves spiritual and intellectual activism: "For Ezra had prepared his heart to seek the law of the Lord, and to do it, and to teach in Israel statutes and judgments"

(Ezra 7:10; see also 2 Chronicles 19:3, 20:33). Meek Nephi, in fact, decried the passivity of those who "will not search knowledge, nor understand great knowledge, when it is given unto them in plainness" (2 Nephi 32:7). Alas, most are unsearching—quite content with a superficial understanding or a general awareness of spiritual things (see Alma 10:5–6). This condition may reflect either laziness or, in Amulek's case, the busyness usually incident to the cares of the world.

Intellectual meekness is a persistent as well as particular challenge. Without it, we are not intellectually open to things that we "never had supposed" (Moses 1:10). Alas, some have otherwise reached provincial and erroneous conclusions and do not really want to restructure their understanding of things. Some wish neither to be shaken nor expanded by new data.

### THE CHAINS OF PRIDE

Just as meekness is in all our virtues, so is pride in all our sins. Whatever its momentary and alluring guise, pride, as Henry Fairlie articulately notes, is the enemy—"the first of the sins" (Henry Fairlie, *The Seven Deadly Sins Today* [Washington, D.C.: New Republic Books, 1978], p. 39).

The meek individual may not, to be sure, always fully decipher what is happening to him or around him. However, even though he does not "know the meaning of all things," he knows that the Lord loves him (see 1 Nephi 11:17). He may feel overwhelmed, but, unlike the proud, he is not out of control. In fact, in some moments it is important for us to "Be still, and know that [he is] God" (Psalms 46:10). Even articulate discipleship has its side of silent certitude!

The "rest" promised by Jesus to the meek, though not including an absence of adversity or tutoring, does, therefore, give us the special peace that flows from "humbleness of mind." The meek management of power and responsibility relieves us of the heavy and grinding chains of pride; however glitzed and polished, they are still chains.

Meekness also protects us from the fatigue of being easily offended. There are so many just waiting to be offended. They are so alerted to the possibility that they will not be treated fairly, they almost invite the verification of their expectation! The meek, not on such a fatiguing alert, find rest from this form of fatigue.

Bruising as the tumble off the peak of pride is, it may be necessary at times. Few of us escape at least some of these bruises. Even then, one must next be careful not to continue his descent into the swamp of self-pity. Meekness enables us, after such a tumble, to pick ourselves up—but without putting others down blamefully. Meekness mercifully lets us retain the realistic and rightful impressions of how blessed we are, so far as the fundamental things of eternity are concerned. We are not then as easily offended by the disappointments of the day, of which there seems to be a sufficient and steady supply.

When we are thus spiritually settled, we will likewise be less apt to murmur and complain. Indeed, one of the great risks of murmuring is that we can get too good at it, too clever. We can even acquire too large an audience. Furthermore, what for the murmurer may only be transitory grumbles may become a cause for a hearer that may carry him or her clear out of the Church.

The meek are unconcerned with prideful preeminence, including considerations of scale. The lowly are not exercised, for instance, over quantitative considerations. The Lord put that concern to rest centuries ago.

*The Lord did not set his love upon you, nor choose you, because ye were more in number than any people; for ye were the fewest of all people:*

*But because the Lord loved you, and because he would keep the oath which he had sworn unto your fathers, hath the Lord brought you out with a mighty hand, and redeemed you out of the house of bondmen, from the hand of Pharaoh king of Egypt.* [Deuteronomy 7:7–8]

### WITH EARS TO HEAR

When the Lord declared, "My sheep hear my voice . . . and they follow me" (John 10:27), it was not only an indication of how profound recognition and familiarity would be at work; it also bespoke another role of operational meekness—listening long and humbly enough for such recognition to occur.

This readiness with ears to hear has been needed in all dispensations, but never more than after the Restoration. The "restitution of all things" (Acts 3:21) ended centuries of deprivation, but the Restoration goes sharply against the grain of heedless secular societies. So, while the truths of the Restoration are "had again," they are useful only "among as many as shall believe" (Moses 1:40–41). Yet those astray include "humble followers of Christ" who err only "because they are taught by the precepts of men" (2 Nephi 28:14). In addition, the adversary's kingdom "must shake" in order that those who will may be "stirred up unto repentance" (2 Nephi 28:19). The meek understand such realities.

Meekness also contains a readiness that helps us to surmount the accumulated stumbling blocks and rocks of offense; we can make stepping stones of them and achieve a deeper and broader view of life. Obviously, Philip had such readiness and meekness when he recognized Jesus as the Messiah of whom Moses had spoken (John 1:45). Obviously, Paul had the broad view, too, when he described Moses as having foregone, by choice, the favored life in Pharaoh's court for a life of service to Jesus (Hebrews 11:24–27). Nevertheless, the stones of stumbling and rocks of offense are real. In fact, these offending rocks (see Isaiah 8:14–15) can prove insurmountable, unless we have the facilitating attribute of meekness with its promise of access to the grace of God.

Even if it stood alone as a benefit, one reason for developing greater meekness is to have greater access to the grace of God. The Lord guarantees that his grace is sufficient for the meek (Ether 12:26). Besides, only the meek know how to draw fully upon his assistance anyway.

Meekness comes trailing a cloud of other beneficial considerations. The prophet Mormon (see Moroni 7:43–44) observed that without meekness there can be no faith, hope, or love. Furthermore, the remission of our sins brings additional meekness along with the great gift of the Holy Ghost, or Comforter (Moroni 8:26). These supernal blessings are not to be enjoyed for any length of time except by those who are meek. As to genuine joy, it is received by none "save it be the truly penitent and humble seeker of happiness" (Alma 27:18).

Preliminarily, we cannot even have true faith, except we are meek and lowly in heart (Moroni 7:43–45). Thus we are able to enjoy greater faith, hope, love, knowledge, and reassurance. We will thus know the answer to what Amulek called the "great question" (see Alma 34:5)—whether there really is a rescuing and redeeming Christ. It is by the power of the Holy Ghost that we know that Jesus is the Christ, that he lived and lives. Thus it is the meek who receive the great answers to the "great question," rejoicing, therefore, over the "great and last sacrifice" (Alma 34:10).

### PREPARING FOR ETERNITY

Since life in the Church illustrates, painfully at times, our own defects, as well as the defects of others, we are bound to be periodically disappointed thereby in ourselves and in others. We cannot expect it to be otherwise in a kingdom where, initially, not only does the net gather "of every kind," but those of "every kind" are also at every stage of spiritual development (see Matthew 13:47). When people "leave their nets straightway" (see Matthew 4:20 and Mark 1:18), they come as they are—though in the initial process of changing, their luggage reflects their past. Hence, discipleship is a developmental journey that requires shared patience, understanding, and meekness on the part of all who join the caravan. Together we are disengaging from one world and preparing ourselves for another and far better world.

Meekness and patience have a special mutuality. If there were too much swiftness, there could be no long-suffering, no gradual soul-stretching, nor repenting. With too little time to absorb, to assimilate, and to apply the truths already given, our capacities would not be fully developed. Pearls cast before us would go unfound, ungathered, and unsavored. It takes time to prepare for eternity.

*For he will give unto the faithful line upon line, precept upon precept; and I will try you and prove you herewith.* [D&C 98:12]

*I will give unto the children of men line upon line, precept upon precept, here a little and there a little; and blessed are those who hearken unto my precepts, and lend an ear unto my counsel, for they shall learn wisdom; for unto him that receiveth I will give more.* [2 Nephi 28:30]

The meek are also less likely to ask amiss in their prayers (see James 4:3). Being less demanding of life to begin with, they are less likely to ask selfishly or to act selfishly.

In so many ways, the wise interplay of our individual agency with God's loving purposes for us is greatly facilitated by our meekness. Were it not so, we would, at best, offer ourselves pridefully to God, but only as we now are—"Take it or leave it," an unacceptable offering. The only individual who might have credibly done that instead meekly submitted himself to the Father's further, shaping will (see Alma 7:11–12).

Meekness could have rescued proud and fearful Judas even after he had left the Last Supper. He could have slipped back in later, quietly and humbly, rejoining his apostolic colleagues, having belatedly determined not to do the dastardly deed. Meekness can rescue us from ourselves even when we are deep in error, even when others have written us off.

## THE SMALL VIEW VERSUS REALITY

Meekness enlarges souls, but without hypocrisy. Contrariwise, "littleness of soul" (D&C 117:11) insures that only a small view of reality will be taken. This narrow view prevailed when Cain slew Abel and then gloried and boasted, "Behold, now I am free" (see Moses 5:33). Free? Yes, free to be "a fugitive and a vagabond" in the stretching desert he had made of his own life (Moses 5:39). Both Cain's desire for Abel's flocks and his being offended at the acceptance of Abel's sacrifice played a part in his fall. Moreover, proud Cain "rejected the greater counsel which was had from God" (Moses 5:25).

The small, myopic view also lends itself, in the Lord's words, to coveting "the drop," while neglecting "the more weighty matters" (D&C 117:8). In all of our getting and grasping we do not seem to grasp, for instance, the implications of this searching question from the Lord:

> *For have I not the fowls of heaven, and also the fish of the sea, and the beasts of the mountains? Have I not made the earth? Do I not hold the destinies of all the armies of the nations of the earth?* [D&C 117:6]

No wonder the Lord also reminds us acquisitive mortals, "For what is property unto me?" (D&C 117:4).

> *I, the Lord, stretched out the heavens, and built the earth, my very handiwork; and all things therein are mine.* [D&C 104:14]

One day he will share all he has with the meek. For every one else, whatever their temporary possessions, the Creator's reversion clause will take effect.

The meek likewise understand still another reality—that, as much as or more than anything else, it is our faith and patience that are to be tried (see Mosiah 23:21). Our trials, however, occur in the context of this precious promise:

> *Thus God has provided a means that man, through faith, might . . . becometh a great benefit to his fellow beings.* [Mosiah 8:18]

Before he became encrusted with power, Saul knew a time when he was "little in [his] own sight" (1 Samuel 15:17). However, meekness did not stay on as his uninvited guest; it quickly departs where it's not wanted. It is so easy for us to become puffed up and to be condescending to others. One devoted public servant who ably served several British Prime Ministers as their private secretary, observed:

*Vanity is a failing common to Prime Ministers . . . ; and I suppose it is natural in view of the adulation they receive but to which they are not, like Kings, accustomed.* [John Colville, *The Fringes of Power* (New York and London: W. W. Norton and Company, 1985), p. 79]

### "MEEK AND LOWLY" MEN

Fortunately, we have fine examples of meekness to help us, and I need go no farther than my own Quorum.

The Acting President of the Council of the Twelve, President Howard W. Hunter, is a meek man. He once refused a job he needed as a young man because it would have meant another individual would have lost his job. This is the same lowly man, when I awakened after a weary and dusty day together with him on assignment in Egypt, who was quietly shining my shoes, a task he had hoped to complete unseen. Meekness can be present in the daily and ordinary things.

The President of the Twelve, President Marion G. Romney, is also a meek man. The scene was a fast and testimony meeting in his home ward, just after he was first sustained by the Church as a Counselor in the First Presidency. Touchingly, meekly, and tenderly, President Romney said to his beloved neighbors that he could obediently sustain whomever the Lord called, even when the person called was Marion G. Romney. All of us who were there loved him all the more! Meekness can be there even in moments of deserved recognition.

Sir Thomas More was a victim of injustice and irony. Generously and meekly, just as he was about to be martyred, he said:

*Paul . . . was present, and consented to the death of St. Stephen, and kept their clothes that stoned him to death, and yet be they [Stephen and Paul] now both twain Holy Saints in heaven, and shall continue there friends for ever, so I verily trust and . . . pray, that though your lordships have now here in earth been judges to my condemnation, we may yet hereafter in heaven merrily all meet together, to our everlasting salvation.* [Anthony

Kenny, *Thomas More* (Oxford and New York: Oxford University Press, 1983), p. 88]

Meekness can be present in moments of injustice and crisis at the hands of lesser men. Jesus meekly endured the lesser spiritual maturity in the Twelve and in his other disciples. He endured this while helping remedy it. He did this without condescension, without despairing, without cynicism, and without murmuring. We have only to look at his prayers to the Father for and in behalf of his disciples to see how perfect his love is (see John 17). Indeed, when his followers deserved censure, they received teaching. Though he sometimes spoke reproving truth to them, Christ spoke the truth in love (Ephesians 4:15).

What a contrast to us mortals! At times we withhold reproof, time, talent, and knowledge from others in order to retain a seeming advantage, an edge. No wonder there could never be compliance with consecration without meekness. For consecration seeks to share—not to withhold.

### THE SERIOUS DISCIPLE

The full witness often does not come "until after the trial of your faith" (Ether 12:6). Those trials may be very focused. President Lorenzo Snow once said to the Twelve of his day, "Every one of us who has not already had the experience must yet meet it of being tested in every place where we are weak" (Abraham H. Cannon journal, April 9, 1890). Indeed, did not the Lord specifically promise the meek that he would make "weak things become strong unto them" (Ether 12:27)?

In those instances of available record, the Lord has displayed much gentleness and tenderness in his tutoring of meek individuals. The pattern usually involves his disclosing more about himself, about his work, and what taking his yoke upon us will mean. He thus expands the horizons of the person being tutored. The Lord likewise usually assigns the individual a portion of the Lord's work to do. The disciple's course involves more lab and fieldwork than lectures.

For the serious disciple, the greater his knowledge, the greater his meekness. The more he strives to become like Jesus and the more he wishes to declare his gospel, the more he rejoices exceedingly when Christ's message is heeded, as did the outreaching sons of Mosiah, who rejoiced that no human soul would perish if they received the gospel.

Unsurprisingly, the Lord's angelic messengers also reflect meek friendship, as did the angel that spoke with Alma:

*Blessed art thou, Alma; therefore, lift up thy head and rejoice, for thou hast great cause to rejoice; for thou hast been faithful in keeping the commandments of God from the time which thou receivest thy first message from him. Behold, I am he that delivered it unto you.* [Alma 8:15]

The meek are such caring realists!

These patterns of gentleness and tenderness are too striking to be accidental. They are even reflected in the voice of the Lord, even in its very timbre, for his is a pleasant, mild, and gentle voice:

*. . . it was not a voice of thunder, neither was it a voice of a great tumultuous noise, but behold, it was a still voice of perfect mildness, as if it had been a whisper, and it did pierce even to the very soul—*[Helaman 5:30]

*. . . yea, a pleasant voice, as if it were a whisper.* [Helaman 5:46]

*. . . it was not a harsh voice neither was it a loud voice; nevertheless, and notwithstanding it being a small voice it did pierce them that did hear to the center.* [3 Nephi 11:3]

The stunning episode atop the Mount of Transfiguration doubtless involved the same pattern of further disclosing, preparing, reassuring, instructing, and blessing with regard to Peter, James, and John (see Matthew 17:1–9). Though we do not have all of the sacred particulars of what occurred there, Peter, James, and John received special blessings and insights as a result of being atop the Mount of

Transfiguration. It was good for them to have been there (Matthew 17:4), but they would not have been in those supernal circumstances except they were sufficiently meek, though further trials and tutoring still lay ahead.

The pattern of calling, blessing, expanding, reassuring, and endowing are reflective of the generosity as well as the gentleness of God our Father and his son, Jesus Christ!

Astonishingly, to those who have eyes to see and ears to hear, it is clear that the Father and the Son are giving away the secrets of the universe! If only you and I can avoid being offended by their generosity.

If we would be with them, whether on a mountaintop or forever, we should ponder anew these sobering words: "For none is acceptable before God, save the meek and lowly in heart" (Moroni 7:44). Besides, can we ever truly and fully accept ourselves until we become more like them?

That you and I may be meek disciples is my prayer on this special day. I salute you as servants of the Lord Jesus Christ and thank him for being our yoke master, for being meek and lowly, and inviting us to learn of him. It is the only way we can truly learn of him—to take his yoke upon us. I say this in the name of Jesus Christ. Amen.

# The Children of Christ

### Neal A. Maxwell

This address will attempt to "survey the wondrous cross" by focusing on the Christology in the book of Mosiah, using not only the words of King Benjamin, Mosiah, Abinadi, and Alma the Younger, but scriptures that lie in the suburbs of Mosiah and other related scriptures. The final focus will be on the requirements for our becoming what King Benjamin called "the children of Christ," which is my text (Mosiah 1:11; 5:9, 11; 26:18).

Left unexplored are other possibilities, such as some our LDS scholars are reconnoitering. For instance, the biblical term *mosiah* was probably a political designation; it also is an honorific title in Hebrew meaning *savior* or *rescuer* (*FARMS Update*, April 1989). Not bad for a bright but unschooled Joseph Smith who, while translating early on, reportedly wondered aloud to Emma if there were walls around Jerusalem (*The History of the Reorganized Church of Jesus Christ of Latter Day Saints*, vol. 4, 1873–1890 [Independence, Missouri: Herald House, 1967], p. 447).

*This fireside address was given at Brigham Young University on 4 February 1990.*

There is so much more in the Book of Mormon than we have yet discovered. The book's divine architecture and rich furnishings will increasingly unfold to our view, further qualifying it as "a marvelous work and a wonder" (Isaiah 29:14). As I noted from this pulpit in 1986, "The Book of Mormon is like a vast mansion with gardens, towers, courtyards, and wings (*Book of Mormon Symposium*, 10 October 1986). All the rooms in this mansion need to be explored, whether by valued traditional scholars or by those at the cutting edge. Each plays a role, and one LDS scholar cannot say to the other, "I have no need of thee" (1 Corinthians 12:21).

Professor Hugh Nibley has reconnoitered much of that mansion, showing how our new dispensation links with the old world. There is not only that Nibley nexus, but also one between him and several generations of LDS scholars.

## SCRIPTURES OF THE RESTORATION

The book of Mosiah begins with a father instructing his sons, just as was done in ancient Israel. Alma the Younger remembered a critical Christ-centered prophecy of his father, you'll recall (see Deuteronomy 6:7; Alma 36:17–18). The book of Mosiah ends as the successor son approaches death, having sought to "do according to that which his father [King Benjamin] had done in all things." As a result, Mosiah's people "did esteem him more than any other man" (Mosiah 6:7; 29:40). So did the Mulekites, who accepted him as their next king, though he was an immigrant among them.

Within the book's sixty-plus printed pages occur not only family and political drama, but some stunning verses of Christology concerning the role, mission, and deeds of Jesus Christ. The Christology of the Restoration, brothers and sisters, restructures our understanding of so many fundamental realities.

A significant portion of King Benjamin's towering sermon was given to him by an angel, and angels speak by the power of the Holy Ghost (Mosiah 3:2; 2 Nephi 32:3). At its center is the masterful sermon about the exclusive means of salvation:

*There shall be no other name given nor any other way nor means whereby salvation can come unto the children of men, only in and through the name of Christ, the Lord Omnipotent.* [Mosiah 3:17; see also Mosiah 4:7–8]

It is not only the divinity but also the specificity of King Benjamin's sermon that marks it. Hence Father Helaman, in sending his two sons, Lehi and Nephi, on a mission to the land of Nephi, exhorted them to "Remember, remember, my sons, the words which King Benjamin spake unto his people" (Helaman 5:9).

In Restoration scriptures, not only is salvation specific, but so also is the identity of the Savior as various scriptures foretell. A savior was to be provided in the meridian of time (Moses 5:57). His name was to be Jesus Christ (2 Nephi 25:19). Christ volunteered for that mission premortally (Abraham 3:27). He was to be born of Mary, a Nazarene, but in Bethlehem—a fact over which some stumbled in the meridian of time (John 7:40–43; see also Micah 5:2, Luke 2:4, Matthew 2:23, 1 Nephi 11:13, Alma 7:10). There would even be a new star celebrating his birth (Helaman 14:5, 3 Nephi 1:21).

And then we learn from the holy scriptures of the sacrifice of the Father's Firstborn premortally; his Only Begotten Son in the flesh was the sacrifice of a Creator-God. The Atoner was the Lord God Omnipotent, who created this and many other planets (D&C 76:24, Moses 1:33, Mosiah 3:5). Therefore, unlike the sacrifice of a mortal, Christ's was an "infinite atonement" made possible, declared King Benjamin, by the infinite goodness and mercy of God (see Mosiah 4:6; 2 Nephi 9:7; Alma 34:10, 12; Mosiah 5:3).

Ironically, the Mortal Messiah would be disregarded and crucified, said Benjamin and Nephi:

*And lo, he cometh unto his own, that salvation might come unto the children of men even through faith on his name; and even after all this they shall consider him a man, . . . and shall scourge him, and shall crucify him.* [Mosiah 3:9]

*And the world, because of their iniquity, shall judge him to be a thing of naught; wherefore they scourge him, and he suffereth it; and they smite him, and he suffereth it. Yea, they spit upon him, and he suffereth it, because of his loving kindness and his long-suffering towards the children of men.*
[1 Nephi 19:9]

This pattern of denigrating Jesus that existed in the meridian of time has continued in our time as noted in this next quotation:

*The sweetly-attractive human Jesus is a product of 19th-century skepticism, produced by people who were ceasing to believe in Jesus' divinity but wanted to keep as much Christianity as they could.* [C. S. Lewis, *Letters of C. S. Lewis* (London: Geoffrey Bles Ltd., 1966), p. 181]

However mortals regard him, there is no other saving and atoning name under heaven! (See Mosiah 3:17, Moses 6:52.)

*O remember, remember, . . . that there is no other way nor means whereby man can be saved, only through the atoning blood of Jesus Christ, who shall come; yea, remember that he cometh to redeem the world.*
[Helaman 5:9]

All other gods, brothers and sisters, fail and fall, including the gods of this world. Currently we are seeing Caesars come and go— "an hour of pomp, an hour of show."

The Christology of Restoration scriptures constitutes the answer to what Amulek called "the great question," which is: Will there really be a redeeming Christ? (See Alma 34:5.)

If, as Abinadi declared, Christ were not risen as the first fruits with all mortals to follow, then life would end in hopelessness (Mosiah 16:6, 7). But he is risen, and life has profound purpose and rich meaning! One day, said King Benjamin, such knowledge of the Savior would spread:

*The time shall come when the knowledge of a Savior shall spread throughout every nation, kindred, tongue, and people.* [Mosiah 3:20]

This spreading is happening in our day at an accelerated rate, brothers and sisters. At a later day, divine disclosure will be total and remarkable:

*And the day cometh that . . . all things shall be revealed unto the children of men which ever have been among the children of men, and which ever will be even unto the end of the earth.* [2 Nephi 27:11]

There will be so much to disclose that we don't now have. All the prophets have testified of the coming of Jesus Christ (Mosiah 13:33). Jesus, the Lord of all the prophets, even called them all "my holy prophets" (3 Nephi 1:13). How could he, as some aver, merely be one of them? Worse still, some consider Jesus only as another "moral teacher." Pronouncements such as Abinadi's underscore Jesus' transcending triumph:

*And thus God breaketh the bands of death, having gained the victory over death; giving the Son power to make intercession for the children of men—*

*Having ascended into heaven, having the bowels of mercy; being filled with compassion towards the children of men; standing betwixt them and justice; having broken the bands of death, taking upon himself their iniquity and their transgressions, having redeemed them, and satisfied the demands of justice.* [Mosiah 15:8, 9]

It is very significant, brothers and sisters, that leaders and founders of other world religions made no such declarative claims of divinity for themselves, though millions venerate these leaders.

No wonder the Book of Mormon was urgently needed for "the convincing of the Jew and Gentile that Jesus is the Christ" (title page). Such testifying is the purpose of all scripture. The Apostle John stated:

*But these are written, that ye might believe that Jesus is the Christ, the Son of God; and that believing ye might have life through his name.* [John 20:31]

Of the Christ-centered plan of salvation, Nephi declared, "How great the importance to make these things known unto the inhabitants of the earth" (2 Nephi 2:8).

Jesus is even described as the Father, because he is the Father-Creator of this and other worlds. Furthermore, he is the Father of all who are born again spiritually (see D&C 76:24). When we take upon ourselves his name and covenant to keep his commandments, we then become his sons and daughters, "the children of Christ" (see Mosiah 5:3–7; 15:1–5; 27:24–29).

In addition, since he and the Father are one in attributes and in purpose, Jesus acts for the Father through divine investiture, sometimes speaking as the Father (see D&C 93:3–5).

The world desperately needs such divine declarations and instructions concerning *why* we are here and *how* we should live—concerning what is right and what is wrong, what is true and what is false. Much needed, too, is the Restoration's verification of the reality of the Resurrection. Much needed, too, is the Restoration's clarification as to the nature of God and man. Likewise, much needed is the Restoration's enunciation of the divinely determined purposes of this mortal existence.

### FEASTING ON ESSENTIAL TRUTHS

The millions who have lived on this planet in the midst of the famine foreseen by Amos, one of hearing the word of God, have never known the taste and nourishment of whole-grain gospel (see Amos 8:11–12). Instead, they have subsisted on the fast foods of philosophy. When Jesus spoke of himself as the bread of life, it caused some to walk no more with him (see John 6:66). No wonder Jesus said, "Blessed is he, whosoever shall not be offended in me" (Matthew

11:6; see John 6:61). To which I add, "Blessed is he who is not offended by the Restoration!"

The pages of Restoration scriptures ripple and resound with so many essential truths! For example, through correct Christology we learn about Christ's premortal pinnacle as the Creator-God and how, even so, only later did he receive a fulness (see D&C 93:12–13, 16). The Lord has told us how important it is to understand not only "what" we worship, but also "how" to worship (see D&C 93:19, John 4:22).

After all, real adoration of the Father and Jesus results in the emulation of them! How shall we become more like them if we do not know about their character and nature?

Said King Benjamin, "How knoweth a man the master whom he has not served, and who is a stranger unto him, and is far from the thoughts and intents of his heart?" (Mosiah 5:13).

Furthermore, unless we understand how the schoolmaster law of Moses was a preparing and a foretelling type, we will not understand dispensationalism, including the place of meridian Christianity in the stream of religious history.

*It is expedient that ye should keep the law of Moses as yet; but I say unto you, that the time shall come when it shall no more be expedient. . . .*

*[For] God himself should come down among the children of men, and take upon him the form of man, and go forth in mighty power upon the face of the earth.* [Mosiah 13:27, 34; see also Mosiah 3:15; 13:29–35; 16:14; Galatians 3:24]

For modernity, brothers and sisters, the relevancy of the message in Mosiah is especially real. For instance, we are clearly indebted to our English ancestors for our precious King James Version. Yet, that nation subsequently suffered from a wave of irreligion. Your academic vice president, Stan L. Albrecht, wrote of that wave of irreligion:

*The pattern of downturn in religious activity in British society . . . made "agnosticism respectable if not universal by the turn of the century.". . . By the early 1900s Arnold Bennett could say, ". . . The intelligentsia has sat back, shrugged its shoulders, given a sigh of relief, and decreed tacitly or by plain statement: 'The affair is over and done with.'"*

*. . . By the 1970s only about 5 percent of the adult population in the Church of England even attended Easter religious services, and the percentage continues to decline.* [Stan L. Albrecht, "The Consequential Dimension of Mormon Religiosity," *BYU Studies*, vol. 29, no. 2, Spring 1989, p. 98]

This next mid-twentieth century expression is from a candid dean of Saint Paul's Cathedral in London:

*All my life I have struggled to find the purpose of living. I have tried to answer three questions which always seemed to be fundamental: the problem of eternity; the problem of human personality; and the problem of evil.*

*I have failed. I have solved none of them and I know no more than when I started. And I believe no one will ever solve them.*

*I know as much about the after-life as you—NOTHING. I don't even know that there is one—in the same sense in which the Church teaches it. I have no vision of Heaven or of a welcoming God. I do not know what I shall find. I must wait and see.* [Dean William Ralph Inge, former dean of Saint Paul's Cathedral, London, England, *Daily Express*, London, England, 13 July 1953, p. 4]

I marvel with you at how the Restoration scriptures are repetitively able to inform us and inspire us; they enthrall us again and again. Ordinary books contain comparative crumbs, whereas the bread of life provides a feast!

Through those scriptures we learn that salvation is specific, not vague; it includes individual resurrection and triumph over death. We each will stand before God as individuals, kneeling and confessing (see Alma 12:13–15, 34–35). The faithful will even sit down, as individuals, with the spiritual notables of ages past, for God has said he will *land their souls, yea, their immortal souls, at the right hand of God in the kingdom of heaven, to sit down with Abraham, and Isaac, and with Jacob, and with all our holy fathers, to go no more out.* [Helaman 3:30; see also Alma 7:25, Matthew 8:11, D&C 124:19]

Thus we will not be merged into some unremembering molecular mass. Nor will we be mere droplets in an ocean of consciousness.

In one way or another, sooner or later, all mortals will plead, as Alma did at his turning point, "O Jesus, thou Son of God, have mercy on me" (Alma 36:18). Thus we are blessed with enlarged perspectives because "through the infinite goodness of God, and the manifestations of his Spirit, [we] have great views of that which is to come" (Mosiah 5:3).

Many in the world today are like some among the Book of Mormon peoples who believed "when a man was dead, that was the end thereof" (Alma 30:18). For others, there are certain existential "givens" as now quoted: "There is no built-in scheme of meaning in the world" (Irvin D. Yalom, Stanford University psychiatrist, "Exploring Psychic Interiors," *U.S. News & World Report,* 30 October 1989, p. 67). "No deity will save us; we must save ourselves" ("Humanist Manifesto II," "Liberal Family," *The Encyclopedia of American Religions: Religious Creeds,* edited by J. Gordon Melton [Detroit: Gale Research Company, p. 641).

No wonder the Restoration is so relevant and so urgent, having come, as the Lord said, so "that faith also might increase in the earth" (D&C 1:21).

Compared to the great, divine declarations being noted this evening, which are central to real faith, what else really matters? Illustratively, two Book of Mormon prophets in referring to a lesser concern, death, used the phrases "it mattereth not" or "it matters not" (Ether 15:34, Mosiah 13:9). Happily, the reality of the Atonement does not depend upon either our awareness of it or our acceptance of it! Immortality is a free gift to all, including to the presently unappreciative (see 2 Nephi 2:4).

Meanwhile, however, even the spiritually sensitive feel less than full joy because, said C. S. Lewis:

*We have a lifelong nostalgia, a longing to be reunited with something in the universe from which we now feel cut off, to be on the inside of some door which we have always seen from the outside, this is . . . the truest index of our real situation.* [C. S. Lewis, *A Mind Awake* (New York: Harcourt, Brace & World, Inc., 1968), p. 23]

In that sense, brothers and sisters, we are all prodigals! We, too, must come to ourselves, having determined, "I will arise and go to my father" (Luke 15:18). This reunion and reconciliation is actually possible. Because of the Atonement, we are not irrevocably cut off.

## GREAT TEACHERS AND LEADERS

The book of Mosiah has so many jewels, including what seem to me, as a political scientist, to be some marvelous principles of politics and leadership. As more and more people on this planet are currently reaching out for a greater voice in their affairs, how relevant and instructive are the words of King Mosiah:

*Now it is not common that the voice of the people desireth anything contrary to that which is right; but it is common for the lesser part of the people to desire that which is not right; therefore this shall ye observe and make it your law—to do your business by the voice of the people.* [Mosiah 29:26]

However, a democracy devoid of spiritual purpose may remain only a process, one within which citizens are merely part of a "lonely crowd," feeling separated from the past including their ancestors.

In contrast, King Mosiah's people had spiritual purpose; they deeply admired his profound political leadership.

*And they did wax strong in love towards Mosiah; yea, they did esteem him more than any other man . . . exceedingly, beyond measure.* [Mosiah 29:40]

Laboring with his own hands, he was a man of peace and freedom. He wanted the children of Christ to esteem neighbors as themselves (see Mosiah 27:4). King Mosiah was deeply anxious that all the people have an "equal chance" (see Mosiah 27:3; 29:38). Yet there would be no free rides, because "every man [would] bear his [own] part" (Mosiah 29:34).

King Benjamin wanted his people to be filled with the love of God, to grow in the knowledge of that which is just and true, to have no mind to injure another, to live peaceably, to teach their children to love and serve one another, and to succor the needy, including beggars (see Mosiah 4:12–30).

Mosiah was certainly not without his personal trials, for Mosiah went through that special suffering known only to the parents of disobedient children. The wickedness of his sons, along with Alma the Younger, created much trouble. Only after "wading through much tribulation" did they finally do much good and repair much of the damage they had done (see Mosiah 27:28). Even later, however, after his sons had repented, before they were to have an enlarged missionary role, Mosiah first consulted with the Lord (see Mosiah 28:6).

Mosiah also faced the challenges of leading a multigroup society: Nephites, Zoramites, Mulekites, Nehorites, Limhites (in Gideon), as well as those covenanters in Alma's group. How varied these interest groups were, and yet how united in love of their leader!

Ponder this indicator of how Mosiah was an open, disclosing, and teaching leader:

*And many more things did king Mosiah write unto them, unfolding unto them all the trials and troubles of a righteous king, yea, all the travails of soul for their people, and also all the murmurings of the people to their king; and he explained it all unto them.* [Mosiah 29:33; emphasis added]

The political leader as a teacher of his people: King Benjamin and King Mosiah are examples of the leader-servant; they followed the pattern of their master, Jesus. Prophets and leaders like Benjamin and Mosiah were charged to "regulate all the affairs of the Church." They did so both with style and with substance. There was love, but also admonishing discipline—with the repentant numbered among the Church and the unrepentant having their names blotted out. Missionary work went well; many were received into the Church by baptism (see Mosiah 26:35–37).

So it was that their people became the children of Christ. The children of Christ in any dispensation willingly make the sacrifice of a broken heart and a contrite spirit (see 3 Nephi 9:20, D&C 59:8, Psalms 51:17). The children of Christ are meek and malleable—their hearts can be broken, changed, or made anew. The child of Christ can eventually mature to become the woman or man of Christ to whom the Lord promises that he will lead "in a strait and narrow course across that everlasting gulf of misery" (Helaman 3:26).

The children of Christ are described by King Benjamin as being submissive, meek, humble, patient, full of love, and—then the sobering line—"willing to submit to all things which the Lord seeth fit to inflict upon [them], even as a child doth submit to his father" (Mosiah 3:19). Significantly, twice in the ensuing book of Alma the very same recitation of these important qualities is made with several added: to be gentle, temperate, easily entreated, and longsuffering (see Alma 7:23; 13:28).

These virtues are cardinal, portable, and eternal. They reflect in us the seriousness of our discipleship. After all, true disciples will continue to grow spiritually because they have "faith unto repentance" (see Alma 34:16, 17; 13:10). These qualities will finally rise with us in the Resurrection. Interesting, isn't it, in contemplating each of the qualities in this cluster, how they remind us of the need to tame our egos? Blessed is the person who is progressing in the taming of his or her egoistic self. King Benjamin, for example, had not the least desire to boast of himself (see Mosiah 2:16). He was unconcerned with projecting his political image because he had Christ's image in his countenance.

We are instructed not only in what we are to become, but also in what we are to avoid. Abinadi noted how Jesus suffered temptation but yielded not (see Mosiah 15:5). Unlike many of us, Christ gave no heed to temptations (see D&C 20:22). This is yet another instructive example to us, his children, for even if we evict temptations we often entertain them first.

The development of these cardinal virtues is central to God's plan for us. Lack of perspective about God's plans is part of the failure of Laman and Lemuel:

> *And thus Laman and Lemuel,* . . . *did murmur because they knew not the dealings of that God who had created them.* [1 Nephi 2:12; see also Mosiah 10:14]

Illustratively, we are advised that on occasion God will chasten his people and will try our patience and faith (see Mosiah 23:21). Is not the question "Why, O Lord?" one that goes to the heart of the further development of faith amid tutoring? Similarly, the question "How long, O Lord?" is one that goes to the very heart of developing patience. Thus we see how interactive all of these things are in the developmental dimensions of God's plan of salvation that culminates in eternal life.

## ACCEPTING GOD'S GREATEST GIFT

Immortality comes to all by God's grace—it is unearned "after all we can do" (2 Nephi 25:23). Full salvation, eternal life, is God's greatest gift (D&C 6:13; 14:7). However, unlike the blessing of immortality, eternal life is conditional. Eternal life, said King Benjamin, is more than endless existence; it is endless happiness! (See Mosiah 2:41.) It was this that was promised to Alma the Younger: "Thou art my servant; and I covenant with thee that thou shalt have eternal life" (Mosiah 26:20).

Eternal life will feature the joys of always rejoicing and being filled with love (Mosiah 4:12), of growing in the knowledge of God's

glory, of being in his presence, of being in eternal families and friendships forever (see D&C 76:62; 130:2; 132:24, 55).

Eternal life also brings the full bestowal of all the specific promises made in connection with the temple's initiatory ordinances, the
holy endowment, and temple sealings—thereby God "may seal you
his" (Mosiah 4:15). In addition, all other blessings promised upon
the keeping of God's commandments will likewise flow in the abundant Malachi measure, so many "there shall not be room enough to
receive [them]"! (See Malachi 3:10.) John declared that the faithful
shall "inherit all things" (Revelation 21:7). Modern scriptures confirm
that the faithful will eventually receive "all that [the] Father hath"
(D&C 84:38). Meanwhile, how much of that promised birthright will
some of us sell and for what mess of pottage?

Comparing the magnitude of this and all the great gifts given
to us of God and our meager service to him, no wonder, said King
Benjamin, we are beggars and unprofitable servants (see Mosiah 2:21;
4:19).

As we accept Christ and become his children, there begins to be
a change—even a "mighty change" in us. As we earnestly strive to
become one with him and his purposes, we come to resemble him.
Christ who has saved us thus becomes the Father of our Salvation,
and we become the "children of Christ," having his image increasingly in our countenances and conduct (see Mosiah 5:7).

The children of Christ understand the importance of feasting
regularly on sacred records that testify of Jesus (see 2 Nephi 31:20;
32:3; Jacob 2:9; JS–M 1:37). Without such records, belief in him and
in the glorious resurrection can quickly wane:

*And at the time that Mosiah discovered them, . . . they had brought no
records with them; and they denied the being of their Creator.* [Omni 1:17]

*There were many of the rising generation that could not understand the
words of king Benjamin, being little children at the time he spake unto his
people; and they did not believe the tradition of their fathers.*

*They did not believe what had been said concerning the resurrection of the dead, neither did they believe concerning the coming of Christ.* [Mosiah 26:1–2]

For those either untaught or unheeding of the essential gospel truths, the lapse of faith in Christ is but one generation away!

So many scriptures point to the reality that Jesus really is to be the specific example for the children of Christ. We really are to emulate him in our lives. Consider these examples:

*Be ye therefore perfect, even as your Father which is in heaven is perfect.* [Matthew 5:48]

*Therefore I would that ye should be perfect even as I, or your Father who is in heaven is perfect.* [3 Nephi 12:48]

*Therefore, what manner of men ought ye to be? Verily I say unto you, even as I am.* [3 Nephi 27:27]

*Ye shall be holy; for I am holy.* [Leviticus 11:44]

*Be ye therefore merciful, as your Father also is merciful.* [Luke 6:36]

*For I have given you an example, that ye should do as I have done to you.* [John 13:15]

*Jesus Christ* [shows] *forth all long-suffering, for a pattern to them which should hereafter believe on him to life everlasting.* [1 Timothy 1:16]

*Christ also suffered for us, leaving us an example, that ye should follow his steps.* [1 Peter 2:21]

*And again, it showeth unto the children of men the straitness of the path, and the narrowness of the gate, by which they should enter, he having set the example before them.* [2 Nephi 31:9]

*Ye know the things that ye must do in my church; for the works which ye have seen me do that shall ye also do; for that which ye have seen me do even that shall ye do.* [3 Nephi 27:21]

*Behold I am the light; I have set an example for you.* [3 Nephi 18:16]

No wonder, in view of these and many other scriptures, that Joseph Smith taught, "If you wish to go where God is, you must be like God, . . . drawing towards God in principle" (*Teachings,* p. 216).

The loving kindness of the Lord that Nephi spoke about is likewise noted in Exodus.

*And the Lord passed by before him, and proclaimed, The Lord, The Lord God, merciful and gracious, longsuffering, and abundant in goodness and truth.* [Exodus 34:6]

In this soaring scriptural declaration, mercy and justice both make their rightful claims, but even so, mercy "overpowereth justice" (Alma 34:15).

Since his qualities are to be emulated by his children, as the Prophet Joseph Smith taught us, it is vital for us to comprehend the character and personality of God if we are to comprehend ourselves (*Teachings,* p. 343). However, as we truly emulate Jesus' example, we will thereby encounter the costs of discipleship through our own micro-experiences. We will come to know what it is to suffer and to be reproached for taking upon ourselves the name of Christ (see Luke 6:22, 1 Peter 4:14). Therefore, our fiery trials, said Peter, should not be thought of as "some strange thing" (1 Peter 4:12).

### THERE IS NO END TO HIS WORKS

As the believing and trusting children of Christ become more Christlike, it will be evident in their daily lives, whether in the treatment of the poor or in the management of their civic affairs (see Mosiah 4:16). Ammon taught, for instance, of how those who become the children of Christ will truly be "a great benefit to [their] fellow beings" (Mosiah 8:18). Alma, Mosiah's successor, learned from the Lord how the illuminated individual can actually evoke faith in other people by "words alone" (Mosiah 26:15, 16; see also 3 Nephi 11:2, D&C 46:13–14).

With his highly developed sense of proportion, King Benjamin said, "Even so I would that ye should . . . always retain in remembrance, the greatness of God, and your own nothingness, and his goodness and long-suffering towards you" (Mosiah 4:11; see also Moses 1:9–10). We who have the Restoration scriptures have further reasons to feel overwhelmed by the greatness of God. We are told that there is no space in which there is no kingdom (D&C 88:37). God's works are without end, and he has created worlds "innumerable . . . unto man" (Moses 1:4, 33, 35). The very heavens and planets do witness that there is a Supreme Creator (Alma 30:44).

Mortal astrophysics confirm the awesome nature of the universe. Astronomers recently indicated they have discovered a collection of galaxies "so extensive that it defies explanation by any present theory." Dubbed "the great wall," these "galaxies form a sheet . . . 3,000 billion billion miles." One scientist said, "We keep being surprised that we keep seeing something bigger as we go out farther" (*The Sacramento Union*, Sunday, 19 November 1989, p. 22).

*And as one earth shall pass away, and the heavens thereof even so shall another come; and there is no end to my works.* [Moses 1:38]

At the Judgment Day, declared Mosiah's successor, everyone at that assemblage will "confess that [God] is God." When one considers history's disbelieving notables who will be there, these lines are subduing:

*Then shall they confess, who live without God in the world, that the judgment of an everlasting punishment is just upon them; and they shall quake, and tremble, and shrink beneath the glance of his all-searching eye.* [Mosiah 27:31; see also Mosiah 16:1, Alma 12:15]

This is while the faithful "shall stand before him" and "see his face with pleasure" (Enos 1:27). His piercing eyes will likewise emanate perfect, overwhelming love, a love, which, alas, few will have reciprocated. The sense of undeservingness will be deep and profound! And thus we have a sense of the rendezvous that lies ahead. There is no end to his works.

Furthermore, Benjamin, Abinadi, Mosiah, and Moroni will be present at the Day of Judgment (see Moroni 10:27), and out of their words we will be judged. At the judgment, we will not only have the prophesied "bright recollection" and "perfect remembrance" of misdeeds, but of happy things as well (see Alma 11:43; 5:18). The joyous things will be preserved, too (see D&C 93:33).

Most of you are too young to appreciate how those of us who are older feel as the sense of memory slips away. I can safely hide my own Easter eggs now.

Among "all things . . . restored" will be our memories (see Alma 11:43; 40:23), including eventually our premortal memories. What a flood of feeling and fact will come to us then, as a loving God deems wise, increasing our gratefulness for God's long-suffering love and Jesus' atonement. What joy upon being connected again with the memories of both the first and second estates!

Meanwhile, during this life, we will continue to experience the unwelcome sense "of having ended a chapter. One more portion of one's self slipping away into the past" (*Letters of C. S. Lewis*, p. 306).

Mary Warnock wrote about how "Anything that is *over* . . . is a lost *possession*. . . . The past is a paradise from which we are necessarily excluded" (Dan Jacobson, "Of Time and Poetry," *Commentary*, November 1989, vol. 88, no. 5, p. 52). And speaking about one writer reflecting on his memories, Warnock said he realized past experiences once shared "are now his alone. . . . The past continually comes to him; but he knows that he can never go back to it" (ibid.). But one day it will all come back!

The children of Christ know now whose they are, whence they came, why they are here, and what manner of men and women they are to become (see 2 Peter 3:11, 3 Nephi 27:27). Still, the children of Christ, like Alma, will "long to be there" in the royal courts on high (Alma 36:22). It is the only destination that really matters. Resplendent reunion awaits us! What is more natural and more wonderful than children going home? Especially to a home where the past, the present, and the future form an everlasting and eternal now! (See D&C 130:7; 38:2; *Teachings*, p. 220.)

Let us do as King Benjamin urged us to:

*Believe in God; believe that he is, and that he created all things, both in heaven and in earth; believe that he has all wisdom, and all power, both in heaven and in earth; believe that man doth not comprehend all the things which the Lord can comprehend.* [Mosiah 4:9]

Meanwhile, how can there be refining fires without heat? Or greater patience without some instructive waiting? How can we develop empathy without first bearing one another's burdens? Not only that burdens may be lightened, but that we may thereby be enlightened by developing greater empathy. How can we increase individual faith without some customized uncertainty? How can we learn to live in cheerful security without some insecurity?

How can there be later magnification without some present deprivation? Except we are thus tutored, how else shall we grow spiritually to become the men and women of Christ? In this brief mortality, therefore, reveries are often rudely elbowed aside by tutoring adversities! Meanwhile, as faithful children, the challenge is: Will we prove ourselves, in King Benjamin's phrase, "willing to submit?" (See Mosiah 3:19.)

Finally, I should like to leave my own witness. In my life, whichever way I turn, brothers and sisters, there looms Jesus, name of wondrous love. He is our fully atoning and fully comprehending Savior, and in the words of scripture, "There is none like unto him."

Whether taught in the holy scriptures or in the holy temples, his gospel is remarkable. Whether it concerns the nature of God, the nature of man, the nature of the universe, the nature of this mortal experience, it is remarkable. His gospel is stunning as to its interior consistency. It is breathtaking as to its exterior expansiveness. Rather than existing without the gospel in a mortal maze, instead I stand all amazed at the wonders of that gospel that we should be privileged to be his children.

Whatever my experiences, the spiritual facts that have emerged from these experiences encompass me. They encompass me and echo the testifying words of King Benjamin as follows, "The goodness of God, and his matchless power, and his wisdom, and his patience, and his long-suffering towards the children of men" (Mosiah 4:6). Everyone of those virtues of God I have counted on, I count on now, I will count on again—whether it is his long-suffering, his matchless power, or his goodness. And so do you! Those are the very virtues that must come in a measure to be ours, my brothers and sisters.

This constitutes the journey of discipleship. We must, like the prodigal son, arise and go to our father and be prepared for that resplendent reunion. We can hasten the journey only insofar as we hasten the process of becoming like him, as the children of Christ going home of which I testify. For his help in my personal journey I plead and for his help for you.

You are the leaven for mankind. And all the winds of political freedom that blow intrinsically carry within them the added prospects that the children of Christ will reach out more expeditiously to their brothers and sisters on this planet with this wondrous message. As we "survey the wondrous cross," as his children, may it be so, I humbly pray, in the name of Jesus Christ. Amen.

# "In Him All Things Hold Together"

### Neal A. Maxwell

I wish to talk about your unfinished journey. It is the journey of journeys and will be described quite differently this Easter night. It is an arduous journey. The trek awaits—whether one is rich or poor, short or tall, thin or fat, black or white or brown, old or young, shy or bold, married or single, a prodigal or an ever faithful. Compared to this journey, all other treks are but a brief walk in a mortal park or are merely time on a telestial treadmill.

## BECOMING MEN AND WOMEN OF CHRIST

Your journey is embodied in an invitation from the resurrected Lord, who himself inquired, "What manner of men [and women] ought ye to be?" Then he directed, "Verily I say unto you, *even as I am*" (3 Nephi 27:27; emphasis added). Making this journey qualifies us eventually as the men and women of Christ.

Confirming this developmental goal, the Prophet Joseph Smith declared, "If you wish to go where God is, you must be like God, or possess the principles which God possesses" (*Teachings*, p. 216).

*This fireside address was given at Brigham Young University on 31 March 1991.*

Peter, likewise, spoke of the manner of persons we ought to be in all godliness (see 2 Peter 3:11).

The scriptures provide the road map for this journey because it is the word of God that will lead the men and women of Christ in a straight and narrow course and land their immortal souls at the right hand of God (see Helaman 3:29–30).

Jesus, our guide and model, had a perfect guide and model himself:

> *Then answered Jesus and said unto them, Verily, verily, I say unto you, The Son can do nothing of himself, but what he seeth the Father do: for what things soever he doeth, these also doeth the Son likewise.* [John 5:19]

Just what Jesus saw "the Father do," including premortally, we do not know, but Jesus was the perfect pupil and he had a Perfect Teacher!

Each of us is at a particular point in the journey, having "come thus far." However, if we are deflected from this journey, we will, instead, become estranged from Christ:

> *For how knoweth a man the master whom he has not served, and who is a stranger unto him, and is far from the thoughts and intents of his heart?* [Mosiah 5:13]

If we are not *serving* Jesus, and if he is not in our *thoughts* and *hearts*, then the things of the world will draw us instead to them! Moreover, the things of the world need not be sinister in order to be diverting and consuming.

For the serious disciple, the cardinal attributes exemplified by Jesus are not optional. These developmental milestones take the form of traits, traits that mark the trail to be traveled. After all, should not Latter-day Saints have a special interest in what is required to become a Saint, virtue by virtue and quality by quality? Hear the words of King Benjamin:

*And becometh a saint* . . . submissive, meek, humble, patient, full of love, willing to submit *to all things which the Lord seeth fit to inflict upon him.* [Mosiah 3:19; emphasis added]

These attributes are *eternal* and *portable!* Being portable, to the degree developed, they will go with us through the veil of death, and still later they will rise with us in the Resurrection when all else stays behind. Meanwhile, so much of our time is ironically devoted to learning and marketing perishable skills that will soon become obsolete. It isn't just the morticians who will have a vocational crisis in the next world, brother and sisters. Please note several additions to these key qualities:

*And now I would that ye should be humble, and be submissive and gentle;* easy to be entreated; *full of patience and* long-suffering; *being* temperate *in all things.* [Alma 7:23; emphasis added]

Unsurprisingly, the disciple's way of using power and authority will reflect these same qualities, for he is to lead by *persuasion, long-suffering, gentleness, meekness, love unfeigned, and kindness* (see D&C 121:41–42). Such should be our leadership style. It is certainly Jesus'!

Numerous other scriptures describe the same, small cluster of spiritual qualities that the men and women of Christ are to strive to achieve in their lives. When significantly developed, these qualities will convey the added "authority of example"! When you and I have seen that authority, we are filled with admiration for it.

Since Christ also declared, "If ye love me, keep my commandments" (John 14:15), clear and specific obligations clearly rest upon us, especially when we ponder this next commandment, which, if we love him, we will strive to keep: "Be ye therefore perfect, even as your Father which is in heaven is perfect" (Matthew 5:48).

The Greek rendering for "perfect" is, by the way, "complete, finished, fully developed." After his atonement and resurrection, Jesus included himself as our pattern. "Therefore I would that ye should be perfect even as I, or your Father who is in heaven is perfect" (3 Nephi

12:48). One of the problems we have in the Church is that we consider perfection in abstraction, and it becomes too intimidating. But when we think of it in terms of the specific, cardinal attributes, and we strive to develop these in a steady process of self-improvement, it is quite a different matter.

Ponder this ancient self-description with its focus on attributes:

*And the Lord passed by before him, and proclaimed, The Lord, The Lord God, merciful and* gracious, *long suffering, and abundant in* goodness *and* truth. [Exodus 34:6; emphasis added]

When Jesus visited his hometown, the people wondered at his gracious words (see Luke 4:22). What is enjoined upon us is thus very specific. The specific qualities are made clear again and again in the scriptures. So is our need to follow the developmental path:

*For I have given you an example, that ye should do as I have done to you.* [John 13:15]

*And again, it showeth unto the children of men the straitness of the path, and the narrowness of the gate, by which they should enter, he having set the example before them.* [2 Nephi 31:9]

These qualities are not only developmental destinations, but, meanwhile, if developed significantly, they also provide us with the balance urgently needed for traveling on the demanding narrow path! It is so easy to fall off one side or the other!

The divine direction is clear: "Behold I am the light; I have set an example for you" (3 Nephi 18:16).

Too often when we seek to excuse ourselves, it is, ironically, "the natural man" we are excusing. Yet scriptures inform us "the natural man" is to be "put off" (see Mosiah 3:19). "He" certainly should not be "kept on" because of a mistaken sense that the natural man constitutes our individuality.

In this process, substance and style interplay constantly—more than we realize! How, for instance, can we be like the Father and Son if we are poor listeners? How can we become "even as [Jesus] is" if we are impatient or proud?

The gospel gives proportion as to both substance and style. For example, it is far more important to be morally clean rather than to be a clean-desk individual. Similarly, it is better to "speak the truth in love," as Paul counsels, than it is to simply speak the truth (see Ephesians 4:15).

These scriptural virtues are intertwined, interactive, and interdependent. We are to be:

1. Meek and humble—not self-concerned, dismissive, proud, seeking ascendancy. Blessed are the meek because they are not easily offended. Besides, those who "shine as lights in the world" have no need to seek the spotlight! (See Philippians 2:15.) The world's spotlights are not only fleeting, but they employ inferior light!

2. Patient—not hectic, hurried, pushy.

3. Full of love—not demanding, dominating, manipulative, condescending, or harsh.

4. Gentle—not coarse, brusque, and vindictive.

5. Easily entreated—not unapproachable, inaccessible, and nonlistening.

6. Long-suffering—not impatient, disinterested, curt, easily offended. There are so many people in the Church, brothers and sisters, waiting to be offended. And it doesn't take long. If one has a chip on his or her shoulder, you can't make it through the foyer, so to speak, without getting it knocked off.

7. Submissive to God—not resistant to the Spirit, counsel, and life's lessons.

8. Temperate (self-restrained)—not egoistic, eager for attention and recognition, or too talkative. In your life and mine, the great moments of commendation and correction have come usually in one-liners.

9. Merciful—not judgmental and unforgiving. Blessed are the merciful, for they shall know the caress of causality as their

forgiving mercy restores others to wholeness! Though God is perfected in the attributes of justice and mercy, we read that, finally, "Mercy overpowereth justice" (Alma 34:15).

10. Gracious—not tactless, easily irritated, ungenerous.

11. Holy—not worldly.

As we think about the process of becoming the men and women of Christ, questions may naturally arise, such as: "Will all the men and women of Christ be alike in every respect?" "Will there be a loss of individuality?" I think not. For instance, the quality of meekness is clearly essential, but there are many individual ways of expressing meekness. Furthermore, what we now defensively regard as constituting individuality is likely to be significantly refined.

An immense developmental clue is to be found in these next words: "Take my yoke upon you, and learn of me" (Matthew 11:29). By being yoked, we can best learn of Jesus' perfected qualities, though only in our comparatively small ways. If we are meek, through our smaller but similar experiences we will come to appreciate Jesus' perfected qualities even more. Then our *adoration* of him produces a desire for *emulation* of him.

The Prophet Joseph, whose own life was lived in a crescendo of self-improvement amid adversity, observed:

> The nearer man approaches perfection, the clearer are his views, and the greater his enjoyments, till he has overcome the evils of his life and lost every desire for sin; and like the ancients, [he] arrives at that point of faith where he is wrapped in the power and glory of his Maker and is caught up to dwell with Him. But we consider that this is a station to which no man ever arrived in a moment. [*Teachings*, p. 51]

The clearer one's views, the more one sees "things as they really are," the greater the happiness!

Thus, beyond the free gift of immortality, "working out our salvation" includes "working out" the development of these eternal virtues in our lives!

Given the tremendous importance of these virtues now and in the world to come, should we be surprised if, to hasten the process, the Lord gives us, individually, the relevant and necessary clinical experiences? We do not usually seek these, however. Yet they seem to come, don't they, even when we do not remember having signed up for a particular course? Sometimes we find ourselves enrolled again in the same course. Apparently we were only auditing before; perhaps this time it can be for credit!

Emerson pleaded, "Give me truths: for I am weary of the surfaces" ("Blight," in *The Complete Writings of Ralph Waldo Emerson* [New York: Wm. H. Wise & Co., 1929], p. 874). While amid so much that is inane, and while surrounded by so many little and superficial things, it is only in the bright light of the restored gospel that we can see the truth as to who we really are and what our possibilities are! As Jacob wrote, we not only see things as they really are, but as they really will be (see Jacob 4:13).

The Lord loves each of us too much to merely let us go on being what we now are, for he knows what we have the possibility to become!

It is all part of the journey of going home. Developmentally, we are all prodigals. When we really "come to" ourselves, spiritually, we, too, will say with determination, "I will arise and go to my father" (Luke 15:18).

This true celebration of the risen Lord of Easter, therefore, is one of emulation as well as of adoration for him. Since he is risen from the grave, let us not be dead as to the things of the Spirit! How can we celebrate the empty tomb with empty lives? How can we celebrate his victory over death by being defeated by the world?

## THE INFINITE ATONEMENT

May I now speak further of Jesus, of the Resurrection, and of the Atonement?

Christ's death and resurrection were specifically foretold in a multitude of scriptures, including this from Isaiah.

*Thy dead men shall live, together with my dead body shall they
arise. . . . and the earth shall cast out the dead.* [Isaiah 26:19]

Ponder how that prophesy was later dramatically fulfilled as
recorded by Matthew:

*And the graves were opened; and many bodies of the saints which slept
arose,*
*And came out of the graves after his resurrection, and went into the holy
city, and appeared unto many.* [Matthew 27:52–53]

As signified by Jesus' personal resurrection and the recognition of
him by friends, immortality is not merely being one droplet in some
floating sea of cosmic consciousness! Resurrection is not being a mere
molecule in an unremembering cloud of drifting molecules! His resurrection was personal and recognizable. So will ours be! Did not the
resurrected ancients go into Jerusalem and appear unto many?

Oh, how we adore Jesus for his atonement! For his free gift of
immortality to all! Consider for a moment, how would we regard
Christ without the reality of his atonement and resurrection? How
would we regard the Sermon on the Mount without the resurrection
of the sermon giver *and* eventually all of us? Without the reality of
God's plan of salvation and Jesus' atonement, how could the meek
truly inherit the earth? How could the pure in heart really see God?
(See Matthew 5.)

No wonder Paul wrote of Christ, "in him all things hold
together" (Revised Standard Version, Colossians 1:17). When, collectively or individually, brothers and sisters, things seem to fly apart for
us at times, what fitting imagery: "In him all things hold together"!
Given the centrality of the doctrine of resurrection, the Restoration
has as one of its main purposes to witness not only of Jesus' resurrection, but that of all mankind.

*And righteousness will I send down out of heaven; and truth will I send forth out of the earth, to bear testimony of mine Only Begotten; his resurrection from the dead; yea, and also the resurrection of all men.* [Moses 7:62]

There are so many ways in which Christ holds all things together. In fact, scriptures further advise, "all things bear record of me" (Moses 6:63).

At Christmastime, for instance, we celebrate a special star that announced Jesus' birth at Bethlehem. Thus, the so-called "little star of Bethlehem" was actually very large in its declaration of divine design! It had to have been placed in its precise orbit long, long before it shone so precisely! Persuasive divine design is underscored in what the Lord has said: "All things must come to pass in their time" (D&C 64:32). His overseeing precision pertains not only to astrophysical orbits but to human orbits as well. This is such a stunning thing for us to contemplate as to our obligations to "shine as lights" within our own orbits and personal responsibilities! (See Philippians 2:15.)

In Jesus there is a unique blend of both meekness and majesty. Though the Lord of the Universe, Christ was meekly willing to live in this world, which he created under the Father's direction. In Paul's words, he agreed to reside on earth as a person of no reputation (see Philippians 2:7).

We sing of his birth, "The stars in the heavens looked down where he lay" ("Away in a Manger," *Hymns*, 1985, no. 206). The onlooking universe was apparently created by him under the Father's direction, involving "worlds without number" (Moses 1:33). Thus the meek Christ child was cradled not only in a manger but was also cradled in the midst of the majesty of his own creations! Even the least of these, when we contemplate the heavens, permits us to see God "moving in his majesty and power" (D&C 88:47). Do we not sing of "All the worlds thy hands have made"? (See "How Great Thou Art," *Hymns*, 1985, no. 86.)

In the Eastern Hemisphere, the special star that signaled his meek birth was recognized by only a few shepherds and several wise men. However, when Christ comes in majesty and power, the sign of his second coming will be such that "all people shall see it together" (D&C 88:93). He declares "all flesh shall see me together" (D&C 101:23). What an impending moment of unparalleled majesty for the Millennial Messiah. Yet it was preceded by the meekness of his Mortal Messiahship.

He created worlds, yet he was regarded as merely being a carpenter's son. He called and inspired Old Testament prophets. Yet Jesus was regarded by some contemporaries in the meridian of time as being less than those very prophets (see Luke 16:29; John 5:45–46; John 8:33, 37–38).

In his mortal ministry, meek Jesus spoke of how he had yet "other sheep" (John 10:16). Still later, when with those "other sheep" of the Nephite fold, he spoke of still "other sheep" (3 Nephi 16:1–3). How many folds and flocks does he have? We do not know. But there are inklings of his majesty, for "by him, and through him, and of him, the worlds are and were created, and the inhabitants thereof are begotten sons and daughters unto God" (D&C 76:24). Yet this Great and True Shepherd, in meekness, revealed to a solitary Samaritan woman that, indeed, he was the Messiah (see John 4:26; Helaman 15:13).

Because Jesus was brilliant beyond our comprehension, he knew even premortally, though intellectually, what he was volunteering to do. Yet he had to experience it all personally—especially the awful agony of Gethsemane and Calvary. He who is "more intelligent than they all" is also more meek than they all! (See Abraham 3:19.) He went meekly forward and partook of the most bitter cup—and did so without becoming bitter!

Jesus descended below all things in order to be able to comprehend all things (see D&C 88:6; 122:8). Thus he is not only a *fully atoning* Savior but is a *fully comprehending* Savior as well!

Christ somehow came to know—just as specifically prophesied—our griefs, sorrows, pains, sicknesses, afflictions, and infirmities (Isaiah 53:4; 2 Nephi 9:21; Mosiah 14:4). He did so, declared Alma, that he might know, according to the flesh, how to succor and to help us in the midst of our infirmities (see Alma 7:11–12).

Only in restoration scriptures—specifically the Book of Mormon—is Jesus' atonement referred to as the "infinite atonement" (2 Nephi 9:7; 25:16; Alma 34:12).

It was "infinite" in several dimensions. First, in what is called the "great and last sacrifice," the sacrifice of a mere animal or an imperfect mortal would not do. It required the sacrifice of an *infinite being*, an eternal and sinless God (see Alma 34:10). Jesus, you will recall, volunteered premortally: "Here am I, send me" (Abraham 3:27). Never has anyone offered to do so much for so many with so few words! As an infinite being, Jesus had the unique power to put down and take up his life.

Jesus' atonement also had *infinite impact* affecting all mankind (see 2 Nephi 25:16). "For as in Adam all die, even so in Christ shall all be made alive" (l Corinthians 15:22).

Third, his atonement involved *infinite suffering*—suffering beyond our comprehension (see D&C 19:18). I will note especially some of his suffering.

The Atonement fulfills many prophesies. Jesus was to be spat upon (see 1 Nephi 19:9), struck, scourged (see Mosiah 3:9). He would be given vinegar and gall (see Psalms 69:21). He would issue a soul cry, the very words of which were prophesied by David in a Messianic psalm (see Psalms 22:1; Matthew 27:46). None of his bones was to be broken (see Psalms 34:20).

We begin to see in the scriptures the weight of the Atonement burdening him shortly before Gethsemane and Calvary:

*Now is my soul troubled; and what shall I say? Father, save me from this hour: but for this cause came I unto this hour.* [John 12:27]

The full weight fell upon him when he entered the Garden of Gethsemane, where he "fell on the ground" (Mark 14:33–36). At one point in the process an angel appeared to strengthen him (see Luke 22:43). The keenest of all intellects to ever grace this planet endured sufferings that were worse than even he, with his unexcelled brilliance, had ever imagined. Hence he was "sore amazed" or, in the

Greek, "astonished," "awestruck" (Mark 14:33). He became "very heavy," which, in the Greek means, "depressed and dejected."

When in the garden, he issued "the Abba cry" (Mark 14:36; Psalms 22:1). It was the most intimate, familial cry of a child in the deepest of distress for his father.

All the cumulative weight of our sins—the whole human family—fell upon him. He, and he alone, bore them! Thus he is able to say, "I have overcome and have trodden the wine-press alone, even the wine-press of the fierceness of the wrath of Almighty God" (D&C 76:107; 88:106). This would include all the penalties that a God who cannot look upon sin with the least degree of allowance would require (see D&C 1:31). Could there be any wrath more fierce than divine wrath? Especially as Jesus encountered cumulative, mortal grossness including the vilest of all human sins? Jesus bore them.

Indeed, Christ was alone, for "there was none with me" (Isaiah 63:3; D&C 133:50). His astonishing, personal triumph was complete. Yet he who premortally had promised he would give glory to our Father kept that promise, saying after accomplishing the Atonement, "Nevertheless, glory be to the Father" (D&C 19:19; Moses 4:2).

Several years ago, Christian physicians, writing in the *Journal of American Medicine*, indicated they felt that, because of the loss of blood when he was scourged, Jesus would have been in serious, if not critical condition before he ever carried a portion of his cross to Calvary. Other scholars say Jesus was likely scourged with a Roman flagellum, something similar to a cat-o'-nine-tails with metallic objects at the end of each thong. If he assumed the usual posture for scourging, it would have been kneeling over before his scourger so that the muscles of his back were tensed and thus more easily torn and shredded. He would have lost much blood in addition to what he lost earlier while bleeding from every pore in Gethsemane.

No wonder he needed help to carry the cross!

Jesus bore all mortal sins, mankind's cumulative total. Thus Jesus, of his suffering, truly could later say that "he descended below all things" (D&C 88:6).

The requirements of divine justice were severe. According to Elder James Talmage, in order "that the supreme sacrifice of the Son might be consummated in all its fulness, the Father seems to have withdrawn the support of His immediate Presence [while Jesus was on the cross], leaving to the Savior of men the glory of complete victory over the forces of sin and death" (*Jesus the Christ*, 3rd ed. [Salt Lake City: The Church of Jesus Christ of Latter-day Saints, 1916], p. 661). What an awful and awesome aloneness! What deprivation, especially after the special and extended closeness of Father and Son!

On the cross, there came from Christ the soul-rending cry, "My God, my God, why hast thou forsaken me?" (Matthew 27:46; see also Psalms 22:1). What awful aloneness! Is it possible that Jesus needed to suffer and experience aloneness not only so his personal triumph would be total, but also so that he might "know according to the flesh" how it is for us to feel forsaken? (See Alma 7:11–12.) In any case, he felt forsaken and alone.

Compared to his feeling forsaken, what are our occasional feelings of being forsaken and alone? Or our feelings of being unnoticed and unappreciated? Or our deprivations?

All this emptying agony preceded the empty tomb, which signified the glorious resurrection. In his comments after the awful atonement, he uses words like "sore" and "exquisite." Jesus tells us that he suffered "both body and spirit" (D&C 19:18–19). He does not even mention having been spat upon, struck, receiving vinegar and gall, being scourged, etc. He does say that he trembled because of pain and would that he might not shrink, that he might not fail to partake fully of the bitter cup and finish the Atonement (see D&C 19:18). As already indicated, he partook of the bitter cup and did so without becoming bitter! Mercifully for all of us, he did not shrink!

*And behold, I am the light and the life of the world; and I have drunk out of that bitter cup which the Father hath given me, and have glorified the Father in taking upon me the sins of the world, in the which I have suffered the will of the Father in all things from the beginning.* [3 Nephi 11:11]

*I have overcome and have trodden the winepress alone, even the wine-press of the fierceness of the wrath of Almighty God.* [D&C 76:107]

Thus he became our *fully comprehending* and *fully atoning* Savior. No wonder we sing of him, *"How great thou art!"* (*Hymns*, 1985, no. 86).

Why did he do it?

*And the world, because of their iniquity, shall judge him to be a thing of naught; wherefore they scourge him, and he suffereth it; and they smite him, and he suffereth it. Yea, they spit upon him, and he suffereth it, because of his* loving kindness *and his long-suffering towards the children of men.* [1 Nephi 19:9; emphasis added]

Ponder the term *loving-kindness*. It is a special word, used in David's plea after he sinned so grievously:

*Have mercy upon me*, O *God, according to thy* loving kind-ness: *according unto the multitude of thy tender mercies blot out my transgressions.* [Psalms 51:1; emphasis added]

Hold that special word in your minds as I read in conclusion these verses about his coming majesty:

*And it shall be said: Who is this that cometh down from God in heaven with dyed garments; yea, from the regions which are not known, clothed in his glorious apparel, traveling in the greatness of his strength? . . .*

*And the Lord shall be red in his apparel, and his garments like him that treadeth in the winevat.*

*And so great shall be the glory of his presence that the sun shall hide his face in shame, and the moon shall withhold its light, and the stars shall be hurled from their places.*

*And his voice shall be heard: I have trodden the wine-press alone, and have brought judgment upon all people; and none were with me;*

*And now the year of my redeemed is come; and they shall mention the* loving kindness *of their Lord, and all that he has bestowed upon them according to his goodness, and according to his* loving kindness, *forever and ever.* [D&C 133:46, 48–50, 52; emphasis added]

Blessed be the Father for his loving-kindness in giving his Only Begotten as Our Redeemer! We do not know, nor could we appreciate if we did, the feelings of the Father as he watched his firstborn go through the Atonement. How great our Father is. Blessed be the Son, Jesus Christ, for his loving-kindness in atoning for our sins. I "scarce can take it in" ("How Great Thou Art"). Whenever you and I witness and experience in a human being impressive loving-kindness, we marvel—and we should marvel. But such highly developed loving-kindness is still not closely comparable to Jesus' loving-kindness. So it is with each of his qualities about which I have spoken tonight. When we are fortunate enough to experience the stirring samples of likeness, these are real and wonderful experiences, but they are not yet fullness. They are not yet the fullness found in Jesus. Even so, he of fullness clearly and kindly beckons us to develop that greater likeness in our lives which precedes fullness. It is that likeness that will give us the light in our lives so that we might, as Paul says, "shine as lights in the world." These are the attributes that convey to us the added authority of example. And as we emulate him, by developing likeness in these attributes, he will bless us and magnify us for his purposes.

My quorum president, President Howard W. Hunter, said twenty-six years ago in April general conference, "He loves the Lord with all his heart, who loves nothing in comparison of him and nothing but in reference to him."

As one of his special witnesses, I testify to you tonight that he is risen. And how marvelous it is, even given the great distance of the trek spoken of earlier, that he beckons us to develop this likeness so that one day we may have fullness with him. It is the journey of journeys. Nothing else is even remotely comparable to it in its importance. There is nothing in comparison of him. Indeed, as Paul said, "in Christ all things hold together."

That is my witness to you on this Easter night, the reality of his mercy, the genuineness of his loving-kindness. He has said to us, "What manner of men [and women] ought ye to be? Verily I say unto you, even as I am" (3 Nephi 27:27). What an invitation! That invitation verifies the possibility of its realization.

I salute you for who you are, but, more important, for what you have the possibilities to become. There is none like him. And as he has said to us in the marvelous imagery of holy scriptures, "I wait for you with open arms." But it is we who must go to him in this journey of journeys.

Finally, I witness to you the reality of the great Atonement. It is the central act of all human history. Nothing else even remotely approaches it in terms of significance. The meek Jesus says: "Here am I, send me." Jesus will come in majesty, and we will hail him for his loving-kindness. If we love him, we must so love one another.

He is risen, and the symbol of Christianity might well be the empty tomb that bespeaks the fullness of the great Atonement of which I testify to you tonight in love and in appreciation and in recognition of who you really are. I bear this witness to you humbly, lovingly, but, most important, in the holy name of Jesus Christ. Amen.

# The Inexhaustible Gospel

Neal A. Maxwell

I give my sincere appreciation to President Lee and to those who have planned these important days for you and for this opportunity to be with you, brothers and sisters. My appreciation goes to Michael Ballam for the beautiful music and, just as important, for the quality of his and his wife's personal discipleship.

The title of my address, "The Inexhaustible Gospel," is intended to convey the vastness and preciousness of that enormous body of knowledge we call the gospel and—if I am at all successful—some of my ever-growing excitement over it.

Before using terms like *truth, knowledge, intelligence, education,* and *wisdom,* I stress at the outset that the scriptural definitions of these terms give us, as Latter-day Saints, an added understanding of these concepts. They differ from those of the world—markedly, in fact. Each is "added upon" by the relevant revelations. These differences are especially worth noting during an Education Week. Please be patient while I attempt to note certain of these distinctions.

*This devotional address was given at Brigham Young University on 18 August 1992.*

For example, our being saved by gaining knowledge obviously refers to a particular form of knowledge, a "knowledge of God" and knowledge of the things of God (see D&C 128:19; *Teachings*, p. 217). Nephi lamented, as you know, over those who "will not search knowledge, nor understand great knowledge" (2 Nephi 32:7). Clearly he was referring to a particular kind of knowledge. In fact, Joseph Smith's translation of Jesus' lamentation—about how those in his time had lost the "key of knowledge"—provides a definition; it adds five words defining what the word *key* means: "the fulness of the scriptures" (JST, Luke 11:53; see also D&C 84:19–20). So we view knowledge differently. Furthermore, Latter-day Saints know that certain knowledge comes only by revelation and, thereby, is only "spiritually discerned" (1 Corinthians 2:14). So we are in some important respects on a different footing from the people of the world.

In addition, brothers and sisters, multiple scriptures make it clear that *knowledge* is meant to be closely associated with other virtues such as patience, humility, charity, and kindness (D&C 4:6; 107:30–31; 121:41–42; 2 Peter 1:5–9).

*Truth* includes, but is not limited to, knowledge that corresponds to reality—things as they were, things as they are, and things as they will be (Jacob 4:13; D&C 93:24). Gospel truth is "morally richer," therefore, than the world's definition of truth, as Terry Warner has written *(Encyclopedia of Mormonism*, vol. 4 [New York: Macmillan Co., 1992], p. 1490). Jesus is "the way, the truth, and the life" (John 14:6). He has "received a fulness of truth" (D&C 93:26). Hence, we are to seek to have "the mind of Christ" (1 Corinthians 2:16). Furthermore, as to the "manner" of people we are to become, it is clear we are to strive to become "even as" Jesus is (3 Nephi 27:27; see also 2 Peter 3:11). If we keep the commandments, the promise is that we will receive "truth and light" until we are "glorified in truth and knoweth all things" (D&C 93:28).

Therefore, gaining knowledge and becoming more Christlike "are two aspects of a single process" (Warner, *Encyclopedia of Mormonism*, vol. 4, p. 1490). This process is part of being "valiant" in our testimony of Jesus. Thus, while we are saved no faster than we gain a certain type of knowledge, it is also the case, as Richard Bushman has observed, that we will gain knowledge no faster than we are saved (*Teachings*, p. 217). So we have a fundamentally different understanding of knowledge and truth—behaving and knowing are inseparably linked.

So defined, the gospel is inexhaustible because there is not only so much to know, but also so much to become! The vital truths are not merely accumulated in the mind but are expressed in life as well.

*Intelligence* is "the glory of God," as we all know. It is defined as "light and truth" (D&C 93:36). The revelations also inform us that if we have "more knowledge *and* intelligence in this life," we will have "so much the advantage in the world to come" (D&C 130:18–19).

I do not pretend to be able to be definitive with regard to this last verse, but, clearly, what we carry forward, brothers and sisters, involves developing our capacity for cognition as well as application. This sets us apart from the world. I hope we understand some of the implications of all these things. Certainly, what we will carry forward is more than what we now term as *IQ* or *databases*. It is the entire being of the individual. Hence our approach to knowledge, truth, and wisdom is markedly different.

What are some of the implications of the foregoing?

First, some of us—and I include myself—sometimes casually speak of education for eternity. Brothers and sisters, it is clear from the verses of scripture that some truths may turn out to have a place in a yet-to-be-revealed hierarchy of truth that the world doesn't understand. The scriptures tantalize us by saying, "All truth is independent in that sphere in which God has placed it" (D&C 93:30). One even wonders if truths, like planets, belong to a particular order (see Abraham 3:9). But we do not now know.

The highest education, therefore, includes salvational truths, bringing us a knowledge of "things as they really are, and of things as they really will be" (Jacob 4:13). This focus can be achieved without leaving the usual educational chores "undone" (Matthew 23:23). Scholars like the president of Brigham Young University, Rex Lee, have surely demonstrated this.

Ultimate orthodoxy—and orthodoxy isn't a popular word nowadays—is expressed in the Christlike life that involves both mind and behavior. Christ's manner of life is truly "the way, the truth, and the life," and he has directed us to pursue his example (John 14:6; see also Matthew 5:48; 3 Nephi 12:48; 3 Nephi 27:27).

Another important implication of what we have been discussing is that all knowledge is not of equal significance. There is no democracy of facts! They are not of equal importance. Something might be factual but unimportant, as Elder Spencer Condie has observed. For instance, today I wear a dark blue suit. That is true, but it is unimportant. The world does not quite understand this. As we brush against truth, we sense that it has a hierarchy of importance. We are dealing with some things of *transcending* importance. Some truths are salvationally significant, and others are not.

Another important insight is that knowledge is intended to travel in a convoy of other Christian virtues. It does not have final meaning by itself. If one possesses some knowledge, as Peter said, but "lacketh" these other qualities, he cannot "see afar off" (2 Peter 1:5–9). A most interesting concept! Precious perspective is missing unless knowledge is accompanied by these other truths.

Other insights bear down upon us as Latter-day Saints. Brilliance, by itself, is not wholeness, nor happiness. Knowledge, if possessed for its own sake and unapplied, leaves one's life unadorned. A Church member, for instance, might describe the Lord's doctrines but not qualify to enter the Lord's house. One could produce much brilliant commentary without being exemplary. One might be intellectually brilliant but Bohemian in behavior. One might use his knowledge to seek preeminence or dominion.

Such are not Jesus' ways, for he asks that perception and implementation be part of the same spiritual process. In Alma's words, we are to "give place" in our lives for the good seed of the gospel to grow—which involves a form of knowing that combines cognition as well as implementation (see Alma 32).

As we all know, Christ does not dominate by his intellect. He leads by example and love. There is no arrogance flowing from his, the keenest of all intellects. He seeks neither to conquer nor to prosper "according to his genius" (see Alma 30:17).

Given these foregoing views of restoration theology as they pertain to knowledge, truth, education, and wisdom, there is, finally, no comfort zone for vanity or hypocrisy. There is no sanctuary for them. Clearly, in such a situation as I have attempted to describe altogether too briefly, a few individuals in the Church end up "looking beyond the mark," missing the already obvious (Jacob 4:14). These few individuals let their minds seek to run far ahead of their confirming behavior. For them, exciting exploration is preferred to plodding implementation. Speculation and argumentation are more fun than consecration for these individuals. Some even try to soften the hard doctrines. What happens, however, is that by their not obeying, they lack knowing, as we are discussing knowing today. Thus, since they cannot defend the faith, a few of them become critics instead of defenders (John 7:17).

As far as salvational truths are concerned, therefore, the secular knowledge explosion in recent years—with all of its many and unarguable benefits to mankind—has not been a bang at all. It has been merely a whimper. It was the Restoration that provided the explosion of salvational knowledge.

I now hasten to add, having said these preliminary things, that the role of secular knowledge is very important. Latter-day Saints should have all the genuine excitement others have in the traditional adventure of learning, including learning secular truths—and we, of all people, should have a little more! In fact, when we are so learning and so behaving, we are truly "about [our] Father's business." This should bring to us a special and genuine zest for learning (see 2 Nephi 9:29; Luke 2:49).

Furthermore, those of us who have spent much of our lives involved with traditional education regard it as one of mankind's most useful, productive, and cost-beneficial enterprises. It is even more beneficial, however, when it has the spiritual dimension added to it. Secular education wisely does not pretend to give us answers to the great "why" questions—any more than you and I, brothers and sisters, would read a telephone directory in search of a plot!

Our different frame of reference should never cause us to preen or to be insensitive to the uncertainty or despair some feel in the world precisely because they believe sincerely that man exists in "godless, geometric space."

I have always had a special appreciation for my friends who, though resolutely irreligious themselves, were not scoffers. Instead, though doubtless puzzled by me and their other religious friends, they were nevertheless respectful. I admire the day-to-day decency of such men and women. Though detached from theology, their decency is commendable.

I now share a lamentation from one character in a story that illustrates the confusion, despair, and pain felt by many. He says,

> Are all men's lives . . . broken, tumultuous, agonized and unromantic. . . . Who knows? . . . I don't know. Why can't people have what they want? The things were all there to content everybody, yet everybody got the wrong thing. . . . It's beyond me. It's all darkness. [PBS production of "The Good Soldier," by Ford Madox Ford, viewed in early 1983]

As if speaking to this very point, the Prophet Joseph Smith observed,

> Knowledge does away with darkness, suspense and doubt; for these cannot exist where knowledge is.
> There is no pain so awful as that of suspense. [Teachings, pp. 287–88]

Joseph, of course, was speaking about a particular kind of knowledge.

Thus our view of education is the same as that Jesus prescribed with regard to our other Christian duties: namely, the weightier matters should receive their deserved prominence without leaving the lesser learning chores "undone" (Matthew 23:23).

The Prophet Joseph also observed, "If you wish to go where God is, you must be like God, or possess the principles which God possesses" (*Teachings*, p. 216). God possesses perfect knowledge, but he also possesses perfect love and mercy. What a contrast he is to those mortals who are bright but bad, who are clever but carnal! Even genius without goodness can be dangerous.

No wonder, therefore, "to be learned is good if [we] hearken unto the counsels of God" instead of setting them aside as if we have somehow outgrown them (2 Nephi 9:29). How can one ever outgrow Christ's example of knowing, behaving, and doing? What happens, however, is that some easily fall into the trap described by Paul, "Ever learning, and never able to come to the knowledge of the truth" (2 Timothy 3:7). One might learn a great deal about the physical characteristics of this planet earth but yet be ignorant of *why* it was created in the first place (see Isaiah 45:18; 1 Nephi 17:36; Moses 1:33,39).

Certainly during Education Week we need to know the plan for the week, what the presentations are, in which room, and at what time. Such information, for the moment, is essential. But compare having that information to knowing the truth about God's plan of salvation!

For mortals, therefore, the gospel is inexhaustible, because "the Spirit searcheth all things, yea, the deep things of God" (1 Corinthians 2:10). Jacob's words are strikingly similar to Paul's: "For the Spirit speaketh the truth . . . of things as they really are, and of things as they really will be" (Jacob 4:13). Unsurprisingly, the scriptural definition of truth matches. It is the "knowledge of things as they are, and as they were, and as they are to come" (D&C 93:24). What vastness!

While encountering and exploring such vastness, we sometimes know more than our tongues can tell. Indeed, knowledge that is "spiritually discerned" is not always easily communicated. But the ultimate place we hope to be in is one where "in the presence of God, . . . all things . . . are manifest, past, present, and future, and are continually before the Lord" (D&C 130:7). What a wondrous God we worship! The Prophet Joseph Smith said "the past, the present, and the future were and are, with [Jehovah], one eternal 'now'" (*Teachings*, p. 220). How different the Lord's "now" is from ours!

In exploring this comprehensiveness and everlastingness, there will be some surprises. Our understanding of some things will be restructured and expanded, especially in the world to come, for "Eye hath not seen, nor ear heard, neither have entered into the heart of man, the things which God hath prepared for them that love him" (1 Corinthians 2:9). In eternity, when the faithful receive "all that [the] Father hath," this will include an enormous enlargement intellectually (D&C 84:38).

However, some divine disclosure can begin even now in mortality:

> *For by my Spirit will I enlighten them, and by my power will I make known unto them the secrets of my will—yea, even those things which eye has not seen, nor ear heard, nor yet entered into the heart of man.*
> [D&C 76:10]

Having been given so many marvelous truths, we are to share them in order that "wise men and rulers may hear and know that which they have never considered" (D&C 101:94; see also 3 Nephi 20:45, 21:8). So much of the gospel we bring is what people have "never considered."

Quite understandably, given its very nature, God's latter-day work will be regarded with much skepticism by many. The Lord foresaw this, saying he would "bring to pass my act, my strange act, and perform my work, my strange work, that men may discern" (D&C 101:95; see also Isaiah 28:21; 29:14, Moffat version).

By accessing the inexhaustible divine data bank—through meekness and righteousness, thereby utilizing the Spirit, scriptures, and prophets—special wisdom is opened to us as the Spirit teaches us of "things as they really are, and of things as they really will be" (Jacob 4:13). President Brigham Young, who had his share of spiritual experiences, said, "When the voice of the Good Shepherd is heard, the honest in heart believe and receive it. It is good to taste with the inward taste, to see with the inward eyes" (*JD* 8:42).

In God's "strange work," his ways of informing mankind are like-wise unusual:

*Therefore he sent angels to converse with them, who caused men to behold of his glory.*

*And they began from that time forth to call on his name; therefore God conversed with men, and made known unto them the plan of redemption, which had been prepared from the foundation of the world.*
[Alma 12:29–30]

Ironically, many refuse to examine gospel truths simply because of *how* God reveals them. These very methods swell skepticism among many. Furthermore, these divine disclosures are not democratically dispensed because such things are "made known unto them according to their faith and repentance and their holy works" (Alma 12:30; see also 2 Nephi 1:10).

However, when people are left alone—without angelic visitations, without divine disclosures, without prophets, without scriptures, without the Spirit—many cease believing. Belief in the basics is the first thing to go, as happened with Book of Mormon peoples who ceased believing in God, in the resurrection, and in a redeeming Christ (Omni 1:17; Mosiah 26:2).

Many in the world hold back from making the "leap of faith" because they have already jumped to some other conclusions—often the Korihor conclusions, which are: God never was nor ever will be; there is no redeeming Christ; man cannot know the future; man cannot know of that which he cannot see; whatsoever a man does is no crime; and death is the end (see Alma 30:13–18). The number of adherents to the Korihor conclusions will grow.

When so positioned, many mortals do not accept the fulness of the gospel. Their reactions to the gospel range from indifference to contempt. Happily, there are some who are meek enough to consider that which they have "never considered" and "never had supposed" (D&C 101:94; Moses 1:10).

When Moses was schooled by the Egyptians, what he learned there did not compare in eternal significance to what he learned from God's revelations, things he said he "never had supposed" (Acts 7:22; Moses 1:10–33).

The great "who," "what," and "why" questions are those on which the transcending revelations focus. "What," for instance, is God doing?

> *For behold, this is my work and my glory—to bring to pass the immortality and eternal life of man.* [Moses 1:39]

"Who" is involved?

> *By him, and through him, and of him, the worlds are and were created, and the inhabitants thereof are begotten sons and daughters unto God.* [D&C 76:24]

God's revelations do not usually give us answers to the "how" and "when" questions, such as details concerning the creation of the earth. Yes, there are revelations such as that on the building of Noah's ark—a revelation not reusable, by the way—and on other tactical matters, but the recurring themes of the revelations are spiritual.

Thus the Creator of the Universe does not choose to dazzle his audiences with data concerning the Creation. Rather, as a Perfect and Loving Shepherd, he is interested in the central needs and concerns of his sheep in his many folds.

These revealed truths carry behavioral as well as intellectual responsibilities. When informed, we are accountable. Solomon, for instance, was widely celebrated for his wisdom (1 Kings 10:1, 6–7). Impressively wise as Solomon doubtless was in many respects, he was not wise enough to keep all God's commandments (see 1 Kings 11:1–14).

Individuals are often otherwise commendable, as was Morianton, who "did do justice unto the people, but not unto himself because of his many whoredoms" (Ether 10:11). In gospel wisdom, knowing and behaving are irrevocably linked!

One basic limitation of worldly wisdom is its lack of longitudinality and of precious perspective. Worldly wisdom cannot "see afar off," and, without a spiritual memory, past mistakes are repeated; folly is resumed! Winston Churchill chose, by the way, as the motto for his last volume of World War II history these words:

> *How the Great Democracies Triumphed, and so Were able to Resume the Follies Which Had so Nearly Cost Them Their Life.* [Winston S. Churchill, *The Second World War,* vol. 6, *Triumph and Tragedy* (Boston: Houghton Mifflin Co., 1953), p. ix]

The world in its search for physical security, for instance, tends to build Maginot Lines while naively neglecting its northern flank. It seeks to control the diseases flowing from sexual immorality but without honoring the principles of fidelity and chastity. The world in its wisdom constantly seeks to accommodate the natural man while gospel wisdom constantly urges us to put off the natural man (Mosiah 3:19). This is a pivotal point, and it makes all the difference!

Being so immersed in the gospel framework, we sometimes fail to realize how illuminating gospel truths are with regard to so many issues of the day. For instance, given the plan of salvation with our need to experience this mortal school, to acquire a mortal body, and then knowing the very preciousness of human life—we see the awful practice of widespread abortion differently. Similarly, struggling to have the "mind of Christ" includes purity of thought and letting virtue garnish our thoughts unceasingly. Hence we view pornography as an awful and enslaving thing. We cannot feel otherwise concerning such practices as abortion and pornography, even if practices such as abortion and pornography are legally and constitutionally protected.

This is not to say we expect others to share our views or even to understand them. Some will not even tolerate our views but, instead, attempt to shame us. If we really are "saints of the Holy One," we will endure the "crosses of the world," and despise "the shame of it"

(2 Nephi 9:18). Whether it is worldly shame or worldly temptations, like Jesus, we should give "no heed unto them" (D&C 20:22; see also Alma 7:11–12).

Salvational truths combine longevity and relevancy; they contain both span and significance! Education that is only "for a season" is narrow; it pertains only to a knowledge of things as they temporarily are, like today's weather forecast or an airline schedule. Temporary facts are useful but terminal. Jesus noted the intensity of the children of this world, but said their operative framework was only "in their generation" (see Luke 16:8).

Given such significant gradations among knowledge, we can resonate to T. S. Eliot's lamentation: "Where is the wisdom we have lost in knowledge? Where is the knowledge we have lost in information?" (T. S. Eliot, *The Rock* [1934], I).

Thus our consuming of certain information is like consuming our daily bread. We need it, but it is perishable. We will soon hunger again (see John 6:47–48, 51). Instead, the bread of life is inexhaustible!

Ultimate wisdom enables us to see Jesus as the Light of the World, but, further, we also come to realize that it is by his light that we are to see everything else! The gospel's bright and illuminating light thereby helps us see God, ourselves, others, the world, and the universe more correctly and more deeply. Indeed, as Paul declared, "in [Christ] all things hold together" (RSV, Colossians 1:17).

For now, though we can mercifully see something of our eventual possibilities, you and I are aware of our present limitations. Tolkien wrote wisely:

*It is not our part to master all the tides of the world, but to do what is in us for the succour of those years wherein we are set, uprooting the evil in the fields that we know, so that those who live after may have clean earth to till. What weather they shall have is not ours to rule.* [Gandalf in J. R. R. Tolkien, *The Return of the King* (New York: Ballantine Books, 1965), p. 190]

Hence we desperately need the gospel's wisdom not only for eternity, but also "for the succour of those years wherein we are set," in order "to do what is in us." Enoch obtained revelation and reassurance and gratefully exclaimed of God, "Yet thou art there" (Moses 7:30). This is what you and I want to know of him: Does he know me, love me, and care for me? We can have the same reassurance given to Enoch.

How intellectually amazing the restored gospel of Jesus Christ is! The gospel is truly inexhaustible! It is marvelous! It is a wonder!

Yet orthodoxy is required to keep all these truths in essential balance. In orthodoxy lies real safety and real felicity! Flowing from orthodoxy is not only correctness but happiness. Orthodoxy is especially vital in a time of raging relativism and belching sensualism. The world's morality is constantly being improvised. Some views are politically correct one day, but not another.

One writer recently observed that the relativistic forces at work

*should warm every atheist's heart. For if God is a socially conscious political being whose views invariably correspond to our own prejudices on every essential point of doctrine, he demands of us no more than our politics require.* [H]*ow would our worship of* [this kind of being] *constitute more than self-congratulation for our own moral standards?*

The writer continued:

*As an atheist, I like this God. It is good to see him every morning while I am shaving.* [Eugene D. Genovese, "Pilgrim's Progress," *The New Republic,* 11 May 1992, p. 38]

Yes, being learned is good! It can supply us with the needed facts and help us develop a facility with facts and a discernment among facts. It can train us to use our minds, to cultivate an intellectual adroitness in connecting various patches of truth and insight. It certainly furthers the calisthenics of the intellect.

Finally, however, you and I should be fully qualified and certified in traditional education and its processes for yet another very good reason: bilinguality. The men and women of Christ should be truly educated and articulate as to secular knowledge but should also be educated and articulate in the things of the Spirit!

I close now by speaking further of Jesus, our Perfect Shepherd. His atoning experience placed upon him the sicknesses, sorrows, griefs, and pains of the human experience in order "that he may know according to the flesh how to succor his people according to their infirmities" (Alma 7:11, 12; see also 2 Nephi 9:21; Isaiah 53:4–5; Hebrews 2:18). He "suffered the pain of all men," women, and children and was "touched with the feeling of our infirmities" (D&C 18:11; Hebrews 4:15). Thus, in the agony of the Atonement, Jesus "descended below all things, in that he comprehended all things" (see D&C 88:6; see also D&C 122:8). How marvelous the "mind of Christ," which we are to try to come to have (1 Corinthians 2:16).

Jesus, our Perfect Exemplar, was astonishingly exemplary even in the hours surrounding the awful but glorious Atonement. The intrigue of Pilate and Herod, for instance, who had earlier been "at enmity" but who "made friends together" because of Jesus, presented opportunities for Jesus to "shrink" from going through with the Atonement (Luke 23:12; D&C 19:18). Herod, who had been desirous "to see [Jesus] of a long season," "hoped to have seen some miracle done by him" (Luke 23:8). Yet Jesus, under heavy questioning from Herod, "answered him nothing" (Luke 23:9; see also Mosiah 14:7). Jesus' integrity and intellect were not for sale! Amid temptation, he maintained his integrity—even in the midst of an opportunity that a lesser individual would have seized to reduce his suffering and to increase the praise of men.

Ironically, when Jesus' enemies came for him, the Light of the World, they came with lanterns and torches (John 18:3). Jesus, who by then might have understandably been so swollen with sorrow and self-concern that there was no time to think of others, nevertheless restored the severed ear of a hostile guard (Luke 22:50–51). Amid irony he kept his poise. He also kept his way, which is not the way of the sword.

Christ spoke only several sentences on the cross. One of them was to insure that his mother, Mary, would be cared for by John (John 19:25–27). Another sentence reassured a thief on an adjoining cross (Luke 23:43). He had empathy amid his agony.

Finally, he maintained his consecration in the midst of the deepest deprivation anyone can know. President Brigham Young taught us that in the course of the astonishing Atonement, the Father withdrew both his presence and his Spirit from Jesus, and, further, even cast a veil over Jesus (*JD* 3:206). Thus Jesus became utterly and totally alone! There then came that great cry of forsakenness! "Nevertheless," Jesus did not "shrink," but, instead, "finished [his] preparations unto the children of men" (D&C 19:18–19). Just as he promised premortally, even when he might have reflected a little credit upon himself for the glorious Atonement, meek Jesus, instead, gave all the glory to the Father (D&C 19:19).

We need not apologize for regarding Jesus as "the way, the truth, and the life" (John 14:6). We need not apologize for regarding salvational knowledge, revealed by him, as being the most precious. Indeed, in Christ "all things hold together," for he is perfect in knowing and perfect in doing. And, most marvelously, he has challenged us to become like him (Matthew 5:48; 3 Nephi 12:48; 27:27).

Of him, I testify! Of his standard of truth and knowledge and behavior, I testify! He is the Light of the World! May we reflect his light in our lives, distinguishing between the things of the moment—including the facts that dissolve—and the supernal, transcending knowledge of spiritual things, the great blessing he has given us through the restored gospel. This is my humble, heartfelt prayer, in the name of Jesus Christ. Amen.

# Wisdom and Order

———◆———

Neal A. Maxwell

Colleen and I appreciate the invitation from President Lee to be with all of you tonight. We have yet to invent better words than those expressive but well-worn words *thank you*, although we can juxtapose adverbs. Hence my major purpose in being with you tonight is simply but gratefully to say "Thank you very much" for all you have done, are doing and will yet do in accomplishing the purposes of Brigham Young University, a special university!

Since I will be speaking to the faculty tomorrow afternoon on matters appropriate to that occasion, these remarks will be somewhat different. I especially include appreciation to those of you who serve in important staff and other functions and to our special guests, the retirees. Staff are less heralded, but, in the words of the Book of Mormon, like Helaman you are certainly "no less serviceable" in the cause! (See Alma 48:19.)

In contrast, while we value nurturing at BYU, we shouldn't be surprised that there are so many countertrends toward depersonalization in today's world. Of the global society in the last days, it was

*This address was delivered at the evening session of the BYU Annual University Conference on 25 August 1993.*

prophesied that the "love of many shall wax cold" (Matthew 24:12). Furthermore, "Peace shall be taken from the earth" (D&C 1:35). There are even wars within as well as between nations, accompanied by a general escalation of violence and confrontation. We also see the prophesied "despair [that] cometh because of iniquity," because we live in an age when "iniquity shall abound" (Moroni 10:22; Matthew 24:12). It is all most regrettable and soberingly foretelling! I, for one, brothers and sisters, see no secular rescue columns on the horizon.

There are many less dramatic expressions of the foregoing trends in our general society, such as the abandonment of personalization by bureaucratization. It is so easy to know people merely as functions. Further isolation is then brought about by function. Many simply pull back into their assigned cubicle and "do their own thing," reluctant to venture forth in unrequired service. Obligations are limited by job descriptions rather than being expanded by the reflexes of the second great commandment. Even entitlements suggest exclusions.

However, such depersonalizing trends need not characterize Brigham Young University. Yes, BYU is a very large community. Yes, some mistakes have been and will be made in the direction of impersonalization. But, no, being big does not automatically mean being impersonal!

Think, for a moment, of just a few of the circumstances in which students here can still experience a frame of reference that remains human sized. For instance, the student wards are deliberately kept small. Students' relationships in a room or in a dorm, can still be personal. Very importantly, their contacts with many of the staff are one-on-one. Likewise, mentoring by faculty is personal. So while students and all of you are part of a large campus community, the impersonalized patterns of the world need not prevail!

In any human situation, whether large or small, each of us can be either a lubricant or an irritant. There isn't much in between. Indifference is an irritation, and neutrality can be seen as muffled hostility.

Now, because you are integral parts of BYU, precious and special assets, may I presume to encourage you briefly to preserve yourselves and your marriages and families in order to serve more individuals and for longer! People-fatigue can overtake us all, especially the conscientious, if we are not wise.

In dealing with the pressures of life, many of you have long since developed your own ways of handling stress and people-fatigue and of rejuvenating marriages, which can become "tired" if we do not nurture them. For you, I shall merely provide some confirmation and encouragement to pace yourselves. You probably have worked things out reasonably well by being aligned with the several scriptures to follow.

Furthermore, each of us has different strengths and faces different circumstances that call for calibrations that are highly individual. Many things in life act upon us over which we have no control, but there is a zone—of differing size for each of us—in which we can act for ourselves, rather than merely being acted upon (see 2 Nephi 2:26). This zone includes a certain amount of disposable time, just as we have disposable income. What we do within that zone is especially up to us to determine.

Basic scriptures can guide us: "See that all these things are done in wisdom and order; for it is not requisite that a man should run faster than he has strength" (Mosiah 4:27). A revelation was given to the Prophet Joseph Smith at a time when he must have been exceedingly anxious to finish the important translation of the Book of Mormon: "Do not run faster or labor more than you have strength and means provided to enable you to translate; but be diligent unto the end" (D&C 10:4).

Thus, the Lord has given us what might be called the "wisdom and order" and "strength and means" tests.

We unwisely often write checks against our time accounts as we never would dare do, comparably, against our bank accounts. Sometimes we make so many commitments, they become like the vines in the allegory of Jacob, threatening to "overcome the roots," including the roots of family relationships, friendships, and relationships with God. Some "pruning-shears" suggestions follow.

On my office wall is a quote from Anne Morrow Lindbergh: "My life cannot implement in action the demands of all the people to whom my heart responds." For me, it is a needed reminder. A few years ago, already weary, I foolishly went late one afternoon to give blessings to three individuals in two different hospitals who were dying of cancer. Not only was I worn out, but, worse, the last person really didn't get much from me. Things had not been done in "wisdom and order." I was running faster than my supply of strength and energy on that occasion. I exceeded my strength. Those blessings would have been better given over two or three days, and I would have had more empathy and energy. Somehow, giving unhurried time is a greater gift even if the minutes or hours are technically the same as when hurried.

Another scripture:

> *And he said unto* [the Twelve], *Come ye yourselves apart into a desert place, and rest a while: for there were many coming and going, and they had no leisure so much as to eat.*
>
> *And they departed into a desert place by ship privately.* [Mark 6:31–32]

Jesus clearly recognized the weariness of his disciples, brought on by their conscientiousness. A renewing retreat can be difficult to arrange. But informal, brief "retreats" can still be fashioned by providing such greenbelts of time between busyness, even if these are only a few minutes long.

Illustratively, after one of the Brethren made a report to President Brigham Young, he was anxious to leave so as not to impose, but President Young said, "Please sit a spell with me. I am weary of men and things." How often do we "sit a spell" with spouse, children, colleagues, or friends? As you know, the original Twelve were counseled that they were not to "serve tables" (Acts 6:1–4). Actually, serving tables is a lot easier. It is visible, measurable, and do-able—compared to opening up the nations of the world or keeping wolves out of the flock. But, if the Twelve were drawn away from their scriptural and constitutional duties, the whole Church would suffer. Being drawn away can happen to all of us, however, almost without our knowing it.

The "wisdom and order" test also recognizes that there are seasons in life when doing certain extra outside civic chores is more appropriate.

While professional responsibilities and formal callings come and go, it is always in season, however, to follow Jesus' commandment: "What manner of men [and women] ought ye to be? Verily I say unto you, even as I am" (3 Nephi 27:27).

Let's all try to watch the Martha-like anxiety, which is genderless. Such anxiety can also deprive us of special experiences if we are too "cumbered about much serving."

Conscientiousness is not an automatic guarantee that we will choose the "good part" that will not "be taken away" from us (Luke 10:38–42).

In a relaxed discussion with several faculty and their partners just last week, it was clear that our most precious remembrances were concerned with "the good part." These had not been taken away from us, whereas many of our once-pressing anxieties were long since forgotten.

Brigham Young, in periods when pressures could have filled him with Martha-like anxiety, instead made Mary-like choices:

> *In my experience I never did let an opportunity pass of getting with the Prophet Joseph and of hearing him speak in public or in private, so that I might draw understanding from the fountain from which he spoke, that I might have it and bring it forth when it was needed. . . . In the days of the Prophet Joseph, such moments were more precious to me than all the wealth of the world. No matter how great my poverty—if I had to borrow meal to feed my wife and children, I never let an opportunity pass of learning what the Prophet had to impart.* [Brigham Young, *Journal of Discourses* 12:269–70]

The yield from Brigham's having "chosen the good part" by so listening "has not been taken from" him or from us!

Husbands and wives, please have one gospel conversation at least once a week—just between the two of you. "Sit a spell," even though it may only last 10 or 15 minutes. A growing intellectual excitement over the gospel can do so much to help counter fatigue and to renew us. So, too, can the joys of quiet, personal Christian service—outside the realm of our formal Church duties.

When we are perplexed and puzzled, and we will be at times, let us ponder Nephi's example: "I know that [God] loveth his children; nevertheless, I do not know the meaning of all things" (1 Nephi 11:17). LeGrand Richards once said of worry: "It's the Lord's Church, so I let Him worry about it." Some of us are not that spiritually poised yet! The Lord knows we "cannot bear all things now" (D&C 50:40). His grace is sufficient for us for each of life's seasons, if we are humble (see Ether 12:27).

Many of our daily choices are not intrinsically hard, but we make them that way. Some choices are matters of preference, not principle. We have a way, at times, of exhausting ourselves and the supply of goodwill while struggling over what are preferences—not principles!

Consider the spiritual poise of Jesus, our Exemplar, in all things. Jesus, who accomplished the most, was never hectically involved. This is all the more marvelous when we realize that so much of his mortal messiahship was crowded into only three very busy years. He had empathy for others even amid his agony in Gethsemane and on the cross. He restored a severed ear. He made certain that his mother, Mary, would be cared for by the Apostle John. He reassured a suffering thief about tomorrow. Self-pity can constrain us severely, but there was none of it in Jesus.

Jesus individualized during what could have seemed to others to be repeated experiences. Even in the midst of his universalness, Jesus, our "great and true shepherd" (Helaman 15:13), cares for each one:

*And the night following the Lord stood by him, and said, Be of good cheer, Paul: for as thou hast testified of me in Jerusalem, so must thou bear witness also at Rome.* [Acts 23:11]

He was especially disclosing to a believing, solitary woman of Samaria:

*The woman saith unto him, I know that Messias cometh, which is called Christ: when he is come, he will tell us all things.*
*Jesus saith unto her, I that speak unto thee am he.* [John 4:25–26]

Will we individualize? Since we are all poised at the edge of another academic year, it would be quite human for us to say resignedly, "Here we go again!" I am so glad Heavenly Father doesn't have such feelings! Even though his course is "one eternal round," as the plan of salvation is executed and re-executed again and again in realms beyond our purview, his love is constant and personal. I am so glad that Jesus did not view each healing as merely one more duty. For him, such a duty was delight.

G.K. Chesterton concluded, "God has never grown tired of making all daisies alike, because God has never grown tired of daisies." Nor must we grow tired of students—or of each other.

Please keep yourselves spiritually and otherwise intact in order to continue as part of this special university. Keeping spiritually intact is of great value, especially when things seem somewhat bleak. Imagine, for instance, what the wrenching feelings of some of Jesus' followers must have been as he was arrested in Gethsemane! Worst still, what was it like for his followers to see him die on the cross? Surely those would be the bleakest hours in Christian history!

Also bleak would have been the time of the Prophet Joseph's imprisonment in Liberty Jail. His followers had been driven from the state of Missouri, and he appeared to be finished. Even so, the Lord told him that "the ends of the earth shall inquire after thy name," (D&C 122:1). What a stunning declaration!

John Taylor said of one who faltered in the bleakness:

*We were driven out of Missouri. . . . I know some men who thought the work was at an end. I remember a remark made by Sidney Rigdon—I suppose he did not live his religion—I do not think he did—his knees began to shake in Missouri, and on one occasion he said, "Brethren, every one of you take your own way, for the work seems as though it ha[s] come to an end."*
[John Taylor, *Journal of Discourses* 11:25]

Then came bleaker Carthage! It looked as though the work of Joseph was finished! Elder George A. Smith gave counsel we should all heed:

*Some men in their hours of darkness may feel—I have heard of men feeling so—that the work is about done, that the enemies of the Saints have become so powerful, and bring such vast wealth and energy to bear against them that we are all going to be crushed out pretty soon. I will say to such brethren, it is very bad policy for you, because you think the old ship Zion is going to sink, to jump overboard.* [George A. Smith, *Journal of Discourses* 17:199–200]

Those of little faith frequently mistake local cloud cover for general darkness.

The motto "The world is our campus" is true of this university, and I rejoice in the way the men and women in its family give so much—sometimes under spartan circumstances. A former member of your faculty and his partner are among the six couples now working in Mongolia in providing humanitarian service.

Likewise, our mission president in the India Bangalore Mission and his wife are part of the BYU family. They serve among a people who number nearly one billion, approaching one-fourth of the human family.

Our mission president in Moscow, Gary Browning, served among the Russian people, who he loved long before it was fashionable to love them. He did so in the midst of some severe physical problems that would have stopped a lesser man, but he simply went on serving.

I think too of Spencer and Shirley Palmer teaching amid spartan circumstances at a University in Beijing, China, in what should be the easy years of retirement. They will be followed by Brother and Sister Paul Hyer, who will enter upon the same service in several months.

Such individuals remind me of how good and decent the members of the BYU family are. But as good as the Y is now, it is going to become much better. Wide as its wingspan already is, it will become much wider. I can only be grateful to have association with all of you as members of that special family.

Again, thank you. May God bless you, I pray in the name of Jesus Christ. Amen.

# "Called to Serve"

Neal A. Maxwell

A s President Merrill Oaks was so kindly introducing me, it occurred to me that I have now had the privilege of being introduced in the Marriott Center by President Dallin Oaks and President Merrill Oaks. I love them both! I did not know their father, but I did know their mother, Stella. She was a very special woman, and one can see her spiritual genes in Merrill and Dallin Oaks.

I am delighted to be with you tonight and to be in the presence of President Rex Lee and his wife, Janet. We sometimes feel a sense of being kindred spirits with certain people when we first get to know them. These friendships are not friendships of initiation, but of resumption. I certainly feel that way about President and Sister Lee, and about others on this stand whom I've come to know, again.

As we approach Easter, with all its glorious significance, we should rejoice in God's great gift of immortality, unearned and universally given—"For as in Adam all die, even so in Christ shall all be made alive" (1 Corinthians 15:22). However, God's greatest gift—eternal life—will be given only to a comparative few: those who

*This fireside address was given at Brigham Young University on 27 March 1994.*

respond to Jesus' invitation, "Come, follow me" (Luke 18:22). It is this invitation to discipleship about which I will speak tonight. The great gift of the Resurrection, therefore, will be "added upon" by the exaltation inherent in eternal life, which is contingent upon the degree of our discipleship.

Consistent with the lovely invocation tonight, I ask for your hearts as well as your ears, because we will consider some of the deep things of God. Such doctrines of the kingdom should not be treated superficially or lightly, so I ask for your pondering as well as your listening.

When Jesus took upon him the heavy, atoning yoke to redeem all mankind by paying the agonizing price for our sins, he thereby experienced what he himself termed the "fierceness of the wrath of Almighty God" (D&C 76:107). The phrase itself makes the soul tremble. Jesus also volunteered to take upon him additional agony that he might experience and thus know certain things "according to the flesh"; namely, human sicknesses and infirmities and human griefs, including those not associated with sin (Alma 7:11–12). Therefore, as a result of his great atonement, Jesus was filled with unique empathy and with perfect mercy.

In turn, however, he who bore the atoning yoke has asked, "Take my yoke upon you, and learn of me" (Matthew 11:29). So the taking of Jesus' yoke upon us constitutes serious discipleship. I speak especially to those of you who are young, saying to you that there is no greater calling, no greater challenge, and no greater source of joy—both proximate joy and ultimate joy—than is found in the process of discipleship. This process brings its own joys and reassurances. Don't, however, expect the world to understand or to value your discipleship. They will not. In a way, they may admire you from afar, but they will be puzzled about the priorities resulting from your devotion.

Shouldering the yoke of discipleship greatly enhances both our adoration and knowledge of Jesus, because then we experience, first-hand, through our parallel but smaller-scaled experiences, a small but instructive portion of what the Savior experienced. In this precious process, the more we do what Jesus did (allow our wills to be "swallowed up in the will of the Father"), the more we will learn (Mosiah 15:7). This emulation directly enhances our adoration of Jesus.

Simultaneously, in this same process, the more we become like Jesus, the more we come to know him. There may even be, more than we now know, some literalness in his assertion "When ye have done it unto the least of these my brethren, ye have done it unto me" (Matthew 25:40). We lack deep understanding of the implications of that remark of Jesus. As with so many things, he is telling us more than we are now prepared to receive.

But back to submissiveness. The Prophet Joseph Smith, writing redemptively to his rebellious brother William, said, "God requires the will of his creatures, to be swallowed up in his will." The Prophet Joseph then pled with William to make "one tremendious [*sic*] effort [to] overcome [his] passions, and please God" (Dean C. Jessee, comp. and ed., *The Personal Writings of Joseph Smith* [Salt Lake City: Deseret Book, 1984], p. 115). Alas, William didn't do it, just as some of us fail to overcome our passions and thereby fail to "please God." We are too busy pleasing ourselves.

In contrast, meek Enoch reached a point in his discipleship, wrote Paul, when Enoch received a testimony that he pleased God (see Hebrews 11:5). Ponder that, brothers and sisters. One can come to the point where he or she knows that they please God.

One mistake we can make during this mortal experience, especially in an academic setting, is to value knowledge apart from the other qualities to be developed in submissive discipleship. Knowledge is very important. Its discovery, its preservation, its perpetuation is one reason we have this special university. Yet being knowledgeable, by itself, while leaving undeveloped the virtues of love, mercy, meekness, and patience, is not enough for full discipleship. Mere intellectual assent to a truth, if it is unapplied, deprives us of the relevant, personal experiences. It's like hearing a lecture without experiencing a lab. It's like being briefed on a field trip but never taking the field trip. There were probably orientation briefings in the premortal world about how this mortal life would unfold for us, but the real experience is another thing!

Thus, although knowledge is clearly very important, standing alone it cannot save us. I worry sometimes in various Church classes that we get so busy discussing the doctrines that talking about them almost becomes a substitute for applying them! One cannot improve upon the sobering words of King Benjamin, who said, "Now, if you believe all these things see that ye do them" (Mosiah 4:10). Such is still the test. Deeds, not words—and becoming, not describing—are dominant in true discipleship!

Of necessity, of course, we are to teach and learn the doctrines. We would be spiritually stranded without them, and, likewise, without the saving and exalting gospel ordinances, because

*in the ordinances thereof, the power of godliness is manifest.*

*And without the ordinances thereof, and the authority of the priesthood, the power of godliness is not manifest unto men in the flesh.*
[D&C 84:20–21]

So it is that discipleship requires all of us to translate doctrines, covenants, ordinances, and teachings into improved personal behavior. Otherwise, brothers and sisters, we may be doctrinally rich but end up developmentally poor!

The celestial attributes—such as love, patience, mercy, meekness, and submissiveness—embody what we are to become. They are not just a litany of qualities to be recited! Awareness of them—even articulate awareness—without their application will not do. Furthermore, these same attributes cannot be developed in the abstract. The relevant experiences are required, even when you and I would try to avoid them. Moreover, our individual developmental schedules reflect God's timetable, not ours. His timetable, if followed, prepares us incrementally for the journey of discipleship and for going home!

Any serious disciple yearns to go home to Heavenly Father and to be welcomed there by Jesus. But the Prophet Joseph Smith declared we cannot go where they are unless we become more like them in the principles and attributes and character they possess (see *Teachings*, p. 216).

Of the many restored truths, God has surely given us "enough and to spare." Soberingly, however, we have been told that unto whom "much is given much is required" (D&C 82:3). I hope we feel the cutting edge of the word *required.* It is used instead of the milder *expected.* Neither does the Lord say, "It would be nice if . . ." The word is *required,* bringing us back again to the need for submissiveness in discipleship.

The gospel's rich and true doctrines combine to constitute a call to a new and more abundant life, but this is a lengthy process. It requires much time, learning through relevant experiences, keeping covenants, and receiving the essential ordinances—all in order to spur us along the discipleship path of personal progression. In the journey of discipleship we lose our old selves. The natural man and the natural woman are "put off," and then we find ourselves having become more saintly (see Mosiah 3:19). We see such saintliness all about us in the Church—quiet, good women and men, not particularly status-full, who are becoming saintly. This is what should be happening in the lives of members of The Church of Jesus Christ of Latter-day Saints.

There are even some noticeable and helpful tuggings—you and I feel them at times—to remind us who we really are. As eternal beings living very temporarily in time, it is often much more than a whisper that tells us we are strangers here and that our ultimate home is someplace else (see "O My Father," *Hymns,* 1985, no. 292).

Walking and overcoming by faith is not easy. For one thing, the dimension of time constantly constrains our perspective. Likewise, the world steadily tempts us. No wonder we are given instructive words from Jesus about the narrowness and the straightness of the only path available to return home: "I am the way, the truth, and the life" (John 14:6). And then he said, "No man cometh unto the Father, but by me." Jesus laid down strict conditions.

We live in a world in which, happily, many others regard themselves as Christians. Some live rich and marvelous lives. But there are some who style themselves as Christians who admire but do not worship Jesus. Some regard him as a great teacher but not as the Great Redeemer. Yes, Jesus is the generous Lord of the Expansive Universe, but, brothers and sisters, he is also the Lord of the Narrow Path! Some people forget his latter lordship.

The ravines on both sides of that narrow path—which, by the way, has much loose gravel on it—are deep and dangerous. Moreover, until put off, the shifting, heavy, unsettling burden of the natural man tilts us and sways us. It is dangerous.

Nor does the natural man or the natural woman go away quietly or easily. Hence, the most grinding form of calisthenics we will ever know involves the individual isometrics required to put off the natural man. Time and again the new self is pitted against the stubborn old self. Sometimes, at least it's so with me, just when at last we think the job is done, then the old self reminds us that he or she has not fully departed yet.

A vital, personal question for each of us, therefore, is, "Are we steadily becoming what gospel doctrines are designed to help us become?" Or are we merely rich inheritors of an immense treasure trove of truth but poor investors in the process of personal development so essential to discipleship?

Significantly, when the Lord described his purposes by saying, "This is my work and my glory—to bring to pass the immortality and eternal life of man" (Moses 1:39), he used the word *work*, even though his is a "marvelous work." For us, becoming even as Jesus is certainly is work (see 3 Nephi 27:27)! Of necessity, this process requires the cross of discipleship to be taken up daily—not occasionally or seasonally.

Sometimes, as we commence taking up the cross, we ignore or neglect the first part of Jesus' instruction. He said, "Deny [yourselves], and take up [your] cross daily, and follow me" (Luke 9:23). This self-denial is especially challenging in a world filled with so many sensual and secular stimuli. Greed and lust, though they have always been friends, have never formed quite the cartel that they have formed now. It is global. It is profitable.

Denying oneself has never been popular as a lifestyle, and it is clearly not today. Self-denial is portrayed by many as too puritanic and too ascetic. Scoffers in this nation have acquired powerful pulpits from which they bray their message, which constantly puts down discipleship and encourages the natural man to think highly of himself and to please himself.

What is it that we are to deny ourselves? The ascendancy of any appetites or actions that produce not only the seven deadly sins but all the others. Happily, self-denial, when we practice it, brings great relief. It represents emancipation from all the "morning-after" feelings, whether caused by adultery or gluttony. True disciples, being concerned with tomorrow, are very careful about today!

Self-denial also includes not letting our hearts become too set on any trivial or worldly thing. Then we can learn the great lessons about the relationship of righteousness to the powers and the joys of heaven.

There's a lot of talk currently in America about empowerment. Certainly economic and political slavery should concern us, and rightly so, but what of being in bondage in other ways? What of emancipation from the enslavement resulting from so many subtle forms of servitude? Listen to these words of Peter: "For of whom a man is overcome, of the same is he brought in bondage" (2 Peter 2:19). So many different things can overcome and capture us.

The fundamental fact is that if we do not deny ourselves, we are diverted. Even if not wholly consumed with the things of the world, we are still diverted sufficiently to make serious discipleship impossible. As a consequence, all the gifts and talents God has given us are not put meekly on the altar to serve others and to please God. Instead, we withhold to please ourselves. Diversion, therefore, is not necessarily gross transgression, but it is a genuine deprivation— especially if we consider what we might have become and what more we might have done to bless and to help others.

Ironically, brothers and sisters, the natural man who is so very selfish in so many ordinary ways is strangely unselfish in that he reaches for too few of the things that bring real joy. He settles for a mess of pottage instead of eternal joy.

By denying the desires of the natural man (to the degree that these exist in each of us), we avoid this diversion, making it easier for us to take up the cross of discipleship. Of course, when it occurs in our lives, emancipation from various forms of bondage brings no celebrating parades, nor does it make the evening news. But it is big news because we *come off conqueror!*

So it is that discipleship, far from being ascetic, is to choose joy over pleasure. It is to opt for the things of eternity over the trendy and appealing things of the moment. Eventually we become readied for the final moment of consecration, when, gladly and completely, we let our wills be swallowed up in the will of the Father. Jesus did this in Gethsemane and on Calvary: "Not my will, but thine, be done" (Luke 22:42). What was God's will? That Jesus complete the Atonement. Even so, Jesus cried out, "Take away this cup from me" (Mark 14:36), and still later, "My God, my God, why hast thou forsaken me?" (Mark 15:34). Yet Jesus yielded.

Is it possible to develop discipleship when one has no initial, inner desires for discipleship? I don't know. Can we plant inner "desires" in someone against their will? External exhortation of such individuals won't usually produce much change. For most of us, however, even when the inner desire is there, it requires periodic sharpening of some outward circumstances to quicken any existing inner desires and to get us to act upon these. It was so with Abraham. Abraham desired a better life, more happiness, and the blessings of the holy priesthood (see Abraham 1:1-2). Outward circumstances were a spur to Abraham's yearnings, but clearly he had firm and basic desires of discipleship.

It's different in the case of prodigals, in the sense that turning away from the world and toward God, toward home, requires of them to make what I call the Great Pivot. This Great Pivot begins slowly and tentatively when the mind perceives *what is* in comparison with *what might be.* This represents the first tentative steps in the process of beginning to develop "the mind of Christ" (1 Corinthians 2:16).

Regarding the varying degrees of progress we have made in our personal development, ponder, if you will, this bit of imagery. What if, brothers and sisters, our individual lack of inner, spiritual symmetry were somehow visibly reflected in our outward physiology? How odd, swollen, and misshapen, or anemically underdeveloped some of us would appear! All intellect and no heart! Earnest and eager, but without a trace of empathy! Egoistic with not a single sinew of mercy! Fixated on pleasing self with little concern for neighbors. Ciphers as to substance, but perhaps with large, mortal wardrobes. Perhaps this latter condition is the flip side of "Look, the emperor has no clothes," in which one would say, "Look, the clothes have no emperor!" People have so many trappings that cover the absence of substance of a spiritual nature—it's all about us in the world's passing parade: "Princes come and princes go; an hour of pomp, an hour of show" (lyrics from *Kismet*).

Of course, our actual degree of inward, spiritual symmetry is somewhat hidden—at least until we get to know each other and to experience each other! So, the lingering question should not be "How many imperfections do I have?" but, rather, "Is my discipleship sufficiently serious that I am working patiently and steadily to overcome those weaknesses, perhaps even changing some of them into strengths?" (See Ether 12:27.)

Sometimes our outward selves are no better indicators of what we're really like than the mortal résumés that are feverishly circulated in the academic and business worlds. Usually these résumés give little reflection of character or conduct. Similarly, one's bibliographies seldom hint as to what kind of neighbor one actually is.

If, however, discipleship becomes a daily duty, this genuinely helps us in developing our spiritual symmetry and character. We then have much less concern, for instance, with things of the moment. The banter in the cafeteria with peers or at the office round table with colleagues would so reflect, and, likewise, family discussions around the dinner table. We would also be much less concerned with our public image and with what "they" think, being, instead, much more concerned with having Jesus' image in our countenance. The one-upmanship we typically see connected with intellectual prowess and other forms of prowess is opposite to what discipleship calls for. Jesus' aim is to lift us up, not to put us down.

Given all you and I yet lack in our spiritual symmetry and character formation, no wonder God must use so intensively the little time available to develop each of us in this brief, second estate. One's life, therefore, is brevity compared to eternity—like being dropped off by a parent for a day at school. But what a day!

For the serious disciple the resulting urgency means there can be few extended reveries and recesses and certainly no sabbaticals—all this in order to hasten God's relentless remodeling of each of us! Parenthetically, I don't know how it is for you, but though the reveries, the special moments come, they are not extended. Soon the drumroll of events, even difficulties, resumes. There is so much to get done in the brief time we have in this mortal classroom.

Considering what we are, compared with what we have the power to become, should give us great spiritual hope. Think of it this way. There are some very serene, blue lakes on this planet situated in cavities that once were red, belching volcanos. Likewise, there are beautiful, green, tropical mountains formed from ancient, hot extrusions. The parallel transformation of humans is much more remarkable than all of that—much more beautiful and much more everlasting!

So it is, amid the vastness of his creations, God's shaping personalness is felt in the details of our lives—not only in the details of the galaxies and molecules but, much more importantly, in the details of our own lives. Somehow, brothers and sisters, God is providing these individual tutorials for us while, at the same time, he is overseeing cosmic funerals and births—as one earth passes away, so another is born (see Moses 1:38). It is marvelous that he would attend to us so personally in the midst of those cosmic duties.

Are we willing, however, to be significantly remodeled even by his loving hands? Enoch was. He marveled over God's vast creations, but when deeply reassured, he fervently exclaimed, "Yet thou art there." God is ever "there"! (See Moses 7:30.) Significantly, Enoch also exclaimed over three attributes of God's character, declaring that God is just, merciful, and kind forever! You and I are counting on those attributes every day, aren't we! And God's using those qualities to bless us should stir us to develop them to operate in behalf of others.

God is very serious about the joy of his children! Why should we be surprised? God desires us to become more like him so we can go home to him. He is a perfect Father!

Where would we be, in fact, without God's long-suffering? Given the divine sorrow each of us here has caused our God and our Savior, what a divine comfort to know that when we "get it all together," it will be mercifully said, "Behold, he who has repented of his sins, the same is forgiven, and I, the Lord, remember them no more" (D&C 58:42). No more reassuring and important words could be said to any of us than these.

What ineffable love! What stunning patience! How wrenching it would be otherwise, having been resurrected, to be forever wincing over having displeased him. Oh, the marvel of his divine mercy and his plan of happiness!

One day, if we are like Enoch, we will, as the man or the woman of Christ, know that we, too, please God. Discipleship's enlarged capacity to serve will bring enlarged joys. No wonder we read lamentations from the Lord about those who do not accept his invitation to discipleship.

*O Jerusalem, Jerusalem, thou that killest the prophets, and stonest them which are sent unto thee, how often would I have gathered thy children together, even as a hen gathereth her chickens under her wings, and ye would not!* [Matthew 23:37]

Or, from the Book of Mormon:

*O ye fair ones, how could ye have departed from the ways of the Lord! O ye fair ones, how could ye have rejected that Jesus, who stood with open arms to receive you!* [Mormon 6:17]

These lamentations measure the deep love Jesus has for us. They underscore the importance of our accepting his invitation to discipleship.

Even so, Jesus prayed for us and for all of his followers not to be taken "out of the world." But instead, he desires that we might be kept from evil (see John 17:15). We stay in the classroom until school is out, and there appears to be "none other way."

It is left to each of us to balance contentment with what God has allotted to us in life with some divine discontent as to what we are in comparison with what we have the power to become. Discipleship creates this balance on the straight and narrow path.

Only a few of you here will remember the old Popeye cartoons in which he proclaimed self-contentedly, "I yam what I yam, and that's all I yam. I'm Popeye, the sailor man." We are beckoned by a very different call—by the Master who asks us to become "even as I am" (3 Nephi 27:27).

Though most of you are young, I continue to be heartened by how far along so many of you already are in your discipleship for your age. I mingle with you, hear about you, and sometimes counsel you. In these and other ways I become aware of your quiet, spiritual triumphs.

An example would be these next words that were spoken recently by the husband of just a little over one year of Jennifer Cracroft Lewis. Her funeral was held here in Provo several months ago. Though grieving over his wife of such a short season, Brother Lewis spoke at the funeral with composure as well as courage:

*I have a testimony of this gospel. I know that the ordinances in the temple that I have partaken of with Jennifer are eternal. This gospel is so great that I will be with her again and I will hold her flesh again as she is resurrected. I have a testimony of this Church, and Jennifer has a testimony of this Church which she bore with me, that Jesus is the Christ. . . . He was resurrected as we will be.*

He continued, saying,

*One of our favorite songs, which we will now sing as a congregation, was "Called to Serve." I believe, as the scriptures have pointed out, that Jennifer, one of the best missionaries I ever had a chance to witness, is called to further service. She has been called home to preach the gospel to those who have not yet received it. I ask that this song be sung with meaning.*

Then, as invited, we all sang "Called to Serve." Weeping and singing were several of Jennifer's missionary companions and her mission president and his wife. I always love to hear that song sung, but I've never heard it sung like that before! Not far from here, on a new headstone, are these words: "Jennifer Cracroft Lewis, September 13, 1968–January 26, 1994, Called to Serve."

This is emblematic of the strength I see and feel in so many of you. God's work here does proceed—here and on the other side of the veil, where those like Jennifer continue to "build up" the kingdom.

Discipleship turns on our spiritual sensitivities. It increases the "aliveness" in each of us. These sensitivities are enhanced, not diminished, with discipleship. It is part of what the scriptures call becoming "alive in Christ because of our faith" (2 Nephi 25:25). In contrast, there's a dullness and a sameness about sin. With discipleship we learn to "act for ourselves," rather than merely letting ourselves be "acted upon" by circumstances.

One of the dangers we face in discipleship is drifting. This can occur when we become "wearied and faint in [our] minds," to use Paul's phrase (Hebrews 12:3). This is one of the tragedies of failing to be serious disciples—not that we become necessarily wicked, but, rather, that those who drift merely exist; they are not truly alive.

No wonder the doctrines must be kept pure. No wonder they must be taught again and again! Furthermore, some doctrines, like faith and repentance, are both principles and also vital processes. Other important doctrines, like dispensationalism, for instance, inform and instruct us, but these do not necessarily develop us personally.

Paul warns those of us on the path of discipleship to be diligent, "lest any root of bitterness springing up trouble you" (Hebrews 12:15). Travel on the straight and narrow path occurs in company with other disciples, imperfect as we all are. Side by side, as we all are, means that there are ways in which we can become offended or even embittered. Given the imperfections of all of us in the Church, offenses will come and disappointments will occur. How we handle these is so crucial. We must be quick to prune any personal sprig of bitterness so that our wills can be truly swallowed up in the will of the Father. When we put off the natural man and the natural woman, we put off jealousy, resentment, and self-pity.

Now, may I close on a personal note to illustrate a dimension of discipleship. Regarding you as graduate students, not as lower-division students, in discipleship, I will speak to you about something we don't usually speak about in the Church.

We sometimes speak of defining moments. These defining moments in our lives usually focus on single episodes that can sometimes be outwardly, as well as inwardly, quite traumatic. Yet these defining moments are usually preceded by small, subtle preparatory moments. Moreover, the defining moments are also followed by many smaller moments that are shaped by the preceding and defining moments.

Here's an illustration. In a long ago May, in 1945, there was such a moment for me on the island of Okinawa at age eighteen. There was certainly no heroism on my part, but, rather, a blessing for me and others during the shelling of our position by Japanese artillery. After repeated shellings that overshot our position, their artillery finally zeroed in. They should have then fired for effect, but there was a divine response to at least one frightened, selfish prayer. The shelling halted. The prayer was accompanied by my pledge of a lifetime of service—a pledge that, though imperfectly, I've tried to keep. With this blessing and pledge, I was nudged toward discipleship without realizing what service would be required. I knew I had been blessed, and I knew that God knew that I knew. I remembered the pledge after the war when my overseas savings gladly went to finance a mission. This mission, of course, was yet another step in the direction of discipleship.

Now, having described for you that defining moment, I want to certify to many subsequent and subtle moments that are at least as important. Unlike the roar and crash of artillery, followed by a delivering silence, these smaller moments involve the Lord's periodic whisperings to my mind. Over the years, and even on this very day, these guide me. They reassure me. They give me, from time to time, in the words of the Prophet Joseph, "sudden strokes of ideas" and, occasionally, the pure flow of intelligence (see *Teachings*, p. 151). These moments are as real for me as what happened on Okinawa. These are inward things, often taking the form of a directing phrase or even a one-liner. I have found with experience what I think you will find: The Lord gives more instructions than he gives explanations.

Probably ten years ago I received a letter from a sensitive and thoughtful missionary in the MTC, asking if I would write his companion a letter of encouragement because his companion was determined to quit and go home, having trouble with the language. Because my secretary was absent, I put the letter down on my desk and thought to myself, "I'll send a letter down in a couple of days."

The Spirit said, "Write the letter now."

I borrowed a secretary, who kindly typed as I dictated. I signed the letter, and I said, "I don't know what's going on, but please go mail this letter right now."

Several days later, another letter came from the MTC from the same earnest companion who had written me before, saying in effect,

*Dear Brother Maxwell:*

*I think you ought to know what happened today. My companion had his bags packed. He was having his exit interview. I went to sit in the outer office and said, "Please, Heavenly Father, let that letter come today," and then I ran down to where the missionaries get the mail, and there it was. I ran back up and knocked on the door and dropped the letter in his lap and said, "I think you ought to read this before you go home." Dear Brother Maxwell, my companion stayed.*

Now, what if I had waited a day? Too late. Promptings often come in short, crisp phrases, impressing upon us a certain duty. They come in other ways to each of us. We know what's happening to us, but we don't know all the implications of it. But God knows. It's a sacred process. We know more than we can tell other people—not only for reasons of confidentiality but for what I will call "contextuality." Those who are not a part of the process are not likely to value and understand its significance. They're not apt to appreciate fully.

The whole process of subtle inspiration and revelation is like this metaphor: An inspired painter working on a large canvas does not report to or ask patrons or friends to react to each brushstroke. Nor does he exclaim after each stroke of his paintbrush well before the canvas reflects any emerging pattern. Yet each stroke the painter registers on the canvas is a part of an inspired whole. Without those cumulative, individual strokes, there would be no painting. But each stroke, if examined by itself, is not likely to be appreciated by itself, least of all by those who stand outside the process, outside of the contextuality.

Our personal spiritual experiences are much like this. They are personal. They are spiritual. Often they are not sharable. Some may be, but it takes inspiration to know when to share them. I recall hearing President Marion G. Romney, who combined wit and wisdom, say, "We'd have more spiritual experiences if we didn't talk so much about them."

So we ponder discipleship tonight. Be assured that God is "in the details" and in the subtleties of the defining moments and the preparatory moments. He will reassure you. He will remind you. Sometimes, if you're like me, he will sometimes reprove you in a highly personal process not understood or appreciated by those outside the context.

In the revelations the Lord speaks of how the voice of his spirit will be felt in our minds. For me, the message is not a whole discourse, but a phrase or a sentence. The Lord says also if we read his words, meaning the scriptures, we will hear his voice. Many here have had private moments of pondering and reading the scriptures when the words "come through" in a clear, clarion way. We know Who it is speaking to us! We've all had the experience of going over a scripture many times without having it register. Then, all of a sudden, we're ready to receive it! We hear the voice of the Lord through his words. So it is in the process of discipleship. There are more meaningful moments than we use profitably, just as in terms of Christian service there are more opportunities around us than we now use. God is ever ready, if only we were always ready.

Brigham Young taught, "There is not a single condition of life that is entirely unnecessary; there is not one hour's experience but what is beneficial to all those who make it their study, and aim to improve upon the experience they gain" (*JD 9:292*). I hope we realize that. We may fritter away our time, but life is always drenched with more opportunities for discipleship than we use. Therefore, all the minutes and the hours and the moments can be, at least incrementally, defining moments.

As one wisely considers the reality of the years, the days, and the moments available to each of us, instead of discipleship being a hectic, anxious thing, it actually causes us to be more calm, more meek and trusting, and more open to God's tutoring of each of us.

He is "in the details" of your lives. He knows you perfectly, just as Jesus knew the woman of Samaria whom he quizzed as to her belief in the Messiah. She said, "I know that Messias cometh . . . : when he is come, he will tell us all things."

And Jesus said, "I that speak unto thee am he."

And she went back to her village all excited and said she'd found the Messiah, and then, significantly, she said to the villagers, "He told me all that ever I did." (See John 4:25–26, 39–42.)

God knows you perfectly. He loves you perfectly. His Only Begotten Son, Jesus, has asked you, "Come, follow me." Thus, in a real and majestic sense, each of us here tonight has been "called to serve"! Of this I testify, in the holy name of Jesus Christ. Amen!

# "Brim with Joy" (Alma 26:11)

Neal A. Maxwell

What a delightful and moving musical presentation! Thank you so very much, choir, for blessing us all so abundantly with your talents. I am grateful, as always, to be privileged to stand at this pulpit.

Each time I have been anxious about rising to the occasion, as I am now. Even though President and Sister Bateman have been welcomed formally, I add my welcome as they assume their duties.

I am so grateful, as you will hear me say in the text of this speech, for a part of mortality that we sometimes overlook: the intertwinings of our lives. I acknowledge the Lord's hand in these intersections. Some here have heard me say that one of the reasons we love each other in the kingdom is that our friendships are not friendships of initiation at all but are, instead, friendships of resumption!

I mention with regard to President and Sister Bateman several intersectings of our lives, beginning in 1975, when President Oaks asked if I would do what I could to influence Dr. Merrill Bateman to take a deanship at Brigham Young University. I found him in Europe,

*This devotional address was given at Brigham Young University on 23 January 1996.*

where he was traveling for an international corporation. I told him it was not a Church call, but that we would be blessed if he would accept, which, happily, he did. He has been such a great friend ever since. Later, I was privileged to be with him and Sister Bateman several times in Japan as they presided over the Asia North Area, providing more intersectings of our lives. Then I watched him perform so well as Presiding Bishop of the Church. In the parlance of management, Merrill is a "quick study"; he does things so well, so quickly. He has the capacity to touch people deeply and quickly.

I am so grateful for these intertwinings of our lives. I could say the same with regard to Elder Eyring. The manner in which our lives have intersected has been such a great blessing to me, and it is likewise so with Bruce Hafen and with so many more. It is a marvelous thing when the Lord gives us these experiences, and, of course, you have them as well.

It should not surprise us, brothers and sisters, that Heavenly Father brings about these intersectings and intertwinings of our lives. So often (after something is over) we will say, "little did I realize" or "I had no way of knowing" in referring to these intersectings. But why should we be surprised? Each of us has circles of friendships, and within those lie the portion of the human family whom God has given us to love, to serve, and to learn from. Hence I feel so blessed to have learned from the Eyrings, the Batemans, the Hafens, and so many others who are here today—both on the stand and in the audience.

Within each of our circles of friendship there lie so many unused opportunities to love, to serve, and to be taught. Indeed, one could apply the scriptural phrase about there being "enough and to spare" (D&C 104:17). None of us ever fully utilizes the people-opportunities allocated to us within our circles of friendship. You and I may call these intersectings "coincidence." This word is understandable for mortals to use, but *coincidence* is not an appropriate word to describe the workings of an omniscient God. He does not do things by "coincidence" but instead by "divine design."

I am one who likes to know of happy ironies and happy intersectings. There are many intersectings, of course, that are not happy. I will mention an episode to you now of which you probably do not know, nor did I until recently.

In 1855 Abraham Lincoln, then a lawyer in Illinois, was asked to participate in a patent infringement case involving McCormick, of reaper fame. Lincoln had been given a $400 retainer and was told he might actually argue the case, so he studied and went to Cincinnati for the trial. A lead lawyer in the case was a man named Edwin M. Stanton—a brilliant Pittsburgh lawyer—who said when Lincoln arrived, "Why did you bring that . . . long armed Ape here . . . ; he does not know any thing and can do you no good" (David Herbert Donald, *Lincoln* [New York: Simon and Schuster, 1995], pp. 185–187). Lincoln stayed at the same hotel as Stanton and the other attorneys, but he was never even asked to eat or to confer with them. Lincoln went home feeling insulted and "roughly handled by that man Stanton" (Donald, *Lincoln*, p. 187).

The years tumbled on, and later Stanton was to join the cabinet of the newly elected president, Abraham Lincoln. There were differences of views, of course, but Stanton came to deeply admire Abraham Lincoln. After the shooting of Lincoln, a few, including Stanton, stood mournfully by his bed as Lincoln was in the process of dying. When Lincoln died, Stanton, who had once described Lincoln as "an Ape," paid tribute to his fallen chief:

> *With a slow and measured movement,* [Stanton's] *right arm fully extended as if in a salute, he raised his hat and placed it for an instant on his head and then in the same deliberate manner removed it. "Now," he said, "he belongs to the ages."* [Donald, *Lincoln*, p. 599]

Would that all rough relationships could have that kind of resolution and generous ending.

Now to my focus today, which will be on the joys and advantages of gospel living, including the place of intertwinings. The focus is on joy, brothers and sisters, because sometimes at your ages we may seem to emphasize the seemingly stern gospel requirements without consistently and helpfully identifying the joys, the blessings, and the advantages of gospel living—both here and now and in the there and then.

I do not mean to imply that the pursuit of all terrestrial objectives is useless and joyless. We can, in pursuing terrestrial objectives, have "joy for a season." Some of the commandments of men, though lesser commandments, may, at times, be aligned with certain gospel values and principles. But keeping the commandments of men is not going to bring us a fullness of joy. In fact, we cannot expect to have a fullness of joy in this life until, as the scriptures inform us, the body and spirit are "inseparably connected" (D&C 93:33). But we can still have much joy and much happiness in life. In fact, God is delighted when His children keep His commandments because then His children are truly happy! And He wants us to be happy. After all, His plan is called "the plan of happiness." Conversely, on occasion, God weeps over the needless suffering of His children (see Moses 7:28, 32–33, 37).

The joys that might have been given to ancient Israel, for instance, evoked Jesus' wrenching lamentation "O Jerusalem" (Matthew 23:37). He offered to ancient Israel more than they were prepared to claim; they were content to live far below their privileges.

As we speak of joy, it is important for us to realize what I recall reading somewhere: "God is serious about joy." Joy is the essence of what He would have us experience.

I continue by asking you a rhetorical question: "What are you actually and specifically deprived of by serious gospel living?"

Ponder these several examples. By complying with the revealed Word of Wisdom, you are much more likely to be deprived of lung cancer, and surely deprived of becoming an alcoholic. You are much more likely to miss out on AIDS if you keep the seventh commandment and refuse to use drugs.

Before you die, my young brothers and sisters, you will thank Heavenly Father many times for the advantages of abstinence! Regarding certain destructive things, abstinence is so much easier than moderation! Meanwhile, you will see those about you who are surfing life's pleasures indulgently. They will eventually crash against the reefs of reality.

By responding to the strong gospel emphasis on education, you will also be deprived of being ignorant.

You will be deprived of that large dose of human despair that "cometh because of iniquity" (Moroni 10:22). You will also miss out on the exhausting and finally futile calisthenics of trying to mold a meaningful morality by using the Play-Doh of permissiveness. It just won't work!

Yes, you will be tested and puzzled, but because of your faith in God's plan of salvation, you will thereby be deprived of cynicism, that corrosive emotion that relentlessly expresses itself in a hundred different ways. By having faith in Heavenly Father's plan of salvation, you will be inspired not only to keep the law of chastity, but you will be able to cope with adversity.

Obviously, you could easily add many more examples of what may for the moment seem to be deprivations that are actually great benefactions, greater than you can now fully appreciate!

I depart from my text to give you an example of the blessings that flow from simple faith in the plan of salvation. About three and a half years ago a young mother, Vicki Nichols, came to my office. Something I had written had apparently helped her, and she wondered if she could visit. As the conversation began, she told me that her husband had recently died of a brain tumor, leaving her with four children. I began to bestow expressions of sympathy, but she, being strong, said, "Brother Maxwell, I am handling that, but I just learned that I, too, have cancer, and I wonder what is going to happen to our four precious children." She is a woman of great faith, strong intellectually, strong spiritually! Sister Maxwell and I felt it a great privilege to be in touch with her from time to time in the intervening several years during which the Lord gave Vicki some prolongation of her time for the nurturing and preparation of those four children. Several days before she died, I called her in Spokane. By now her voice was very weak. She said something like, "You will understand how wrenching the prospect is of my leaving the four children," expressing the kind of feelings that only a loving mother could have. However, because she understands the plan of salvation, Vicki said, "Brother Maxwell, can I tell you something? I am so torn at the prospect of prolonged separation from my children, but I want you to know that, nevertheless, I have a sense of anticipation about going through the veil of death." It was a privilege to speak a few days later at Vicki's funeral. The oldest of her children, Traci, is about sixteen, a wonderful daughter. As related to and remembered by me, soon after Vicki died, the oldest daughter gathered together her three siblings and they talked about their mother and the gospel's plan of salvation. What a simple, yet powerful act of faith!

There is no adversity that can set aside God's plan of salvation. It is an immense blessing to know about the plan, to believe in it, and to have faith in it.

The advantages of abstention have been referred to already. Consider, however, the devout Jewish rabbi, Harold Kushner, who was once chided because he abstained from eating pork. He turned the tables on his enquirers and said, "Isn't it incredible? There are five billion people on this planet, and God cares what I have for lunch" (Rabbi Harold S. Kushner, "The Human Soul's Quest for God," *Brigham Young Magazine*, February 1995, p. 26). With your knowledge of the expansive plan of salvation, you could say, "Yes, the God of 'worlds without number' cares about what each of us on this tiny planet says and does, including how we treat our parents, our friends, and our roommates."

A major point about joy is that joy is obviously of a higher order than mere pleasure. Pleasure is perishable. It has a short shelf life. Mere pleasure is not lasting because it is constantly feeding on itself. Thus the appetites of the natural man, though frequently fed, are never filled. For instance, even as gluttony digests its latest glob, it begins anticipating its next meal. The same pattern prevails with regard to the praise of men, to lust, and to greed. Strange as it seems, so far as the carnal pleasures are concerned, the very act of their consumption insures the cancellation of their satisfactions. They just do not last!

Joy, on the other hand, is lasting. It involves the things that really matter, such as being forgiven and forgiving another. One true test of ultimate value has to do with whether or not something is lasting. Of so many human endeavors, even those celebrated with great excitement, the child's question in one of Southey's poems stands as a stark reminder: "But what good came of it at last?" (Robert Southey, *The Battle of Blenheim* [1798], st. 11). This criterion is not one to which the things of the flesh can successfully respond.

The carnal pleasures cannot finally deliver. In fact, there is a scripture in the Book of Mormon declaring that the adversary lets his followers down at the last day (see Alma 30:60). He can't finally deliver. It is Jesus who is the Great Deliverer!

No wonder, therefore, the pleasurable things of the day and the things of the moment—such as having political power and social sway—are so fleeting. They are unrelated to true joy and to the everlasting things. Mere popularity, for instance, is not only transitory, it can also be dangerous. Wise President N. Eldon Tanner cautioned us, "This craving for praise and popularity too often controls actions, and as [people] succumb they find themselves bending their character when they think they are only taking a bow" (N. Eldon Tanner, "For They Loved the Praise of Men More Than the Praise of God," *Ensign*, November 1975, p. 76). A wise and special man!

Sometimes, therefore, it is wrong to belong:

*Nevertheless among the chief rulers also many believed on* [Christ]; *but because of the Pharisees they did not confess him, lest they should be put out of the synagogue:*

*For they loved the praise of men more than the praise of God.* [John 12:42–43]

The synagogue, of course, is a metaphor for any lesser, mortal belonging that can divert or dilute our efforts, first of all, to build up the kingdom of God (see JST, Matthew 6:38).

I like the way Malcolm Muggeridge spoke of his changing perspective:

*Now, the prospect of death overshadows all others. I am like a man on a sea voyage nearing his destination. When I embarked I worried about having a cabin with a porthole,* [and] *whether I should be asked to sit at the captain's table, who were the more attractive and important passengers. All such considerations become pointless* [because now] *I shall soon be disembarking.* [Malcolm Muggeridge, *Things Past*, ed. Ian Hunter (New York: Morrow, 1979), p. 166]

One of the great blessings the gospel gives us is the lens through which we can see with proportion. Special perspective comes from the marvelous and overarching principles of the gospel.

For some reason, the last month or so, my mind has turned to a colleague of many years ago at the University of Utah. Dr. Reed Merrill was a distinguished educational psychologist. He had, for instance, done pioneering work in establishing the process of licensure associated with clinical psychology, as well as important work in educational psychology. However, he had been inactive in the Church and inattentive to spiritual things, though a good person. Then, in the early 1980s he was stirred spiritually by the Lord. I could see it when he came to visit me twice. He wrote two powerful letters regarding the comparative emptiness of his secular discipline with the fullness of the gospel of Jesus Christ. These observations meant a lot because they came from a man of unquestioned intellect and integrity. Other catalytic things were happening, unbeknownst to me, including his daughter's service on a mission, to say nothing of a wonderful wife.

Reed called me sometime before his daughter's sealing, asking if I would perform her sealing. I said, "I would be delighted." I think I had an intervening trip overseas, but asked, "Reed, will you be there?"

With his typical integrity, he said, "Neal, you know me well enough to know I won't be there unless I am fully worthy to be there." When the morning came for the sealing in the Salt Lake Temple, I waited with particular anticipation. Then Reed came down the corridor of the temple. We embraced, and he said, "Neal, I made it!" He had come home! Subsequently, he taught in his high priests group and in various classes. It was a spiritual renaissance in his life, a marvelous thing to see. How wonderful it is when anybody comes home!

Yesterday, when I reviewed my handwritten notes used ten years ago at Reed's funeral, they included words of gratitude for what I called, even back then, "the intersections of our lives"—Reed's and mine. The most important thing to be said about Reed Merrill when he departed from this life was that he exited "in spiritual crescendo." Such things bring joy!

Some of what has preceded has been related to the natural human desire you and I have to belong and to have people notice and care. My plea is not to downplay that basic fundamental need, because it is there for a reason. Instead, I ask you to distinguish between belonging in a proximate way and belonging in an ultimate way. One can, for instance, belong to a churning, changing group in an airport transit lounge. Yet this is not belonging. One can, instead, begin to sense that he or she belongs to God and that we are part of something that is very, very special and very, very large. This is another great blessing that comes from the gospel that gives us perspective.

If you and I were left, instead, to draw conclusions or generalizations from our small, personal databases, we would not be very wise. But we can access the divine database through the scriptures and prophetic utterances, acquiring perspective about "things as they really are" (Jacob 4:13). Otherwise, our generalizations won't be worth much more than the one I encountered years ago: "All Indians walk single file, at least the one I saw did!" We can end up being so provincial and so parochial. I love these lines from G. K. Chesterton, the brilliant Catholic writer:

*How much larger your life would be if* [you] *could become smaller in it. . . . You would begin to be interested in* [others]. *You would break out of this tiny . . . theatre in which your own little plot is always being played, and you would find yourself under a freer sky, in a street full of splendid strangers.*

[G. K. Chesterton, *Orthodoxy* (Garden City, New York: Image Books, 1959), pp. 20–21]

The gospel tells us who those "splendid strangers" are. It gives us a sense not only of the immensity and the vastness of God's work, but also of the great personalness of His work as well.

Since a real sense of belonging does matter, one of the great things you and I can do for family and friends is to contribute regularly to their storehouses of self-esteem by giving deserved and specific commendations and encouragement.

Another thing we can do when we see the chaff in the lives of friends (as compared with the worthy kernel of their characters) is, "with the breath of kindness," blow the chaff away.

What is interesting is that joy has a way of renewing itself, and the ripple effects of joy are constant and ever emanating; joy has a momentum of its own.

Another great advantage of joy, contrasted with pleasure, is that joy overrides routine, which, otherwise, could make us bored. We don't know, for instance, how many times Heavenly Father has been through the plan of salvation before with other of His children elsewhere before our particular sequence on this planet. God even hints at the repetitiveness of His redemption when He says, "[My] course is one eternal round" (see 1 Nephi 10:19; Alma 7:20; D&C 3:2). Yet God is never bored by what might seem mere routine. Why? Because of His perfect love for His children! What He calls "my work and my glory" brings abundant and pure joy! (see Moses 1:39).

Therefore, because God loves us, He seeks with such vigor and long-suffering to separate us from our sins, which He hates! This process of separation is one reason why much of the pain and suffering must be borne, a necessary thing if we would share in His ultimate joy.

A fascinating thing about joy and love, with which you are surely familiar, is that when we enlarge our capacity to love, other people become real individuals, not merely functions. Gospel duties cease to be mere routine and become, instead, doors to delight. Every doctrine of the gospel is a door to delight that, when opened, exposes us to a vista of things we have not yet fully comprehended.

I love Brigham Young and am grateful this university bears his name. Hear what he says about love:

> There is one virtue, attribute, or principle, which, if cherished and practised by the Saints, would prove salvation to thousands upon thousands. I allude to charity, or love, from which proceed forgiveness, long-suffering, kindness, and patience. [*JD* 7:133–34]

A marvelous insight!

Charity initiates and sustains all the other spiritual qualities in much the same way that courage sustains these qualities at the testing point.

There was a time, however, in the earlier life of Brigham Young, when he was not so insightful or articulate. Before he joined the Church, being untouched by the restored gospel, Brigham was apparently somewhat discouraged about life. As a young man he disapproved of much of what he saw in the world; he wondered what life held for him. Then his loving brother, Phineas, gave Brigham some prescient counsel: "Hang on, [Brigham], for I know the Lord is agoing to do something for us" (sermon of Heber C. Kimball in minutes, 8 January 1845, Brigham Young Papers, Historical Department, The Church of Jesus Christ of Latter-day Saints). Did he ever! The rest is Moses-like history!

In the process of his personal development, Brigham had to be patient and submissive. As a result, he harvested and then gave to us so many insights, some of which are stunning, including the one I shall now read, as if he were speaking to each of us here today:

> When the Latter-day Saints make up their minds to endure, for the kingdom of God's sake, whatsoever shall come, whether poverty or riches, whether sickness or to be driven by mobs, they will say it is all right, and [they] will honor the hand of the Lord in it, and in all things, and serve Him to the end of their lives, according to the best of their ability. . . . If

*you have not made up your minds for this, the quicker you do so the better.*
[*JD* 1:338; emphasis added]

You can see Brigham's soul enlarged "without hypocrisy" and his intellectual and spiritual stretching in the powerful insights he shared so generously with us. Brigham Young's joy was not at the mercy of men or circumstance. Likewise, you and I need to be able to utter those words "it is all right." Even when we are confronted with things we cannot fully understand, we can know that God does understand and that He loves us. Brigham's example helps us to appreciate the need not to be too much at the mercy of our moods or too much at the mercy of circumstances.

Another thing about joy: Joy not only helps us do our gospel duties but it increases our individuality. It is sinners who reflect such a stale sameness. Righteousness lends itself to individuality. Think, in contrast, of poor Lemuel, who "hearkened unto the words of Laman" (1 Nephi 3:28). He was Laman's satellite. One wonders if poor Lemuel ever had any thoughts of his own.

As we see righteousness in someone like Brigham Young or Eliza Snow, then we see a flowering of individuality and an immense use of talents and integrity. But we have to be patient and educate our desires. As President Joseph F. Smith counseled:

*God's ways of educating our desires are, of course, always the most perfect. . . . And what is God's way? Everywhere in nature we are taught the lessons of patience and waiting. We want things a long time before we get them, and the fact that we wanted them a long time makes them all the more precious when they come. In nature we have our seedtime and harvest; and if children were taught that the desires that they sow may be reaped by and by through patience and labor, they will learn to appreciate whenever a long-looked-for goal has been reached. Nature resists us and keeps admonishing us to wait; indeed, we are compelled to wait.* [*GD*, pp. 297–98]

Our patience, brothers and sisters, is the flip side of God's long-suffering. The more our desires, therefore, become like the Lord's, the greater will be our joy.

We will also avoid the problem Paul cited of members who fainted in their minds and who grew weary. We have a special promise concerning how to avoid getting weary intellectually. The Doctrine and Covenants says if we are faithful and if we will share the gospel, we "shall not be weary in mind" (D&C 84:80). What a great blessing! We avoid weariness. We avoid boredom. These are more of the many advantages of the gospel.

When Nephi was reactivating people, he was commended for his unwearyingness (see Helaman 10:4). But his unwearyingness reflected the joy he had in the significant labor he was performing. As Nephi regenerated others, he renewed himself! Likewise, when you and I extend genuine empathy to someone else, we are emancipated from the full weight of our own cares. Then our souls, too, are enlarged without hypocrisy. Heavenly Father is anxious to give us "all" that He has. He delights to honor His commandment keepers, but He can only give us blessings based upon our obedience to the principles upon which they are predicated.

One way of looking at the "thou shalt not" commandments, therefore, is that these are prohibitions which help us avoid misery by turning us away from that which is wrong. Once we become settled in terms of the direction in which we face, and once the telestial sins are left behind, the focus then falls upon the sins of omission. Committing these robs us of joy.

Our Heavenly Father accentuates the development of what are presently neglected taste buds of our souls. Just as important are the taste buds that have been burned over by sin. He desires that we regenerate these, because they will give us joy.

Another thing God does is emancipate us from our provinciality, as noted earlier. Then, to use the prophetic words of scripture, we come to consider things that we "never considered" before (D&C 101:94). This emancipation gives us perspective.

I have often tried to describe, though feeling inarticulate, how the gospel creates excitement in us. In that connection may I share this attempt with you?

*No wonder, given its intellectual expansiveness, we are still inventorying the harvest basket of the Restoration! Having dashed about the wonder-filled landscape of the Restoration, exclaiming and observing, it should not surprise us if some of our first impressions prove to be more childish than definitive. Brushing against such tall timber, the scent of pine is inevitably upon us. Our pockets are filled with souvenir cones and colorful rocks, and we are filled with childish glee. There is no way to grasp it all. Little wonder some of us mistake a particular tree for the whole of the forest, or that in our exclamations there are some unintended exaggerations. We have seen far too much to describe. Indeed, we "cannot say the smallest part which [we] feel"* (Alma 26:16).

Such is my inadequate way of saying to you how I feel about the excitement and the expansiveness of the gospel and the joy that it brings, especially when individuals are becoming the men and women of Christ. You are in that process. Heavenly Father doesn't want us, as His spirit sons and daughters, to be mere automatons, dutifully jumping over what seem to be arbitrary hurdles. Instead, He wants us, His children, being empowered to choose for ourselves, to choose joy instead of misery.

Joy will come in a thousand ways—when we see a relationship mended or enriched as between spouses and siblings and friends. The apostle John understood all this and wrote, "I have no greater joy than to hear that my children walk in truth" (3 John 1:4). Children who walk in truth can access the Spirit; they can receive personal revelation.

In closing I tell you of an experience illustrative of the principle just noted, as I recall its being described to me. In 3 Nephi 26:14, meek Jesus, the Resurrected Lord of the Universe, lets children teach their parents greater things than He, Jesus, had taught their parents.

NEAL A. MAXWELL **269**

This occurred through the process of revelation. It is a verse that I hope you will read.

Around a year ago, Dan and Nan Barker in Arizona, who had been blessed to adopt four children, had their three-year-old boy say, "Mommy, there's another little girl who is supposed to come to our family."

The mother said, in effect, "We're already so blessed to have all of you."

The boy continued, "She has dark hair and dark eyes. And she lives a long way from here."

The mother asked, "How do you know this?"

To which the boy replied, "Jesus told me, upstairs."

To which the mother said, "We don't have any upstairs."

The parents, being taught by the child, got in touch with an international adoption agency. Several months ago, Sister Maxwell and I were privileged to be in the sealing room of the Salt Lake Temple. There, sealed to Nan and Dan Barker, was a little girl with dark hair and dark eyes from Kazakhstan in the former Soviet Union.

Revelation is one of the great realities of gospel living, and it is so productive of joy.

For so many reasons, therefore, I am not surprised that Brigham Young would say, "If you want to enjoy exquisitely, become a Latter-day Saint, and then live the doctrine of Jesus Christ" (*JD* 18:247).

The phrase "alive in Christ" describes individuals whose aliveness is enhanced by their righteousness. We are the most joyful when we are the most alive. And Jesus, because He was the most empathic, most loving, most forgiving, and the most appreciative individual to ever live on this planet, has a perfect fullness of joy. No wonder He instructs us, "What manner of men [and women] ought ye to be? Verily I say unto you, even as I am" (3 Nephi 27:27). He wants us to have great joy. No wonder, too, His lamentation "O Jerusalem" was so stark and sad.

When we reach a point of consecration, our afflictions will be swallowed up in the joy of Christ. It does not mean we won't have afflictions, but they will be put in a perspective that permits us to deal with them. With our steady pursuit of joy and with each increasing measure of righteousness, we will experience one more drop of delight—one drop after another—until, in the words of a prophet, our hearts are "brim with joy" (Alma 26:11). At last, the soul's cup finally runs over!

May you be sufficiently committed to be "alive in Christ," even in the turbulent last days in which you will live. For, indeed, whatsoever afflictions you may have, they can be "swallowed up in the joy of Christ" (Alma 31:38). Then you will be able to say with Brigham Young, even though things perplex and vex you even beyond your capacity to resolve them at times, "It is all right." Thereby you will be acknowledging the hand of God. For His hand is a loving hand, stretched out to love and to lead us, if we will, into a fullness of joy. Of this joy that awaits us, I testify in the name of Jesus Christ. Amen!

# The Pathway of Discipleship

———◆———

Neal A. Maxwell

Thanks to all of you for coming to your various assembly points tonight. I feel deeply touched by what has been said and even more by your presence and what you represent. I am not able to respond adequately to the outpouring of love and faith in my behalf except to try to be better and do better. I want you to know how deeply appreciative I am of that love and those expressions of faith in my behalf.

I am pleased Elder Henry B. Eyring could be here. He is serving as commissioner of Church education, and it will be under his leadership, in my opinion, that the Church Educational System will become even more of a system than it has ever been in the past. The two phrases that come to mind from scriptures are "knit together" as never before and "fitly framed together" as never before (see Colossians 2:2, Mosiah 18:21, Ephesians 2:21).

For Brother Stan Peterson, who watches over our wonderful seminary and institute system, I express deep appreciation. It is, in my judgment, one of the two or three most effective programs in the

*This fireside address was given at BYU on 4 January 1998.*

entire Church. I am grateful President Bateman is here and for his wonderful leadership of a wonderful university. He will be part of this knitting together in ways that will yet have to be determined, but it will be a special thing.

I am delighted Sister Janet Lee is here tonight. She is the gallant wife, as you know, of our valiant President Rex Lee, a special man.

These wonderful stake presidents and their wives on the stand represent so many stake presidencies throughout the Church who love the youth and young adults of the Church in special ways. I am grateful to be in their midst.

I take note of the fact that Sister Maxwell and I were privileged to meet at the University of Utah Institute of Religion. What a special day it was for me to meet her. I must confess I can't tell you what the lesson was that day, but I will always be grateful for that blessing, among the many, that the Church Educational System has given to me. Colleen has been wonderful as a nurturer and as an encourager—in the last year in particular.

So tonight as we are bound together by the satellite system, let that be symbolic of how we are bound together in the entire Church Educational System and, even more, in the increasingly expansive brotherhood and sisterhood of the kingdom of God on the earth. So let us focus tonight on our shared discipleship amid this shared mortal experience—a subject dear to my heart and about which I know a little more than I did a year ago.

When striving disciples reflect deeply upon this mortal experience, certain realities become even more clear. This includes a clarifying and particular reality, which is my theme for tonight: We are immortal individuals whose constant challenge is to apply immortal principles to life's constantly changing situations. Seen in this way, life's varied situations are more sharply defined. With this perspective we can improve our daily performances because we have fixed our gaze on eternity and its great realities.

Though we share immortality, our individual traits, talents, trials, opportunities, and circumstances vary widely. Even so, it is ever the case that whatever the particular, passing mortal situation, all of the individuals involved are immortals with immense possibilities. C. S. Lewis put this so well when he said:

*It is in the light of these overwhelming possibilities, it is with the awe and the circumspection proper to them, that we should conduct all our dealings with one another, all friendships, all loves, all play, all politics. There are no* ordinary *people. You have never talked to a mere mortal. Nations, cultures, arts, civilisations—these are mortal, and their life is to ours as the life of a gnat. But it is immortals whom we joke with, work with, marry, snub, and exploit.* [C. S. Lewis, *The Weight of Glory and Other Addresses* (New York: Macmillan, 1980), p. 19; emphasis in original]

It is a profound quote.

I readily recognize that you will be living in an increasingly secularized society in which people simply don't see other humans in this true light. Many don't even believe in an individualized resurrection. I grant, too, that some also assume that there is an absence of immortal truths and absolute principles. As a result, these people prefer to view humans as being without real behavioral boundaries. Given such disbelieving views, it is no wonder that the ways of the natural man quickly prevail. Whether by giving way to materialism or to the things of the flesh, these individuals live without a knowledge of and a commitment to Heavenly Father's plan of salvation.

An eminent Japanese thinker recently looked at our pleasure-centered Western society and wrote insightfully of a dilemma growing out of this sense so many mortals have of planlessness and purposelessness. He wrote:

*If there is nothing beyond death, then what is wrong with giving oneself wholly to pleasure in the short time one has left to live? The loss of faith in the "other world" has saddled modern Western society with a fatal moral problem.* [Takeshi Umehara, "The Civilization of the Forest: Ancient Japan Shows Postmodernism the Way," *At Century's End: Great Minds Reflect on Our Times*, ed. Nathan P. Gardels (San Diego: ALTI Publishing, 1996), p. 190]

Nevertheless, as striving disciples, our strategic focus must fall on the interaction of immortal individuals and immortal principles as applied to life's changing tactical situations. It is vital, therefore, for you and for me, in the words of Jacob, to see things "as they really are" and things "as they really will be" (Jacob 4:13). It's interesting that those who have eyes single to the glory of God are those who see the most of reality.

But this road of discipleship about which we are speaking tonight is not easy. It requires sturdy, all-weather souls who are constant in every season of life and who are not easily stalled or thrown off course. Likewise, even with this accurate view of the mortal experience, we still need time and the wise use of our moral agency. We still need God's long-suffering to help us. We need all of these combined in order to gain experience in life amid this ongoing process. And amid this ongoing process you and I can actually come to know for ourselves, like Alma of old, who "fasted and prayed many days that I might know . . . of myself" (Alma 5:46), that these immortal principles are true.

We can also come to know, through obedience, how much God loves us as his immortal children. It happens just as President Brigham Young said it would:

*How shall we know that we obey* [God]*? There is but one method by which we can know it, and that is by the inspiration of the Spirit of the Lord witnessing unto our spirit that we are His, that we love Him, and that He loves us. It is by the spirit of revelation we know this.* [JD 12:99]

If we can get that witness for ourselves that we are his and that he loves us, then we can cope with and endure well whatever comes in the varied tactical situations of life.

Of course, there are going to be puzzling moments. Nephi, paralleling what Brigham Young said, had this reaction when he was perplexed: "I know that [God] loveth his children; nevertheless, I do not know the meaning of all things" (1 Nephi 11:17). We cannot always fully or glibly explain everything that is happening to us or around us, but knowing that God loves us is absolutely crucial. Then, as immortals possessed of immortal principles, we can overcome the mortal trials and we can put the pressing things of the day in precious perspective.

Besides, the divine attributes of love, mercy, patience, submissiveness, meekness, purity, and others are those attributes we have been directed to develop in each of us—and they cannot be developed in the abstract (see 3 Nephi 27:27, Mosiah 3:19). These require the clinical experiences—those things through which we are asked to pass. Nor can these attributes be developed in a hurry. Thus the scripture says, "All these things shall give thee experience, and shall be for thy good," referring to the mix of mortal experiences, immortal individuals, and immortal principles (D&C 122:7). And when that interplay occurs, and we see things through the lens of the gospel, then we can see things more clearly and navigate the road of discipleship.

Another thing will happen: We will become much more aware of and alive to the many possibilities for doing good that are present in life's daily situations. Even the moments that seem humdrum are full of possibilities. Nothing is really routine.

I speak tonight, therefore, not only of life's large defining moments but also of the seemingly small moments. Even small acts and brief conversations count, if only incrementally, in this constant shaping of souls, in this strategic swirl of people and principles and tactical situations. What will we, for instance, bring to all of those moments small and large? Will we do what we can to make our presence count as a needed constant in such fleeting moments, even in micro ways? Do you and I not sometimes say appreciatively of individuals who have helped us, "They were there when we needed them"? Will we reciprocate?

The daily discipleship of which I'm speaking is designed to develop these very attributes that are possessed to perfection by Jesus. These attributes emerge from a consciously chosen way of life; one in which we deny ourselves of all ungodliness and we take up the cross daily—not occasionally, not weekly, not monthly. If we are thus determined, then we are emulating yet another quality of our Lord, of whom we read: "And there is nothing that the Lord thy God shall take in his heart to do but what he will do it" (Abraham 3:17). True disciples are meek but very determined.

To underscore further what is being presented tonight concerning the mortal experience, one way of looking at the "thou shalt not" commandments is that these prohibitions help us to avoid misery by turning us away from that which is enticing but harmful and wrong. However, once we are settled in terms of the direction of our discipleship and the gross sins are left firmly behind—"misery prevention," it might be called—then the major focus falls upon the "thou-shalt" commandments. It is the keeping of the thou-shalt commandments that brings even greater happiness. True, as the scripture says, "Wickedness never was happiness" (Alma 41:10), but neither is lukewarmness full happiness. Failing to be valiant in Christian discipleship will leave us without significant happiness. Therefore, our active avoidance of wickedness must be followed by our active engagement in righteousness. Then we can come to know true joy—after all, man is that he "might have joy" (2 Nephi 2:25).

It is very often the sins of omission that keep us from spiritual wholeness because we still lack certain things. Remember the rich, righteous young man who came to Jesus asking, "Good Master, what good thing shall I do, that I may have eternal life?"

"Keep the commandments."

"All these things have I kept from my youth up."

And then came Jesus' searching response: "One thing thou lackest: go thy way, sell whatsoever thou hast, and give to the poor . . . : and come, . . . and follow me." (See Matthew 19:16–21 and Mark 10:17–21.)

A customized commandment thus came for that man. It was something he needed to do, not something he needed to stop doing, that kept him from wholeness.

Furthermore, certain taste buds of our souls may have been burned over by sin, and our Father desires that we regenerate these taste buds of the soul by means of repentance. Our Heavenly Father also desires the development of what are presently the many other neglected taste buds of our souls. These, when they are really developed, will bring even greater happiness and true joy. If it were not so, how could we anticipate with Paul the music and scenery that "eye hath not seen, nor ear heard" (1 Corinthians 2:9) and be prepared to enjoy it except we have cultivated these taste buds of great refinement?

Wickedness is not the only mortal failure. Yes, the avoidance of wickedness remains ever important, but the sins of omission also represent a haunting failure. How often, may I ask you, do we speak about the need for repentance concerning our sins of omission? Or how often do we make personal confessions of them to God?

There is a memorable scriptural phrase about our need to have "faith unto repentance" (see Alma 34:15–16). Faith unto repentance covers both sins of commission and sins of omission. And so the faith of discipleship about which I speak briefly tonight isn't simply for life's crises, though they will come. Rather, it is especially needed to ensure our regular repentance. After all, the scriptures are filled with thou-shalt commandments and with so many exhortations for us to do good. James, for instance, speaks of pure religion, urging us to visit and bless the variously deprived (see James 1:27). Significantly, James also declares that those who would do lasting good should themselves also *be* good—"unspotted from the world" are his words.

This is no small point. We live in a world, for example, in which some individuals do some good but do so while breaking the seventh commandment—chastity before marriage and fidelity after. If we really want to do much good, we must also *be* good. Instructively, in the Book of Mormon we read about a political leader, Morianton, who dealt justly with his people but not with himself. Why not? "Because of his many whoredoms," the scriptures say (Ether 10:11). This is a fascinating insight regarding the ecology of the soul.

The promptings for us to do good come from the Holy Ghost. These promptings nudge us farther along the straight and narrow path of discipleship. The natural man doesn't automatically think of doing good. It isn't natural. How many people worry about the car behind them or the person below them? The natural man just doesn't do it. For us, however, these promptings enlarge our awareness of other people's needs and then prod us to act accordingly. This is why, I believe, when the Lord speaks of enlarging the soul, he adds, in the Doctrine and Covenants, that it must be done "without hypocrisy" (D&C 121:42). Our personal righteousness, more than we know, governs how much good we can do.

It is sadly true, as we all know, that many on this planet hunger for bread, but many also hunger deeply to experience the reassuring eloquence of example. This represents a desperate need that is incumbent upon us to provide as part of our discipleship.

You and I all know individuals who do much quiet good by following the scriptural injunction about lifting up the hands that hang down (see Hebrews 12:12, D&C 81:5). Some of those hands that hang down once grasped the iron rod and then let go, having simply given up. Hence, those hands need to be reached for because they will not be proffered by such discouraged individuals.

But it takes faith to persist in doing good, particularly quiet good, for which there is no recognition. Otherwise, why bother? Therefore, faith in Heavenly Father's plan of salvation is needed not just for life's turbulent, traumatic moments but also for daily life's seemingly small but nevertheless defining moments.

Will we, for instance, remember our true identity as we move through daily life? How much sin occurs because people momentarily forget who they really are?

Will we, for instance, always remember that our behavior must be connected with our beliefs? It must be done without hypocrisy.

The unrelenting reality, brothers and sisters, is that we are never very far away from the need for "faith unto repentance," including repentance of our sins of omission. Such faith unto repentance is not just for next year or next month or next week, but also for tomorrow.

One of the seemingly small things involves being more willing than we sometimes are to give the needed conversational correctives instead of engaging in "conversational cloak holding" by merely going along silently with the prevailing tide of discussion.

I recall reading of General George C. Marshall, whom President Franklin Roosevelt appointed to be his chief of staff early in World War II. Roosevelt was a very persuasive, informal man. During one of their first meetings, desiring to be friendly, perhaps even palsy-walsy, he called General Marshall "George," to which the reply came, "It's General Marshall, Mr. President" (David McCullough, *Truman* [New York: Simon & Schuster, 1992], p. 534). Think about the courage that simple act took—but it helped to define a relationship that, by the way, became a rich relationship.

The small conversational correctives matter so much. If we have that quality, we will appreciate what General Robert E. Lee reportedly did on one occasion. Asked for his opinion of a military colleague, Lee replied candidly but generously, after which the questioner said, in effect, "Well, he doesn't speak so highly of you." General Lee replied, "Sir, you have asked me for my opinion of him, not his opinion of me." Lee had, as one writer described another leader, "furnished his mind . . . with fixed principles" (Walter Bagehot, "Memoir of the Right Honourable James Wilson," *The Works of Walter Bagehot*, ed. Forrest Morgan [Hartford, Connecticut: Travelers Insurance, 1889], 3:384). If you and I can process life's tactical situations through a mind furnished with fixed principles, integrity is the result.

Conversations and decisions in which we engage, even if they seem small, expose the heart and the mind and their furnishings. Brigham Young once said, "You cannot hide the heart, when the mouth is open" (*JD* 6:74).

We can be of so much service to others in many thou-shalt ways. Of course, the problem is that rendering such service takes time, and we are all so busy. Some situations may call for service that somehow seems to be beneath us. Besides, we have other things to do. The "thou shalts" are so convenient to put off. Who will notice the procrastination anyway? After all, we are not robbing a bank. Or are there forms of withholding that constitute stealing?

Consider a conversation again—and this conversation was arranged for by an angel:

*And the angel of the Lord spake unto Philip, saying, Arise, and go. . . .*

*And he arose and went: and, behold, a man of Ethiopia, an eunuch of great authority under Candace queen of the Ethiopians, who had the charge of all her treasure, and had come to Jerusalem for to worship,*

*Was returning, and sitting in his chariot read Esaias the prophet.*

*Then the Spirit said unto Philip, Go near, and join thyself to this chariot."*

[Notice the significant language:] *And Philip ran thither to him, and heard him read the prophet Esaias, and said, Understandest thou what thou readest?*

*And he said, How can I, except some man should guide me? And he desired Philip that he would come up and sit with him.* [Acts 8:26–31; emphasis added]

How many times are we too busy to "come up and sit" with someone who needs conversation? You and I have divine promptings all the time encouraging us to do good, but we often deflect them instead of doing like Philip, who "ran thither."

We sometimes give needed physical cloaks to warm people and to cover them, and it is good that we do. How often do you and I also give what the scriptures call the "garment of praise" (Isaiah 61:3)? The "garment of praise" is often more desperately needed than the physical cloak. In any case, as we all know, these needs are all around us, every day. There are so many ways we can "lift up the hands which hang down, and strengthen the feeble knees" (D&C 81:5).

We can also be generous when there are interpersonal differences of opinion. Generosity and fairness are marks of character. Compared to his early days in Parliament, Winston Churchill later developed his capacity to be generous, including to his rivals. This was seen in his tribute to the just-deceased Neville Chamberlain, whom he had earlier replaced as prime minister. Churchill had once described Chamberlain as looking at foreign affairs through a "municipal drain pipe." Nevertheless, on the occasion of the tribute for Chamberlain, Churchill said, "In one of the supreme crises of the world [our colleague was] contradicted by events." In that same speech Churchill praised Chamberlain, saying, "The only guide to a man is his conscience; the only shield to his memory is the rectitude and sincerity of his actions. . . . With this shield, . . . we march always in the ranks of honour" (Tribute to Neville Chamberlain, House of Commons, 12 November 1940). How generous of Churchill. "Contradicted by events" was intended to explain Chamberlain's gross and naïve failures regarding the rise of Hitlerism.

In each of life's situations, large or small, therefore, if you and I will bring fixed principles and strive to be more like Jesus, including emulating his generosity, then we will be living abundantly and not just existing. The Book of Mormon has those fascinating phrases about our moral agency whereby we are to act for ourselves and not merely be acted upon (see 2 Nephi 2:16, 26; Helaman 14:30).

Now, since we are not always free to choose just when and how all of life's interactions will occur, we are nevertheless free to choose our responses to these moments. Since we can't compute beforehand all our responses, it becomes vital to set our course as immortals on the basis of immortal principles to be applied as reflexively as possible. Besides, there may be no time in which to ponder how we will respond anyway. If, for example, one determines that he will keep the seventh commandment, then his applying this fixed principle will result in temptations either being deliberately avoided in the first place or in being quickly deflected. All of this can be achieved without great thought, risk, or needless anxiety. In fact, I would go so far as to say to you tonight, my brothers and sisters, that if we are truly attached to immortal principles, some decisions need to be made only once, really, and then righteous reflexes can do the rest. Absent such fixed determinations, however, one can be tossed to and fro by temptations that then require case-by-case agonizing.

The same could be said of honesty in business or integrity in human relationships. Each day interactions occur relentlessly, involving people, principles, and circumstances.

One of the things we can do to help us develop those reflexes is to further develop our scriptural literacy so that, as Nephi prescribed, we can "liken all scriptures unto [ourselves]" (1 Nephi 19:23). Each day challenges arise, responses are given, and decisions are made.

Will it be in the setting of fixed principles, however, as has been emphasized?

To this, the rising generation of youth and young adults in the Church, I say that scriptural memories, spiritual memories, can be lost in a generation:

*And also all that generation were gathered unto their fathers: and there arose another generation after them, which knew not the Lord, nor yet the works which he had done for Israel.* [Judges 2:10]

In just one generation!

When the scriptures are either not available or are not searched and believed, then two things happen—a loss of belief in God and a loss of belief in the Resurrection: "They had brought no records with them; and they denied the being of their Creator" (Omni 1:17).

*Now it came to pass that there were many of the rising generation that could not understand the words of king Benjamin, being little children at the time he spake unto his people; and they did not believe the tradition of their fathers.*

*They did not believe what had been said concerning the resurrection of the dead, neither did they believe concerning the coming of Christ.* [Mosiah 26:1–2]

Those vital things always go first, and they can go within a generation, unless we truly are feasting upon the scriptures. Feasting on the scriptures, combined with the gift of the Holy Ghost, will "show unto you all things what ye should do" (see 2 Nephi 32:3–5).

I testify to you tonight that the scriptures give us nourishment for every season of life and the Holy Ghost can prompt us in all moments so that we can, in fact, be blessed with insight and reassurance.

What can deter our feasting on the scriptures? Jesus warned, "The care[s] of this world . . . choke the word" (Matthew 13:22). They surely do. Still worse, those choked with the pleasures of the world have no time for scriptures. Some actually have pleasure in unrighteousness. Here again we see the natural man gravitating toward the cares and the pleasures of this world.

In that cumulative process, today's small inflection for good adds to what becomes tomorrow's mountain of character. A bad inflection, however, of a defining moment gouges a little more in what later becomes the eroded gully channeling us so swiftly into the "gulf of misery" (see 2 Nephi 1:13). More than we realize, life's experiences of boredom, exhilaration, deprivation, conflict, compromise, mistakes, successes, resentments, loving, excluding, belonging, repenting, and forgiving swirl about us constantly. How will immortal principles be applied by immortal individuals to these swirling situations?

This is why the plan of salvation, which is so extremely important, came with the Restoration—so we can understand life and the discipleship being described tonight. If people misread life, this leads to murmuring, rebellion, and irreligion. Of Laman and Lemuel we read, "They knew not the dealings of that God who had created them" (1 Nephi 2:12). Decades later in the Book of Mormon, it was said once again, as if it were a part of the institutional memory of the Nephite and Lamanite people, that Nephi's brethren "understood not the dealings of the Lord" (Mosiah 10:14).

Without gospel perspective in our lives, we just won't "get it" either. Special moments will come and go unused and unnoticed. How we manage those moments in daily life ends up either developing character or disintegrating character.

These moments of truth may be small, but they give us a chance to express character. Mercifully, when we make mistakes we can recover and learn from them by "faith unto repentance." We cannot, of course, relive a particular moment in our lives, but we can use it as a spiritual spur to remake ourselves. We need not let yesterday hold tomorrow hostage.

People always matter, of course, but the more I think about this interplay of immortal individuals and immortal principles, it is almost as though the particular tactical situation merely serves as a temporary, focal catalyst for what is really going on. Some other tactical situation might have served just as well. In any case, it is for each of us as immortals to make of these moments in daily life that which eternal principles would have us make of them.

I am the first to acknowledge that we, as Church members, have a tremendous challenge being equal to our theology and our opportunity. We fall short. If we stumble, let us arise and continue the climb. The Lord will bless us because we are possessed of truths about "things as they really are, and . . . things as they really will be" (Jacob 4:13). These truths beckon us, even in our imperfections, to be better.

I share with you tonight, as I near the end of my remarks, what seems to me to be a profound window of divine disclosure through which we are permitted to look. As is the case with many scriptures, there are many multiple meanings. I wish to note one from that moment in which Enoch, in the presence of the Lord, was permitted to see the trauma of the people in the time of Noah. The principle to be noted is that we do not always weep alone:

> *And it came to pass that the God of heaven looked upon the residue of the people* [the Noachians], *and he wept; and Enoch bore record of it, saying: How is it that the heavens weep, and shed forth their tears as the rain upon the mountains?*
>
> *And Enoch said unto the Lord: How is it that thou canst weep, seeing thou art holy, and from all eternity to all eternity?* [Moses 7:28–29]

And then came the marvelous response from God:

> *The Lord said unto Enoch: Behold these thy brethren; they are the workmanship of mine own hands, and I gave unto them their knowledge, in the day I created them; and in the Garden of Eden, gave I unto man his agency;*
>
> *And unto thy brethren have I said, and also given commandment, that they should love one another, and that they should choose me, their Father; but behold, they are without affection, and they hate their own blood; . . .*

*Wherefore,* [continued the Lord] *for this shall the heavens weep, yea, and all the workmanship of mine hands.*

*And it came to pass that the Lord spake unto Enoch, and told Enoch all the doings of the children of men; wherefore Enoch knew, and looked upon their wickedness, and their misery, and wept and stretched forth his arms, and his heart swelled wide as eternity; and his bowels yearned; and all eternity shook.* [Moses 7:32–33, 40–41]

An absolutely supernal, marvelous insight! Our Father in Heaven is so tender even for his most mistaken children.

Enoch began to rejoice when God told him of Jesus' coming in the meridian of time and told of the Atonement. He rejoiced again when God told him of the great latter-day Restoration.

Not always, but more than we know, when we are confronted in the human circumstance with the difference between *what could be* and *what is,* we do not weep alone!

I have felt to add these concluding thoughts in friendship and counsel to you.

Do not, my young friends, expect the world to esteem the seventh commandment—chastity before marriage and fidelity after. Some people in the world will fret genuinely over the consequences of its violation, such as staggering and unprecedented illegitimacy and marital breakdowns. However, sexual immorality per se will still not be condemned by the secular world as long as the violators have any commendable qualities at all or as long as they are, in some respect, politically correct. We will have to keep the seventh commandment because it is spiritually correct, not because we will get much support from society's other institutions.

A second suggestion: As you pursue your discipleship and observe the human scene, do not be surprised or unnerved by the natural man's relentless push for preeminence and power. It really reflects the premortal psychodrama. Nor should you be surprised over the efforts of so many to cover their sins or to gratify their vain ambition.

Be grateful, therefore, for the gospel's emphasis on meekness. Be careful of the natural man's milder expressions—craving for credit and rustling for recognition. Alas, so often the hearts and even the moral agency of others can be crushed in the search for self-glorification.

We have just celebrated the birth at Bethlehem. Another individual sought the role of Redeemer, saying, "Send me, I will be thy son, and I will redeem all mankind, that one soul shall not be lost . . . ; wherefore give me thine honor" (Moses 4:1). Brothers and sisters, God would have never permitted a different babe to be born at Bethlehem, of course; nor would he have permitted the destruction of the agency of mankind with all its implications for a very different mortal experience. What happened, as you know, is that precious Jesus stepped forward and said, "Father, thy will be done, and the glory be thine forever" (Moses 4:2). He was the babe who was born at Bethlehem!

Remarkable restoration windows such as these are provided for our instruction in this dispensation—if we will ponder over them and make their insights a part of our discipleship.

Lastly, I again express publicly my gratitude for God's having granted me a "delay en route." However long, I know it has not been given merely for loitering or sightseeing along the pathway of discipleship. Perhaps the delay includes moments like tonight, when I can express my love for you, my confidence in you, and my testimony of Jesus, whose work this is. He has shown the meaning of the mortal experience by the eloquence of his example and by his having shown the way to us in every particular, including his gallantry during the agonies of the Atonement, of which he declared, "And would that I might not drink the bitter cup, and shrink" (D&C 19:18). Not shrinking is more important than surviving, and Jesus is our exemplar in every way. I salute him for the eloquence of his example. I express my everlasting gratitude to the Father for the superb plan of happiness and, with you, my appreciation for the promptings of the Holy Ghost and plead that each of us might not deflect these but might receive them as indicators of how much more we could do if we were more serious disciples. For these things I express my gratitude and my desire to give the honor and the praise and the glory to the Father and the Son and the Holy Ghost.

I take heart in the rising generation's capacity to move the people of this planet spiritually in ways not achieved before. You are indeed a generation of destiny, young adults of promise. I do so in love and appreciation, expressing my witness to you in the power and authority of the holy apostleship and in the name of Jesus Christ. Amen.

# Sharing Insights from My Life

—————◆—————

Neal A. Maxwell

I t is a special time for you as students in terms of the calendar, brothers and sisters. A new semester has started. Obviously it is the end of one year and the beginning of another. Soon it will be the end of a century, and a whole new century will open up before you. And you really are, as we enter upon that new century, part of the hope of Israel. So I am grateful for President Bateman's invitation to be with you in this time of transition, and I will, with some encouragement from my wife and some others, wax a little bit autobiographical today, which I typically don't do.

My life has been, fortunately—for me at least—intertwined with Brigham Young University for nearly 28 years: either as Church commissioner of education, as a member of the board of trustees, as chairman of the executive committee, or off and on as the grand-father of several students here. No wonder, therefore, that I feel that President Bateman and the faculty and administration are truly colleagues.

———————

*This devotional address was delivered at BYU on 12 January 1999.*

Furthermore, you as students continue to be, at least to me, another royal generation being raised up for the purposes of the Lord in your individual lives. Yes, you have some personal imperfections of which you are aware, probably painfully at times. But you are also drenched in personal gifts, talents, and abilities of which you may be less aware. So though longevity is one reason for giving some advice today, the other reason for so doing is because of your immense possibilities carved out of this particular time in human history.

It surprises me that I have lived nearly three-fourths of the 20th century. Such a span is not comparatively a long time, considering the able and spritely septagenarians and octogenarians among whom I labor. Yet it is still a significant time span. Certainly at times in the spring of 1945, as an 18-year-old infantryman on Okinawa, it did not look very likely to me that my life would span three-quarters of this century. Nevertheless, experiences undergone and lessons learned have combined over the years to heighten my gratitude to God for the gift of life. I have lived through a depression, a world war, and a cold war, and have long since entered my anecdotage—and you will not be entirely spared from that latter symptom today.

In the passing years I have developed much appreciation for the institution of the family. Other institutions simply cannot compensate fully for failing families. If we will hold fast to the Church's proclamation on the family, we will see that we hold the jewels, as it were, that can enrich so many other things. Let the world go its own way on the family. It appears to be determined to do that. But we do not have that option. Our doctrines and teachings on the family are very, very powerful, and they are full of implications for all the people on this planet.

Though I murmured as a young man at times with chores, I have acquired in the space of this passage of time a hardened view of the spiritual necessity of work. Even if work were not an economic necessity, it is a spiritual necessity. If I have any concern about your generation, speaking collectively, it is that a few of our wonderful youth and young adults in the Church are unstretched—they have almost a free pass. Perks are provided, including cars complete with fuel and insurance—all paid for by parents who sometimes listen in vain for a few courteous and appreciative words. What is thus taken for granted, however innocently, tends to underwrite selfishness and a sense of entitlement. Selfishness and a sense of entitlement don't need any transfusions in our society today. I know that having said those things to you now, and having spoken plainly, there are some here who have worked exceedingly hard and need no comment from me on that score. As I look at the rising generation, the gospel of work, which is part of the fullness of the gospel, will need more attention, not less.

I am excited to report to you that I am enjoying the scriptures more than ever. I have read a lot in my life—thousands of books, I'm sure. But rarely do I encore reading except for the holy scriptures. Therefore, I am even more anxiously engaged in the restored gospel than ever because the restored gospel is so engaging. It really does get a grasp on our minds, and there is no end to the exploration that one can make of it. It is, as I said from this pulpit years ago, an "inexhaustible gospel." To be anxiously engaged really does mean that we are engaged intellectually as well as spiritually, and life in the kingdom, as you all know, is also very engaging. So although some people at my stage of life might say, in effect, "Been there. Done that," not I. I feel instead this sense of anxious engagement in something that I have yet to take the full measure of. As I look back across the sweep of this century, I feel that very strongly.

Now, as already indicated, I am going to be somewhat autobiographical today. I mention first of all a small episode involving a large principle. The principle is the need for us to avoid the rush to judgment. This episode occurred just after I returned home from World War II. During months overseas while in the service, I had saved money to go on a mission. This was part of keeping my promise to the Lord made back in May of 1945, to which I will refer later. Back then I naïvely and foolishly thought I could pay God back, and of course I am more and more in His debt with the passing of time.

In any event, when I was discharged, I wanted to go on a mission right away. But our bishop did not call me at once. Finally, somewhat audaciously, I went to his home one night and told him I wanted to go on a mission. I had the money, and I didn't want to wait. Only then did he proceed to process the call. I impatiently wondered back then why he seemed so slow. Only decades later did I learn from the good man who was then his ward clerk that my bishop had felt, since I had been overseas for quite a while, I shouldn't be rushed into the mission field.

Oh, how quick we are sometimes to judge with so little data! And these experiences are in each of our lives, and they are illustrative of large issues, if we will but learn from them. I am so grateful to that ward clerk who, at least 40 years later, sent me a note one day saying he'd heard I'd mentioned this tapping on the bishop's door at night, and he thought I ought to know the bishop's feelings. The rush to judgment continues to be the reflex of the natural man and the natural woman if we do not guard against it carefully.

Another insight that seems to recur again and again in confirmation is that the todays of life constitute the holy present. We can't fix the past. We may be able to repent of it, but we can't change past events. We *can* fashion the future, and we do that by using what someone has called the holy present, which indeed it is.

I share with you again a simple little insight that may help you at certain junctures in your lives. It is that you must not mistake passing local cloud cover for general darkness. They are very different things, and for us to distinguish local cloud cover, which will soon be blown away, for general darkness is a terrible thing, especially with the restored gospel, which is so full metaphorically of light. We must not be mistaken about this.

I have likewise learned that illness can be a tutoring and sanctifying experience as well as a debilitating thing. There await each of us clusters of circumstances and experiences, and if we see "things as they really are," to use Jacob's felicitous phrase (Jacob 4:13), we'll be able to understand that illnesses may be debilitating but are also very tutoring, and we will be open to what they can convey to us. Such is spiritually very, very important.

In modern revelation we are told very frankly, brothers and sisters, that "when we obtain any blessing from God, it is by obedience to that law upon which it is predicated" (D&C 130:21). I don't know how it is for you, but I have felt so often in my life so greatly blessed for what little obedience I have given. My conclusion with regard to that verse is that the Lord's ratio of blessings to our obedience is a very generous ratio indeed. He is so quick to reward us, so quick to reassure us, and so anxious to take delight when we serve Him. So if you puzzle over that verse, as I have in life, including in recent times, the only bottom line I can give you is that the ratio of blessings to our minuscule obedience is a very, very generous ratio indeed.

I have also watched enough of human history and tried to be something of a student of public affairs to recognize passing movements, fads, and things of that kind. There are political fashions over which people become so excited, and they feel so threatened by them. They tend to equate them with the scriptural phrase "the kingdom of the devil" (2 Nephi 28:19). The kingdom of the devil, brothers and sisters, must be regarded as a collective, generic designation. We must not confuse it with any of its subsets, as ominous and bad as they may be for their season in human history. We must not confuse the subsets with the whole of it.

Once again the Book of Mormon and modern revelation give us the guidance we need so that we are not taken out of our places by too much concern over what on the landscape of history may after all be a very temporary thing, real and menacing though it may be. In the Book of Mormon is a verse I wish I fully understood, but which I draw to your attention. It is 2 Nephi 28:19, which says "the kingdom of the devil must shake." It is a very intriguing verse. I do not presume to know what this redemptive turbulence will be like, but it will be such that a few people now caught up in that generic kingdom of the devil will be "stirred up" and find their way out and into the kingdom of God. I don't know how that will happen, but it will happen. I rather imagine, and this is sure speculation, that there will be in this redemptive turbulence some jarring inconsistencies brought to the fore—jarring enough that they will cause some people who are caught up in the subsets to leave and find the truth. As prophesied in the Book of Mormon, full of portent for Latter-day Saints, there will be real turbulence.

Then, in like manner, as I have watched a few personal friends over the years go through the ebb and flow of faith, I have wondered about the underlying causes. What happened? And again and again a verse in the Book of Mormon is the most satisfactory explanation. It is an interrogative in Mosiah 5:13: "For how knoweth a man the master whom he has not served, and who is a stranger unto him, and is far from the thoughts and intents of his heart?" This describes what usually happens: otherwise basically decent people simply get caught up with the cares of the world. If instead of drawing closer to the Master we become a stranger to Him, then we have lost our way. The decent people to whom this happens haven't engaged in major transgression, as a rule, but they have distanced themselves from the Savior and He has become a stranger to them. If, on the other hand, we really are drawing closer to Jesus and we are becoming however incrementally more like Him, then we are progressing. To use another Book of Mormon phrase, we must be "willing to submit to all things which the Lord seeth fit to inflict" (Mosiah 3:19). Whenever our wills are increasingly subsumed by His—the Book of Mormon calls it "swallowed up in the will of the Father" (Mosiah 15:7)—then we really are on the road to discipleship. But that can't happen with the sort of superficiality with which some approach discipleship.

I am going to preach a hard doctrine to you now. The submission of one's will is really the only uniquely personal thing we have to place on God's altar. It is a hard doctrine, but it is true. The many other things we give to God, however nice that may be of us, are actually things He has already given us, and He has loaned them to us. But when we begin to submit ourselves by letting our wills be swallowed up in God's will, then we are really giving something to Him. And that hard doctrine lies at the center of discipleship. There is a part of us that is ultimately sovereign, the mind and heart, where we really do decide which way to go and what to do. And when we submit to His will, then we've really given Him the one thing He asks of us. And the other things are not very, very important. It is the only possession we have that we can give, and there is no resulting shortage in our agency as a result. Instead, what we see is a flowering of our talents and more and more surges of joy. Submission to Him is the only form of submission that is completely safe.

This ought to be more obvious to us than it is sometimes, brothers and sisters, because developmentally, as well as doctrinally, all the other commandments hang, as Jesus said, on the two great interactive commandments. Let me read them to you now because they are so vital.

*Jesus said unto him, Thou shalt love the Lord thy God with all thy heart, and with all thy soul, and with all thy mind.*

*This is the first and great commandment.*

*And the second is like unto it, Thou shalt love thy neighbour as thyself.*

*On these two commandments hang all the law and the prophets.*

[Matthew 22:37–40]

Now we don't think about it enough in the Church, but the first commandment is first for a reason. And the second commandment is second for a reason. True, the second commandment is like unto the first, but it isn't the first commandment. We worship the perfect object of that first commandment, God, because of His spiritual supremacy. We do not worship our neighbors. We are to love them but not worship them. This recognition of God's supremacy on all counts is why that commandment is first and why it is completely safe for us to submit to Him. Besides, at a university it is not inappropriate to remind you that that first commandment includes all of our heart, soul, and mind. The mind must surrender to God, too. It is my impression, looking about the world, that there are comparatively more knees bent in reverence to God than there are minds bent in reverence to Him. That human stubbornness tends to show up in terms of our unwillingness to submit our minds to Him.

C. S. Lewis put it well when he said, "We are bidden to 'put on Christ,' to become like God. That is, whether we like it or not, God intends to give us what we need, not what we now think we want"

(*The Problem of Pain*, chapter 3, paragraph 18). Hence it is so vital for us to be submissive because we'll be puzzled when He gives us what we need in order to become more like Him and the Son, unless we are submissive in mind.

Now that grand key, therefore, is why we will have missed the train if Jesus is a stranger and far from the thoughts and intents of our heart. Because of his intellectual submissiveness, Enoch learned about what Paul called "the deep things of God" (1 Corinthians 2:10). I love that phrase of Paul's. Enoch personally saw the tears of the Lord. He personally heard the Lord's lamentations about the human family. God recited how He has given us our agency, commanded us to love and to choose Him and likewise love one another. Here again are the two great commandments. Yet we mortals so often choose evil or let the cares of the world crowd out the important things.

Instead of choosing God and His ways, we get busy with the cares of the world, and that is when neighbors get excluded, too. So obeying that first great commandment permits us to acknowledge and love the Lord and to accept His love of us, brothers and sisters, including the timing and shaping of us. Remember Nephi's meek acceptance of God's will: "I know that [God] loveth his children; nevertheless, I do not know the meaning of all things" (1 Nephi 11:17). We don't know the meaning of all things, but we know that God loves us, and that is sufficient to get us by and through anything.

We have a lot of people who partially keep the second commandment more than they truly keep the first. The trouble with just focusing on the second commandment to the exclusion of the first is that we may momentarily do some good deed for a neighbor, but it may not mean that we have worshipped God with all our mind. The first commandment sets the high tone, the divine standard. If it were not so, then, as the scriptures say, "Every man walketh in his own way, and after the image of his own god, whose image is in the likeness of the world" (D&C 1:16). That first commandment is the linchpin for everything else. Even self-centered people find themselves doing good, keeping the second commandment at times, but it is almost a kind of sidebar thing, as though they really have other things to do but are going to do a modicum of service here and feel good about it. We must not, therefore, overlook how crucial that first commandment is.

Furthermore, regarding that commandment, mortal choices need not necessarily be wicked in order to do harm. Some choices are diversions more than they are transgressions. As a result of these diversions, the sins of omission mount up. And they constitute a real deprivation because of what we withhold from our fellow human beings. Perhaps it is unintentional, but without that first commandment, some things get omitted.

In contrast, the Lord's reach for us is so redemptive and constant. His arm, we are told in the Book of Mormon, extends all the day long (see 2 Nephi 28:32). And the prophet Mormon spoke in powerful lamentation of those who did not respond even so (see Mormon 6:16–22). Yet Jesus waits with open arms to receive you, and if we are fully faithful at a much later date, we can eventually know at the entrance to His kingdom that sublime moment the prophet Mormon described when we could be "clasped in the arms of Jesus" (Mormon 5:11). There, the Lord Himself, by choice, is the gatekeeper, "and he employeth no servants there" (2 Nephi 9:41). This is why King Lamoni's father surely had it right. In His halting initial faith he said to the Lord, "I will give away all my sins to know thee" (Alma 22:18). That sacred deep act of discipleship is so crucial. I love, therefore, this statement of the Prophet Joseph Smith. I find it encouraging, as you doubtless have in terms of your discipleship. The Prophet Joseph said:

*We consider that God has created man with a mind capable of instruction, and a faculty which may be enlarged in proportion to the heed and diligence given to the light communicated from heaven to the intellect; and that the nearer man approaches perfection, the clearer are his views, and the greater his enjoyments, till he has overcome the evils of his life and lost every desire for sin; and like the ancients, arrives at that point of faith where he is wrapped in the power and glory of his Maker and is caught up to dwell with*

*Him. But we consider that this is a station to which no man ever arrived in a moment. [Teachings, p. 51]*

King Benjamin said of that moment, that when we reach it, we will "have no more disposition to do evil" (Mosiah 5:2). And we can tell in our hearts and with the help of our conscience how we are doing on the basis of those two criteria. This means, frankly, that our sins of omission, at least speaking for myself, need more attention and appreciation and more repentance. They don't involve, as said earlier, transgression, but they are a matter of deflection.

Perhaps it is true in discipleship as it is in athletics that the legs go first. Good spiritual legs such as those of ancient Joseph, in the face of temptation from Potiphar's wife, are so crucial. In that terse verse we read of Joseph that he "fled" (Genesis 39:12). It takes courage to run away from evil, and good legs. And those same good legs are needed for us to lengthen our stride and to continue. That's why we sing the song "Do not weary by the way" ("If the Way Be Full of Trial, Weary Not," *Deseret Sunday School Songs* [Salt Lake City: Deseret Sunday School Union, 1909], no. 148). And if we don't worry by the way, we will pass life's daily quizzes, not just the major exams. And that takes good legs.

We must keep things in proportion. Remember Thomas B. Marsh and the dispute over milk? He had let the issue grow out of proportion, and it caused him to focus jealously on the minor imperfections of the Prophet Joseph. This led to his excommunication. Happily, Thomas B. Marsh came back.

At that same time, Lorenzo Snow, a contemporary, said that he noticed the minor imperfections in the Prophet Joseph, but he was grateful that the Lord could use him even so to do such a significant work (see Neal A. Maxwell, *"But for a Small Moment"* [Salt Lake City: Bookcraft, 1986], p. 127). This made Lorenzo Snow grateful because there was then some hope for himself.

One of the realities of the kingdom is that we work with each other in the midst of our imperfections. We see those imperfections as well as the traits and talents that God has blessed us with. And during this process of life together in the community of Saints, we watch each other grow. It is not surprising when we see each other grow as a result of the opportunities in the kingdom. And it isn't usually just one muscle that is developed. On the other hand, we see people in the Church for whom adversity is an anesthetic and for whom suffering is a sedative. And in that soil the root of bitterness can spring up. I wish I could say to you that suffering teaches automatically, but it doesn't. To paraphrase Anne Morrow Lindbergh: If suffering inevitably taught us, the human family would be a very wise family indeed (see *Hour of Gold, Hour of Lead* [New York: Harcourt Brace Jovanovich, 1973], p. 214). It takes meekness to learn from suffering.

Some here know that for 25 years I have felt one of the precious verses in all scripture about discipleship was the one given to the Prophet Joseph in Liberty Jail: "All these things shall give thee experience, and shall be for thy good" (D&C 122:7). That premise is that experience is valuable, and the only way to have it is to have it. And whether it involves adversity or whatever, then we are blessed. Notice these lines from Paul: "Knowing that tribulation worketh patience; And patience, experience; and experience, hope" (Romans 5:3–4).

You may ask, "There is no other way?"

And I answer, "No, there is not. There is no other way." And thus, in this discipleship about which I am speaking, it is so essential that out of these experiences we form character. It is much easier in this life to be a character than to have character. And we see characters before us in the media all the time. To have character is a special and wonderful thing, but to develop it is not a pain-free process. The Prophet Joseph said:

> *I am like a huge, rough stone rolling down from a high mountain; and the only polishing I get is when some corner gets rubbed off by coming in contact with something else, striking with accelerated force . . . all hell knocking off a corner here and a corner there. Thus I will become a smooth and polished shaft in the quiver of the Almighty.* [*Teachings*, p. 304]

It doesn't happen in a day, and you and I see these collisions between members and challenges. Those who are meek handle them, and they become smooth and polished.

I love a line from the prophet Moroni and say it to my posterity, some of whom are here today. I can't express it any better. He said:

> *Condemn me not because of mine imperfection, neither my father,*
> *because of his imperfection, neither them who have written before him;*
> *but rather give thanks unto God that he hath made manifest unto you*
> *our imperfections, that ye may learn to be more wise than we have been.*
> [Mormon 9:31]

What a marvelous, meek way for one generation passing on to relate to the one that is rising. Thus I return again to the words *anxiously engaged.* They do not mean hectically engaged. They do not mean frantically engaged. Rather, they reflect a deep, quiet commitment—some anticipation of what lies ahead. We must be willing to let our gears of commitment be hammered and shaped so that they mesh with life's opportunities in ways that are crucial.

We are so blessed with a rich theology, so blessed with the Church that is full of ordinances and doctrines and all of those things that make it so engaging and so easy to be anxiously engaged.

Now there is a problem that we have to face. C. S. Lewis called it "the tether and pang of the particular" ("The Brook," *The Pilgrim's Regress* [Grand Rapids, Michigan: Wm. B. Eerdmans Publishing Company, 1974], p. 198). He was describing life's local situations with which we must deal.

I was talking with a widow of just one month who is left with several children. Her young husband died of cancer. She was not whining. She was not complaining. She was just describing for me the tether and pang of the particular and what it is like to be a single parent and to have to do all things on her own. Such is the tether and pang of the particular. Again that marvelous Book of Mormon tells us that we have got to be content with the things allotted to us.

Whatever the circumference of our tether is, we ought to be content with that and live within the tether and pang of the particular.

Now, as I prepare to close, you face a time in which there is a significant amount of social decay in our society. Some of its roots lie in the 1960s. You can easily see why the Book of Mormon described people as having "become weak, because of their transgression, in the space of not many years" (Helaman 4:26). It doesn't take very long. For you to be strong is absolutely crucial, brothers and sisters.

I hope you will forgive me if I say something your parents might like me to say, because I can do it better than they. I can remember three or four times when I was a little feisty and independent before marriage—not as to behavioral or doctrinal things, just more assertive—and while my parents saw that, they respected my agency. I knew how they felt, but they backed off a little bit. There was almost a sacred zone there where they could say, "You know how we feel."

I found myself loving and respecting them all the more. If some of you may be in that situation now or subsequently, and see in your wonderful parents a willingness to back off a little bit because they honor your agency, honor them. Back off a little bit, and out of that will come the kind of negotiation you'll come to expect a little more when you are on the other side of that equation. Lehi described himself as "a trembling parent" (2 Nephi 1:14). I think that is not too graphic. Even with good children there are times when you will know that trembling as a parent. Get some experience with this sacred zone, therefore, by honoring parents now who may be wise enough to back off a little bit, and you back off a little bit in such a way that there is an accord such as you would like to have.

Now I close with two experiences. As a teenage boy I watched my six-week-old sister, Carol, struggle with what seemed to me to be lethal whooping cough at a time when there were no antibiotics. I came home one night from having been a grease monkey at a Greyhound bus depot and saw the light was on. It was about four o'clock in the morning. I knew it meant trouble. As I came in, Carol was laid out on the round dining room table, and Dad was waiting for a neighbor to come to join in blessing her. I thought she was gone. It seemed to me she had quit breathing. Then I watched the power of the priesthood, and I watched her start breathing again. That experience let me know the reality of the priesthood at a very young age. Our prayers for her were answered.

Have I had some prayers that were not answered? Yes, and so have you. Sometimes the reason is that we may ask for something without enough faith, or we may in fact ask for something that isn't expedient or that isn't right. For us to get used to the fact that all prayers are not automatically answered is one of life's growing experiences.

Despite the constant turnover in the experiences and generations of students, let me try to make this second story relevant. It took place during the fighting on Okinawa in May of 1945. Enemy artillery had been searching for our little mortar squad for several days, and the shells had been going over us. We felt fairly secure. But they must have moved their artillery pieces because they dropped a shell right between my hole and the foxhole of my friend. I'm sure I was not the only one praying, but I did pray mighty hard, and I made some promises to the Lord about how I would seek to serve Him if indeed He chose to spare me. I'm still trying to keep that promise. Some prayers are answered dramatically, as with Carol and the prayer in the foxhole. With others we must importune and wait. But if we do that, there will come to us in those waiting moments special things.

Let me mention without naming anyone the experience last night of being with a wonderful matriarch. In the last three years this wonderful lady and good friend of Colleen's and mine has lost a husband, a daughter, a son, and two brothers. At 8:30 this morning, her remaining son had brain tumor surgery. As I watch that family, so settled, so established, I can see that they know what Nephi knew: "I know that [God] loveth his children; nevertheless, I do not know the meaning of all things" (1 Nephi 11:17). The feeling I felt watching that family circle and their many friends was that this family is okay. They will make it, whatever the results of the surgery may be.

If we are meek enough and we are willing to submit enough, then we can be like our friend's marvelous young son last night after his blessing. He was secure. This is a son who, when his first wife died a few years ago, was seated with the family in the first two rows at the funeral. When it was his turn to praise his wife, he passed the young baby to someone else on that row and then came to the pulpit and gave a wonderful sermon, as if speaking at his wife's funeral was something he did twice a month.

Such intrinsic spirituality has grown in him and in his family. This family could indeed have a conversation with Job and hold their own.

Thank you for letting me be autobiographical. Please, submit your will to God. It is the only gift you've got to give. And the sooner it is placed on the altar, the better it will be for all.

I love you. I have great hopes for your generation. Thank you for this chance to bear my witness to you today. This is the Lord's work. There is nothing else that even approaches it in significance. And you have been called to carry it forward today in a time of opportunity such as we have never seen before. God loves you that much, of which I gladly testify in the name of Jesus Christ. Amen.

# "Free to Choose"?
# (2 Nephi 2:27)

———◆———

Neal A. Maxwell

Thank you so much, President Samuelson. You're blessed to have this wonderful man as your president. But I miss him at Church headquarters—greatly and personally! It's always easy to praise Sharon because she represents, as does my wife—as do so many others—the faithful women of this dispensation, without whom this work simply could not be done. They are the kind of souls who are high yield and low maintenance.

I appreciate the special rendering of Merrill Bradshaw's composition, having had the privilege of spending a little time with him just a couple of hours before he died. I appreciate, likewise, Steve Cleveland's prayer. This is a man who cares about what happens on the basketball court, but first he's a disciple. For that I love him the more.

Unsurprisingly, I have become more keenly conscious of the passage of time. Several evenings ago a 13-year-old granddaughter was on her way, all made up, to be in a school play, and I found myself saying, "Kansas, this isn't Dorothy anymore!" I am unresentful of the

*This devotional address was given on 16 March 2004.*

passage of time and am still well within the sound range of the kettle drums representing the cacophony of mortality. Yet I sometimes seem to hear, ever so faintly, the distant sounds of beckoning trumpets as these waft in upon me.

I plead for the Spirit to help me. But you must help, too, because of the format of this presentation, which will feature a conversational style and which assumes you will be active, though inward, responders. I hope the Spirit will arc between us so that there is a rapid and shared understanding (see D&C 50:10). In any case, I hope you feel my love and openness and forgive in advance my falling short.

The vital revelations about the agency of man—the freedom to choose—inevitably and simultaneously portray the perfect generosity and perfect justice of God. In the key words that soon follow, we see how deeply serious God is about human joy. The Prophet Joseph Smith declared, "If men do not comprehend the character of God, they do not comprehend themselves" (*Teachings*, 343). In no respect, brothers and sisters, is this more true than with regard to comprehending God's mercy and justice and His commitment to our freedom to choose.

The doctrine of our freedom to choose is set forth sparsely and is not fully presented in the precious Holy Bible. But we have key phrases that have been given to us in the Restoration scriptures:

1. "I [have given] unto man his *agency*" (Moses 7:32; emphasis added; see also D&C 101:78; Moses 4:3; JST, Genesis 3:4).

2. "Thou mayest *choose for thyself*" (Moses 3:17; emphasis added).

The gift sounds reassuring and really good, doesn't it? I am free to choose—just as things ought to be! Certainly you and I can handle it—almost effortlessly!

3. "That ye may live and move and do *according to your own will*" (Mosiah 2:21; emphasis added).

The granting of agency is so complete and personal, isn't it? So breathtaking! Thus there is initial exhilaration. But a disquieting and accompanying realization also emerges:

Satan "sought to destroy the agency of man," bringing on the war so vigorously fought in the premortal world (Moses 4:3; see also Revelation 12:7).

But never mind, you and I are still free, though admittedly we're on a path requiring daily decisions as we

4. "act *according to [our] wills* and pleasures, *whether to do evil or to do good*" (Alma 12:31; emphasis added).

Do my viscera feel a catch coming? Otherwise, why does the divine candor seem so stern? Including in these next words:

5. "Whosoever doeth iniquity, *doeth it unto himself*; for behold, ye are free" (Helaman 14:30; emphasis added).

Evaporated by now is the earlier "no-hands" naïveté about how "I am free to choose." Still, I am free to choose, even if I can *neither be immune from the consequences* of my wrong choices nor avoid accountability (see Romans 14:12; D&C 101:78).

At this point you and I may feel a little nudging. Yes, our freedom to choose is truly a shining and shimmering gift, but it is also one that can cause some shivering at times. Is this why we are sometimes almost afraid to decide certain things? Are we afraid we might make a mistake? But "no decision" *is* a decision! Hence this soul sigh: Choosing is no picnic after all.

But we are not alone!

The chilly wind one sometimes feels is more than offset by the warming reality that each of us has within us: the guiding *light of Christ.* We can actually distinguish between good and evil (see 2 Nephi 2:5; Moroni 7:16, 19). We can repent! Further, *the gifts of the Holy Ghost* can guide us and reassure us. And those gifts include peace and joy and love—of which there is such a terrible shortage in the world! Such is the precious and pervading sunshine of the Spirit (see Galatians 5:22; James 1:17; Moroni 10:8, 17).

Mercifully we are therefore not left alone! Nevertheless, we are at risk!

Back now to the more crisp and revealed words about choosing!

6. "[You will receive] according to *[your] desire*" (Alma 29:4; emphasis added).

7. "[And you will receive] according to *[your] wills*" (Alma 29:4; emphasis added).

I'm not sure we grasp how the final judgment will reflect our choices! But my desires and choices really will be honored! How manifestly just of God! How trembling for me! There is the anxiety protruding once again. Are my desires sufficiently educated to choose wisely (see Alma 13:3, 10)? Could the further education of my desires be the most important form of continuing education?

So it is that the chilly dawn of realization is further felt: Real choosing bristles with alternatives, enticements, defining moments, accountability, counterfeits, and consequences!

8. Why then do some actually choose to remain *"willingly . . . ignorant,"* such as of impending Messianic events (2 Peter 3:5; emphasis added)? Yes, some seem to say, "My mind is made up, so don't confuse me with cosmic facts. Instead, let me compartmentalize my life and my choices."

One cannot stay, however, on that naïve plane of understanding very long when he or she reads these next sobering words. They are so ripe with implications. They inform us that some rebels are simply

9. *"not willing* to enjoy that which they might have received" (D&C 88:32; emphasis added).

That cold wind is really blowing at the edges of my mind now. Foregoing enjoyment? But why? Knowingly turning down something vastly better? Why?

So this is a real war—with real casualties—in which there can be no real pacifists. No wonder, brothers and sisters, there's been such a long shelf life of the wry quip we've all heard about "free agency and how to enforce it." In effect, some seem almost to ask, "Is this gift returnable?"

10. "For, behold, *the devil . . . rebelled against me . . . ; and also a third part of the hosts of heaven* turned he away from me *because of their agency*" (D&C 29:36; emphasis added).

Lucifer was very angry then, and he is very angry still—choosing to strive to make "all men [to] be miserable like unto himself" (2 Nephi 2:27).

Wait a minute!

One-third deliberately chose *not* to undergo the mortal experience by choosing not to go on choosing? It seems so. It all began such a very long time ago, since

11. "it must needs be that the devil should tempt the children of men, or they could not be *agents unto themselves*" (D&C 29:39; emphasis added).

Thus his very temptations become vexing verifications that we're free to choose.

12. "Wherefore, the Lord God gave unto *man* that he *should act for himself*. Wherefore, man could not act for himself save it should be that he was *enticed by the one or the other*" (2 Nephi 2:16; emphasis added).

Hmmm! So it's worse still. The choices are not to be made among passive alternatives but among vibrant, alluring choices! Why can't we just glide through life and cherry-pick what we want? Why must there be "an opposition in all things" (2 Nephi 2:11)? It seems so relentless at times!

13. "That *every man may act in doctrine . . . according to the moral agency which I have given unto him*, that *every man* may be *accountable* for his own sins in the day of judgment" (D&C 101:78; emphasis added).

Well, by now any earlier and superficial exhilaration has fully departed. And we see instead unsmiling accountability standing astride every path, every choice.

Time now to let go of this format with my informal and conversational insertions and to review!

Again, what are the ground rules?

Well, the revealed record shows that Lucifer clearly chose to seek his personal preeminence, chose to be angry when he was rejected, chose to lead others astray, and chose misery, not joy. His followers in turn chose to rebel, chose to respond to his false allures, and turned their collective backs on the second estate!

But there's this ground rule: The Prophet Joseph assured us, "The devil *could not* compel mankind to do evil; all was voluntary. . . . God *would not* exert any compulsory means, and the devil could not" (*Teachings*, 187; emphasis added). Such is our situation.

Professor C. Terry Warner has written that individuals

*cannot avoid being both free and responsible for their choices. Individuals capable of acting for themselves cannot remain on neutral ground, abstaining from both receiving and rejecting light from God.* [In Daniel H. Ludlow, ed., *Encyclopedia of Mormonism*, 5 vols. (New York: Macmillan, 1992), s.v. "agency," 1:26; see also 2 Nephi 2:27–29; 10:23]

If we even just glance at spiritual history, no wonder there is this touching lamentation from long-suffering Jesus, or Jehovah. When speaking of ancient Israel, He said, "How oft would I have gathered you as a hen gathereth her chickens, and ye would not" (3 Nephi 10:5). "How oft"? The "how-oft question" is one of the most haunting in all of eternity (see also Luke 13:34).

It is matched by what the Lord of the vineyard can justifiably say at the end of the salvational day. Reading these words often makes me weep. As He surveyed all that He had tried to do—leaving us free—and all the yield that might have been, and having given us our freedom to choose, He, the Lord of the vineyard, tenderly asked: "What could I have done more?" (Jacob 5:47).

Oh, the special character of God! Oh, His perfect love and patience! Captured eloquently, I think, by President J. Reuben Clark, Jr., who said:

*I believe that in his justice and mercy* [God] *will give us the maximum reward for our acts, give us all that he can give, and in the reverse, I believe that he will impose upon us the minimum penalty which it is possible for him to impose.* [*CR*, October 1953, 84]

So here we are: comprehending the character of God and comprehending that there could be no joy without agency.

I wonder what it means—and perhaps you do, too—when I read the related verse about how Lucifer does not understand about "the mind of God" (Moses 4:6). The details have not been revealed to us. But could it possibly involve Lucifer's catastrophic failure to comprehend the inviolate interplay of agency and joy?

Once more, therefore, the act of choosing is more than nodding assent or passive shoulder shrugging. It reflects real choices made over time that form definite patterns. Even our prayers are much affected by our choices. If we have made good choices, we are much less likely to ask "amiss" (2 Nephi 4:35) in our prayers but instead can ask according to that "which is right" (3 Nephi 18:20). And then the promise is there for us to begin to claim more and more. The choices and prayers can be such that we *can* ask, and what we ask for can be "done even as [we] asketh" (D&C 46:30).

Again, there can be no agency avoidance. *No* decision *is* a decision. Delay is a delusion, and that delay always discards the holy present. It simply throws it away.

Again, choosing to be obedient is a choice. Jesus chose to let His will be "swallowed up in the will of the Father" (Mosiah 15:7). It was a deliberate choice—a choice, of course, that blessed all mortals mightily and everlastingly. Being obedient is a way *of* life, but it is also the way *to* eternal life.

With you I have reflected over that spiritually intriguing phrase "compound in one" and about our freedom to choose. It tells us that without being able to choose among alternatives, life would be no life at all. Things would "remain as dead" with no "sense nor insensibility" (2 Nephi 2:11). And we are told God's creation would have served "no purpose" (2 Nephi 2:12). Very strong language! Thus for a few moments today we have been discussing a very strong doctrine indeed!

Do I mean of God's creation there would be no beautiful Grand Canyon to behold? Who would have the sensibility to appreciate it? No mother's glow over her baby's first smile? Who would have the capacity for such joy? Do I mean there would never be individuals of holiness to admire? Who could have been free to choose holiness or to admire it? Oh, the annihilating "compound in one"!

I marvel, as many of you know, at the extent of the cosmos— this encompassing vastness and personalness. It is incredible to even contemplate. But it is not as grand as God's gift to us of the freedom to choose. There are literally now, science says, more stars in the universe than there are grains of sand in every beach, every desert, and every ocean floor on this planet (see Allison M. Heinrichs, "The Stellar Census: 70 Sextillion," *Los Angeles Times*, 26 July 2003, A19; see also Carl Sagan, *Cosmos* [New York: Random House, 1980], 196). Scriptural words are not just elegant, extravagant language. Besides, souls matter more than stars. And He wants us to have joy. We cannot do that unless we are free to choose. But neither can we have that joy unless we are willing to be spiritually submissive day in, day out, and unless we exercise that grand and glorious freedom to choose in which people truly matter more than stars.

I testify to you that though the grandness of this doctrine is beyond our comprehension, it is not beyond our attention and exploration. We are, in fact, in the position of having been given revelations that were then far beyond the Prophet Joseph Smith, bright as he was. Yet he was their enunciator and their declarer. We worship a God whose character is so stunning and who wants us to come home. But He will not force us. *He will not force us.*

God bless you, my young friends, in your daily choices, in the inflections of your decisions, and in the thoughts that traverse your minds. May there be for all of us, including myself, an alignment with Him that brings us home. Home where, as He says, He will give us "all that he hath" (Luke 12:44). There isn't any more—of which I testify in the name of Jesus Christ, amen.